Enhancing Teaching and Learning

A Leadership Guide for School Library Media Specialists

by Jean Donham

Neal-Schuman Publishers, Inc.

New York   London

Published by Neal-Schuman Publishers, Inc.
100 Varick Street
New York, NY 10013

Copyright © 1998 by Jean Donham

Library of Congress Cataloging-in-Publication Data

Donham, Jean
    Enhancing teaching and learning : a leadership guide for school library media specialists / Jean Donham
        p.   cm.
    Includes biographical references and index.
    ISBN 1-55570-328-3
    1. School libraries—United States. 2. Instructional materials centers—United States. I. Title.
Z675.S3D65   1998
027.8'0973—dc21   98-18950
                                                                    CIP

Contents

PART II: THE LIBRARY MEDIA PROGRAM

List of Figures

Preface

Enhancing Teaching and Learning: A Leadership Guide for School Library Media Specialists is a guide for effecting change in a library media program by integrating it into the school's instructional program. The need to be simultaneously proactive and responsive presents a challenge. On the one hand, the library media professional has an agenda for developing information literacy, advocating for reading, and facilitating effective uses of information technologies. Advancement of this agenda demands leadership. On the other hand, that agenda can only be effectively accomplished when it is integrated into the curriculum, and such integration requires collaboration between the library media professional and the teaching staff. The result of the interaction between the library media program and the other components of the students' school experience is *synergy*—the effect is greater than the sum of the parts. When the library media program is integrated with curriculum, with parents, with the community, each of those interactions serves to increase the impact on students. However, when the parts work in isolation from one another, their potential effectiveness is diminished.

Two key words in the American Association of School Librarians/Association for Educational Communications and Technology (AASL/AECT) *Informative Power: Building Partnerships for Learning* are leadership and collaboration. These two words serve to temper one another. Leadership suggests a proactive role where the library media program gives direction to the school's curriculum and instruction. Indeed, such leadership is necessary and appropriate, particularly in implementing an information literacy curriculum and guiding effective use of information technology within the school's curriculum. Collaboration, on the other hand, requires working together as equal partners with the teaching staff. The library media specialist must exert leadership, yet still be collaborative and collegial.

There is a tendency in all professions to become egocentric and to see one's specialty as the center of its universe. In medicine, the family physician sees his role as central to patient care, while the surgeon sees herself taking the lead in case decisions. In education, a school administrator is often perceived as the pivotal instructional leader of the school. Language arts and reading teachers are often seen as central to student success because reading and writing are essential for success in all curricular areas. Such perceived centrality is particularly easy for the school library media program because it interacts with all curricular areas and all grade levels in the school, has ties to the community, and is closely associated with the school administration. Yet, it is important to maintain respect for the expertise of classroom teachers, the position of school administrators, and the beliefs and values of the community at large. Striking the balance between collaboration and leadership is a key to successful implementation of an effective library media program. My hope is that this book will provide guidance to library media professionals to find the appropriate balance—one where the library media program is at once affected by and affects its surroundings.

The library media program then must function in context with its environment. Dictionary definitions of the word *context* carry such concepts as *environment, surroundings,* and *external conditions.* To work within context will mean that there must be adequate flexibility in the program to adapt to those conditions. Schools vary in how they are organized, in how they are managed, in what they believe about teaching and learning, and in what needs their students have. There can be no specified number of minutes per day for teaching in the library media center, no predictable number of meetings a library media professional attends, no simple formula for the facility, the staffing, or the activities. This is not to say that the library media program merely responds to its surroundings; indeed, I recommend a more proactive posture, but proactive within the parameters of the school, working in concert with its culture.

During my 13 years as a district-level library media and technology coordinator, I observed a variety of implementations of the fundamental principles of effective school librarianship. No two schools in that district had identical library media programs, yet each was effective in meeting local needs. There is not just one right way to carry out a successful library media program. Certainly there are nonnegotiable elements. There must be an information literacy curriculum; teachers and library media specialists must collaborate to integrate information literacy into the curriculum; there must be support for a collection of resources that meets the needs of students and teachers; facilities must accommodate a variety of simultaneous activities; students must have good access to the resources of the library media center. Yet the implementation of these elements in any given school must be adapted to suit the local school culture; what works in a multi-age, continuous progress setting may not fit a more traditional school, and within parameters certain adaptations must be made. Where to "draw the line" of acceptability is the key decision library media professionals face.

Enhancing Teaching and Learning is divided into two parts. Part I addresses the components of the school environment—the students, the curriculum and instruction, the principal, the school district, the community. I devote a separate chapter to each of these five components in order to show how the library media program can interact with these elements to enhance learning. In Chapter 1, questions considered include: What conditions of students' lives affect their learning? How does the library media specialist's role in working with children differ from that of the teacher? What direct interactions occur between the library media specialist and students that enrich the student's learning experience? Chapter 2 considers how the curriculum and instruction are changing and how the library media program can help improve learning. Understanding the work of the principal can give the library media specialist strategies for working effectively with administrators, as discussed in Chapter 3. Beyond the school itself is the school district, which influences many decisions within the school. The impact of site-based decision making is discussed in Chapter 4, as well as the roles and relationships for the library media specialist within the district structure. Chapter 5 focuses on the school's community at large, and the relationship between the school library media program and the community of parents, other service agencies, and local businesses.

Part II addresses specific strategies that may be particularly helpful in allowing the library media program to go beyond being a warehouse to being an active player in teaching and learning. Planning with teachers for instruction is one way the library media specialist can become a part of instruction. Chapter 6 describes such collaborative planning. Scheduling is a mechanism for organizing the library media program within the school day. Various scheduling models and their benefits will be considered in Chapter 7. Chapter 8 discusses strategies for collection development and maintenance, with an emphasis on the collection's relationship to curriculum. Chapter 9 explores both aliteracy and illiteracy. What is the role of the library media program in reducing both? How do the library media program's efforts related to reading align with efforts in the classroom? Technology is pervasive in the school. Its place as a component of the library media program is the topic of Chapter 10. The information processing skills curriculum is addressed in Chapter 11: What needs to be taught? How should it be taught? How can these processes be taught within a meaningful context driven by real information needs? Chapter 12 addresses instructional assessment, with emphasis on assessing students' development of information processing skills. Finally, evaluation of the school library media program is discussed in Chapter 13.

The AASL/AECT Guidelines for Library Media Programs identify three elements of the library media program: learning and teaching, information access and delivery, and program administration. Each of the following chapters ends with a list of suggested action strategies related to these program elements. These strategies are intended to help library media specialists implement the national guidelines by providing leadership and working collaboratively with other educators in the school.

I wrote *Enhancing Teaching and Learning: A Leadership Guide for School Library Media Specialists* to help library media specialists implement their programs collaboratively. In addition, I urge you to use material from the book in your discussions with administrators, parents and other interest groups, and school leaders on integrating the library media program into the school curriculum.

Acknowledgments

This book grew out of years of experience and study, both of which were influenced and aided by several people. Two important mentors for me have been David Loertscher and Al Azinger. David gave me models that helped me communicate a vision for school library media programs and Al taught me how to lead. The library media specialists in the Iowa City Community School District invested energy and talent to bring that vision to life in schools where they have made important differences in teaching and learning. I am especially grateful to Denise Rehmke, Anne Marie Kraus, Susan Richards, Barbara Becker, Victoria Walton, Barbara Stein, Mary MacNeil, Mary Jo Langhorne, and Deb McAlister for the examples and ideas they shared as I wrote.

This project required that someone believe that I had something to offer the profession. Two important people expressed confidence and supported the project: Virginia Mathews, who was persistent in her encouragement, and Charles Harmon, who supported the work.

My family sacrificed to allow me to focus on this project. For three years, they gave me time and space to work. Many hours of what could have been family time together was instead time I spent thinking, reading, researching, writing. My sons, Joel and Andrew Donham, grew from being boys to young men while this project dominated our household. Their father, Kelley Donham, helped me by filling the parenting gaps this work created.

Robert van Deusen listened to my thinking aloud about each chapter and then read the drafts to see whether the writing matched the thinking. June Gross read each chapter and gave me her responses about the message. Eric Rector applied a skillful editor's pencil and Jennifer Sprague created the index.

In this book, a quotation from Robert Reich says, "Rarely do Big Ideas emerge any longer from the solitary labor of genius." This book, like all other work I have done in my life, is the product of collaboration with others. The synergy that comes from many people sharing ideas and working together is what produced this book, and that is its topic as well.

PART I:

The Environment

Chapter 1

Students

This chapter

- describes conditions of youth attending American schools and how those conditions affect their learning
- describes the nature of motivation and its effect on learning
- relates the library media program to the needs of students
- identifies action strategies for working with students

Denise: ambitious . . . hard-working . . . hoping to become an engineer . . . eager to please her teachers . . .
Jana: pretty . . . popular . . . chatty . . . wants to be liked . . .
Kate: angry . . . outspoken . . . hostile . . .
Michael: quiet . . . shy . . . tense . . . anxious . . .
John: bright . . . inquisitive . . . success-oriented . . .
Peter . . . Tom . . . Angelique . . . Joel . . . Manuel . . . Kerri . . . Andrew . . .

A chapter about students is an appropriate beginning for a book about the library media program. While the library media center has many constituencies—teachers, parents, the community at large—its primary goal is to help students become effective users of information. To accomplish that goal, the library media program must be sensitive to young people's cognitive and affective needs.

The relationship between adults and youth can be fragile. Power and authority, levels of self-confidence, and implied and explicit expectations complicate the relationship. An adult's unintended cue can direct a less-than-confident student away from the library media center.

Young people's assumptions about authority figures or their desire for independence can prevent them from seeking help. Many students see the library media specialist as *different* from the teacher—sometimes less threatening. However, some may find the library media specialist more intimidating because they have had relatively few interactions. Each interaction with a student determines whether that student will want to return to the library media center. The situation is analogous to a salesperson in a retail store where the quality of interaction will determine whether the customer will return. Effective "customer relations" requires understanding and appreciating the nature of the customer. This chapter focuses on the most important library media program "customer"—the student.

Students entering school library media centers seek help and resources for a variety of reasons, and each student brings a different level of confidence. One hope students share is that they will find what they need and have access to friendly, knowledgeable, and sincere help. The library media specialist is in a unique position for building relationships with students. Teachers set expectations for student performance. Library media specialists help students meet those expectations. Library media specialists enjoy a special relationship of "team player" with students. Those students who feel disenfranchised from the school culture may benefit particularly from the special nature of that relationship. The library media specialist shares the students' goal of "getting the assignment done" or "finding the answer," as compared to the teacher's role of "giving the assignment" or "asking the question." The library media specialist has an unusual opportunity to facilitate learning.

CONDITIONS OF AMERICAN YOUTH

The conditions of American young people vary dramatically. In affluent families, children have their own computers, modems, videocassette recorders, and other resources. Other students have none of these resources in their homes. In each school, considering students' economic and family conditions is a first step toward being responsive to their needs. It is also helpful to understand the conditions of young people in the nation; this knowledge helps educators relate the condition of local youth to others. Schools tend to be insular, yet students will move to other communities, just as students will arrive from other communities.

In 1993 the U.S. Census Bureau reported that 22.7 percent of children in America lived in poverty. National Center for Educational Statistics (NCES) data from 1994 show the national dropout rate, based on persons ages 14 to 34 who were not in school and had not completed high school, was 11.2 percent. NCES data also indicate that the difference in dropout rates was 11 percentage points when comparing high-income families to low-income families. While library media specialists, like all educators, have concerns about young people, some of these realities lie beyond the library media program. Indirectly, the library media program may encourage a student to stay in school. The library media center may be a refuge for a student with a special interest in technology who is otherwise unmotivated in school. Occasionally, a media center can be a haven for someone who feels socially alienated elsewhere in the school.

The library media program can also have an impact by improving access and helping increase opportunities for learning; by considering level of difficulty and ethnic representation in collection development; by teaching information skills; and by responding to out-of-school influences, particularly those from television.

IMPROVING ACCESS

The increase in numbers of "latchkey" children who were regularly unattended at home after school has given rise to latchkey programs sponsored by parent groups and school districts to keep children at school longer hours, both before and after the regular school day begins. In many settings, library media specialists have been reluctant to extend their hours to offer access to children in these programs, perhaps because of the library media specialist's contract or the availability of support staff. However, the library media center ought to be accessible to children whenever they are at the school. This may require library media specialists to give up some control of the facility. Providing some operations training to latchkey program staff and having them operate the center before and after school can extend access. If there is no existing latchkey program, the library media specialist might advocate extending the library media center hours to accommodate those children who have essentially no safe place to go after school. While it is tempting to say, "But that is not my responsibility," there is a need for a safe and productive way for children to use the hours from the end of the school day until the time parents come home from work. Library media center resources offer opportunities for making those hours safe and productive. Collaboration with other community agencies, especially the public library, may pave the way for homework help or arts activities in the library media center as well. The library media center can no longer be seen as a facility that operates for children only from 8:30 a.m. to 3:00 p.m. and then withdraws concern for their learning.

School library media centers need to forge close alliances with local public libraries to identify solutions for extending access; bringing public library staff to school library media facilities for "rush hours" may be one creative solution. Adjusting the work hours of staff to include early morning, late afternoon, or early evening hours may be a solution. Electronic access can sometimes be a solution; however, this solution is only viable if students have computers and modems at home. It is wise to find out who owns computers and modems before online access is identified as the solution; otherwise, the inequity between "haves" and "have nots" may increase rather than decrease. Neighborhood centers or other facilities where students can do homework also offer means for providing access to information resources with the cooperation of the school library media program.

The needs of secondary school students call for careful policy making for both school hours and after-school hours. Extended hours increase access for some secondary school students. However, in 1992 almost 30 percent of high school students were working (Smith, 1994, p. 136). Open access to the library media center during the school day may be the only opportunity for these students since their jobs may fill their after-school hours. After-school time is also heavily booked for students involved in extracurricular activities—music, drama, and athletics, for example.

Access to the library media center is a two-way concern. The library media center must have an open-access policy; teachers must also have a policy of open access, that is, they must allow students to leave their classrooms and their study halls to go to the library media center. Although it is common for high school teachers to allow students some time in class to work on assignments, it is sometimes difficult for students to move to the library media center to access resources they might need. Concerns for orderliness in the halls and accountability for students' whereabouts can conflict with providing school-day open access. Solutions to that conflict require the systemic thinking of teachers, administrators, and the library media specialist. Library media specialists must advocate for open access and encourage school policies that facilitate it. As secondary schools investigate block scheduling or initiatives to expand the length of class periods, eliminate study halls, and make other modifications in the schedule, library media specialists must be alert and assertive in protecting student access to the library media center when they need it.

Block scheduling is one school innovation that has been found to have an impact on access for secondary students. Block scheduling involves lengthening classes to 90 minutes or more each day, and reducing the number of classes meeting each day. This longer block of time can increase access, as teachers organize the longer time period into several activities, one of which may be accessing the library media center (Baker & Turner, 1996). Schools have reported a major increase in library media center use with block scheduling (Galt et al., 1996). Using the block-scheduled class time, students who may not previously have had access to the library media center have access when time is booked for their classes.

Access to the library media center is one way to address concerns about equity among students in terms of use of computers. In 1995 a study of American consumerism revealed a clear distinction in personal computer ownership across income categories (Times Mirror Center, 1995). Households that reported owning a computer for more than two years were "upscale," that is, annual income was over $50,000. Those households accounted for 52 percent of home computer ownership, while 29 percent of home computers were found in households with an annual income between $30,000 and $50,000. Only 19 percent of computer owners reported an income below $30,000. In the same survey, of those who had acquired a computer within the previous two years, 36 percent earned over $50,000, while 38 percent earned between $30,000 and $50,000, and 26 percent earned less than $30,000. These increases in purchase among middle and lower income families may predict more equity of access in the future. However, the gap will exist for some time. It is also important to note that in this survey, analysis of how computers were used showed variation among groups. The more recent purchasers tend to use their computer more for game playing whereas those who have owned computers longer tend to use theirs for productivity. So, while computers are becoming more widely available in homes, their purposes—entertainment versus productivity—may indicate less equity for learning than ownership might suggest. Access to the library media center's computer resources during and beyond the school day can narrow the equity gap.

The advantage students enjoy when they have access to a computer at home is evident to all teachers who collect homework and observe students' levels of sophistication in using electronic information resources. In an information-based environment—and that is what school is—skill in using the computer as an information and communication tool is highly advantageous.

COLLECTION DEVELOPMENT TO MEET STUDENT NEEDS

Some clearly identifiable conditions call for consideration in collection development. Data from the 1990 census revealed that almost 14 percent of children ages 5–17 spoke a language other than English at home. This figure represents an increase of approximately 40 percent in ten years. While political climates change and the current wave suggests interest in establishing the predominance of English as the language of the nation, nevertheless, schools continue to have children arriving at their doors speaking Spanish, Chinese, Japanese, Vietnamese, and a score of other languages. Providing materials that help these children develop their skills in English is an important contribution of the library media program. Also important is providing materials in formats and styles that facilitate English-as-a-second-language students' learning content across all curricular areas. Marketing the library media center to these students is a critical part of advocacy. Electronic resources that offer voice as well as text may be particularly helpful to their language development.

One in five American children between the ages of three and seventeen are reported by parents to have had a developmental delay, learning disability, or behavioral problem during childhood (National Commission on Children, 1991, p. 31). Children from single-parent families are two to three times as likely to suffer these problems as children living with both parents. The differences are attributed to the stress of family conflict, and the disruption and deprivations associated with living with only one parent. The need for materials that fit the cognitive and affective realities of students is keen. Materials that include not only text, but also graphics, charts, and tables are essential for conveying information. Electronic resources with sound and motion to augment textual information may be needed by some students. Library media specialists must provide materials directly to students and to teachers for use with students. Only 30 percent of fourth-grade public school students scored at or above the proficiency level in reading on the 1994 National Assessment of Educational Progress. This measurement underscores the need for materials at various levels of difficulty, when half or more students in some settings are not at basic reading proficiency levels. Attention to readability of materials may be especially important at the middle school and high school levels.

Materials also need to show sensitivity to students' lives. In 1991 about 33.4 million children, or half of all U.S. children, lived in a "traditional nuclear family" (that is, a married couple and their biological children), according to the U.S. Census Bureau. About 15 percent of children lived in "blended" households that included at least one step-parent, step-sibling, or half-sibling; another 13 percent lived in "extended" families in which one or more adults other than the biological parents were present in the household. United States Commerce Department data show that approximately 28 percent of all U.S. children lived with only one parent in 1994. These variations in families call for sensitivity when selecting materials.

INSTRUCTION TO MANAGE TELEVISION INFLUENCE

The societal concern about the "information age" has stimulated renewed interest in the library media curriculum; increasingly, there is respect for the importance of developing skill in accessing, interpreting, and evaluating information. Information processes are taking their place in school curricula in the company of problem solving, critical thinking, and decision making. One pervasive source of information and entertainment is television. The average number of hours of television viewing per week for children (ages 2–11) and teens (ages 12–17) are approximately the same—nearly 22 hours per week (McGill, 1994). During the 1993–1994 season, the ten highest-rated programs among children ages 2–11 were sitcoms airing during prime time. Such television viewing does not challenge students to think critically or creatively. Very high levels of television viewing (35 hours or more per week) negatively correlate with academic achievement (Chen, 1994). A moderate amount of television viewing (10–15 hours per week) has been reported as positively related to academic achievement. The crux of the issue may be what programming children watch and how it is used to advance learning. Television has valuable programming to offer; however, viewing 35 or more hours of television per week does not indicate selective viewing.

Concerns are often raised about the effect of inappropriate televised material on young people. Heintz describes an interesting study of teenagers having "massive" exposure (three hours per night for five consecutive nights) to prime-time, sexually oriented programming. Such viewing was found to influence the moral judgment of 13- and 14-year-olds. Specifically, the teens who had been exposed to such programming rated a series of sexual indiscretions and improprieties as "less bad" and described the victim as "less wronged" than did teens who had not seen the programs (Heintz, 1994). The power of the medium is evident, but it needs to be channeled into productive uses, especially for youthful audiences. Overall, research findings indicate a positive association between television violence and aggressive behavior (Smith, 1996).

A significant body of research indicates that parents can influence the effects of television programming on their children by intervening or even by watching with their children. Research suggests that parents can inoculate children against television's possible negative consequences and amplify its positive effects in the following ways (Abelman, 1984):

- *perceived reality*: If parents explain the unreal nature of televised presentations, the negative effects should be minimized.
- *consequences*: If parents associate consequences with acts portrayed on television, the impact of behaviors associated with positive consequences is strengthened while the attraction of acts associated with negative consequences should be minimized.
- *motives*: If parents interpret the reasons for an action as principled, more learning should occur.
- *evaluation*: If parents express approval or disapproval, this should increase or decrease performance because it cues the child to parental attitudes.

Yet, while parents can use television for teaching, research clearly indicates that few parents involve themselves in their children's consumption of television. See, for example, the work of J. McLeod et al. (1972) and Bradley S. Greenberg et al. (1972). This lack of parental intervention signals the need for schools to develop students' skills as critical, thoughtful consumers of television. In the state of North Carolina, media literacy is included in both the communication skills and information skills curricula. All Canadian provinces except Quebec are developing mandated media literacy curricula, either as a cross-curricular subject or within language arts (Pungente, 1996). But in most communities, instruction for media literacy exists only due to the energy and initiative of a single teacher, not because of a coordinated, community-wide programmatic plan of implementation. Library media specialists can be advocates for media literacy education. Developing critical viewing skills is parallel to critical reading skills; in this media age, such skills need to be taught with equal or greater emphasis.

In summary, many environmental conditions affect students. Educators cannot simply throw up their hands in dismay and say, "I can't fix all that is wrong with society." Granted that the library media center cannot resolve all the difficulties in young people's lives, some actions may improve students' opportunities to succeed. The hard task is determining what *can* be done within the school to address equity, attention, or involvement in lear,ning. Advocacy and sensitivity are dispositions for an effective school library media specialist to create a student-friendly environment, acquire materials that match students' needs and interests, and attempt to increase opportunities for all students.

MOTIVATION FOR LEARNING

Motivation Theory

A classic work in motivation is Maslow's (1971) hierarchy. He theorized that human needs fall into a hierarchy and that the higher needs arise only after lower needs have been met. At the lowest level are physical and organizational needs, that is, the basic needs for security and survival. Above these basic needs are social needs, the need for esteem and for a sense of belonging. As social needs are met, intellectual needs, such as the need for knowledge and understanding, emerge. Above these are the aesthetic needs met by the appreciation for life's order, beauty, and balance. At the top of the Maslow's hierarchy is self-actualization. He described the self-actualized person as one motivated by needs to be open, to love others and self, to act ethically, to express autonomy, and to be curious.

Students need approval, affiliation, and achievement. Some students are approval-dependent; they conform because they need the assurance from others that their performance is at an acceptable level. Other students have less need for approval and are motivated by their own need for achievement or affiliation. A corollary to the achievement need is the need to avoid failure. Motive will affect the risks one is willing to take; for example, often students who are driven by a fear of failure will be less willing to take risks, to try new strategies or tasks. Similarly, students high in the need for affiliation perform in ways that they perceive to be respected by their peers.

Individuals who generally attribute their successes and failures to their own behavior are said to have an internal locus of control, while those who generally attribute their success and failure to luck, task difficulty, or some action of others are said to have an external locus of control. Self-concept as a learner also appears to affect a student's achievement motivation. The student with an internal locus of control for success and a positive self-concept as a learner ("I can succeed because I have the ability and I can exert the effort.") has a better chance for high achievement than the student with an external locus of control ("I can't succeed because the teacher doesn't like me.").

In his contentious book *A Nation of Victims; The Decay of the American Character*, Sykes (1992) posits that as a society we have adopted a stance of externalizing control, making martyrs of ourselves, and accepting no responsibility for any of our culture's social, political, or economic woes. If his perspective on culture is accurate, schools have a larger societal milieu challenging them as they try to help students see that they are responsible for their own achievement.

Motivation Strategies

A substantial body of research exists related to intrinsic and extrinsic motivation. Intrinsic motivation refers to the perception that an activity is engaged in because it is rewarding. Extrinsic motivation, on the other hand, is the perception that one engages in an activity for some external reward (for example, students read a set number of books to win a special prize, such as a pizza). The research literature contains more than 100 studies that conclude that extrinsic rewards are often ineffective, and in fact can be detrimental in the long run. In one typical experiment, Lepper, Greene, and Nisbett (1973) observed three- to five-year-old preschool children coloring with felt-tip pens. The researchers observed that the children enjoyed playing with the pens. Next they asked the children to draw with the markers. The researchers promised some children a "Good Player Award" for drawing pictures. Other children drew pictures without the promise of a reward. Two weeks later the researchers returned and observed the children's inclination to draw with the markers. Those children who had been promised an award spent only half as much time drawing as they had originally. Those who did not receive awards showed no decline in interest. Many studies follow this pattern with similar outcomes—ultimately a decline in motivation to do the task is associated with external rewards.

The literature identifies three types of reward contingencies (Dickinson, 1989). *Task-contingent* rewards recognize participation; the preschool coloring activity is an example, where children were rewarded just for participating in the task. *Performance-contingent* rewards are provided only when the student completes a task. In studies, rewarded students were less inclined to perform the task later than were the students who had not been paid (Deci, 1971). Every parent who has paid a son or daughter for sidewalk shoveling knows how likely it is that sidewalk shoveling will be done voluntarily in the future. *Success-contingent* rewards are given for good performance. Dickinson maintains that extrinsic rewards can be effective when they are contingent upon successful performance and when the standard for success is attainable. Paul Chance offers some suggestions for judicious use of rewards and urges that educators remain aware that extrinsic rewards can have adverse effects on student motivation (Chance, 1992):

- When possible, avoid using rewards as incentives. For example, don't say, "If you do X, I'll give you Y." Instead, ask the student to perform a task and then provide the reward for having completed it.
- Remember that what is an effective reward for one student may not work for another. Effective rewards are things that students seek—positive feedback, praise, approval, recognition; they relate to the needs of each student.
- Reward success and set standards so that success is within the student's reach. To accommodate differences among students, reward improvement or progress.

DeCharms (1968) designed a program to change motivation in children from external to internal with favorable results in their achievement. The students learned their own strengths and weaknesses, chose realistic goals, and assessed their own progress toward their goals. The program stressed personal responsibility. He reported that children in the study improved in both their achievement motivation and their actual achievement. In a follow-up study, he found that the improvements had persisted and indicated that the participants showed evidence of being likely to graduate from high school (DeCharms, 1970). Educators want students to believe that they have some internal control over their own prospects for success. What teachers and other school adults say and do influences the attribution patterns that students develop, and ultimately influences their achievement (Bal-Tar, Raviv, & Bal-Tar, 1982). One important aspect of DeCharms's work was the effort to help students assess their own strengths; within the body of research on intrinsic and extrinsic motivation, many studies emphasize the difference that self-concept makes in motivation. Children with a high self-concept tend to attribute their success to their own ability and are less dependent on extrinsic motivation—they are self-rewarding (Ames, 1978).

Kohn has studied motivation extensively. He states that internalization of motivation is crucial to developing enduring habits and behaviors. To that end, he declares that extrinsic reward and punishment systems are counterproductive (Kohn, 1993). He states:

> In general, the more kids are enticed to do something for a reward, whether tangible or verbal, the more you see a diminution of interest the next time they do it. That can be explained partly by the fact that praise, like other rewards, is ultimately an instrument of control, but also by the fact that if I praise or reward a student for doing something, the message the child infers is, "This must be something I wouldn't want to do; otherwise, they wouldn't have to bribe me to do it" (Brandt, 1995, p. 15).

Kohn recommends, instead, three ways to motivate students. First he suggests that the work students do must be interesting. He poses this question: "Has the child been given something to do worth learning?" His second recommendation has to do with the school community. Students should feel part of a safe environment in which they can ask for help. Finally, he raises the issue of choice. He urges teachers to give students opportunities to choose what they will do, how, and with whom.

The Library Media Program and Motivation

A similar position on motivation is taken by Silver and his colleagues who have identified four human needs that hearken back to Maslow: success (the need for mastery), curiosity (the need for understanding), originality (the need for self-expression), and relationships (the need for involvement with others) (Strong, Silver, & Robinson, 1995). Under the heading "Independent Learning," the "AASL/AECT Information Literacy Standards for Student Learning" (1998) include three standards that closely parallel the needs identified by Silver:

- Pursue information related to personal interests (curiosity).
- Appreciate and enjoy literature and other creative expressions of information (originality).
- Strive for excellence in information seeking and knowledge generation (success).

Silver and his colleagues describe motivation strategies for helping students address each of these needs. To respond to the need for mastery, students need to have the criteria for success clearly articulated—what does successful performance look like? Student success is enhanced when the teacher models successful performance and labels the parts of that successful performance. For example, when asking students to take notes on what they have read, by modeling the note-taking process for them and thinking aloud during the demonstration, the library media specialist can show them what the process looks like when executed well.

One strategy related to curiosity is to provide incomplete or contradictory information that compels the student to explore information resources. Another way to pique curiosity is suggesting topics for research that relate to students' personal lives. Giving students choice in deciding what they will investigate also supports curiosity.

The need for self-expression calls for students to have a variety of media available for projects and activities in response to assignments. Developing multimedia, desktop publishing, or dramatic productions are examples of ways to build creativity into students' work that will increase their motivation by appealing to their desire to be original. Another strategy to respond to the need for creativity is to expand the audience for student work—use cable television to send student work out into the local community, use the World Wide Web as a publication forum, or identify interest groups or other classes within the school as audiences for student work.

Finally, to respond to students' need for relationships or social in-

**AN EXAMPLE OF ENHANCEMENT IN ACTION:
THE LEARNING LAB**

A high school social studies teacher uses the library media center as a "learning laboratory" for his American Studies classes. Students work as teams for a three-week project in which they spend every class period in the library media center. Each team has responsibility for studying a dimension of American life (such as sports, politics, prohibition, entertainment, transportation, economics, religion) in the 1920s. Their goal is to investigate and work as if each team were a department of a magazine staff. The final product will be a magazine that brings together the work of all teams. This unit motivates students. The library media center has created a collection that will respond to these students' needs; they will be successful in their search for information. They have access to the necessary hardware and software for desktop publishing to create the end product. The library media staff provides the support to students as they work in this "learning lab" atmosphere. Curiosity is the key to this project; the students generate their own information questions— they have control over their work. The end product allows for originality as students design the magazine; in this case students use Pagemaker (Adobe) for the final project. They count on each other for the work. The time the project takes allows group members to develop meaningful relationships and identify the substantive contributions that each member can make.

teraction, cooperative learning strategies and group projects with accountability shared among all members of the group are ways to cultivate student interest.

The library media program can be a valuable asset to the teacher and everyone else in the school who is seeking to cultivate motivation through success, curiosity, originality, and relationships. As a "learning laboratory," the center becomes the ideal space to support curiosity with its resources, to encourage relationships with its ambiance, and to support creativity with its multimedia.

The Learning Lab example in the box differs from what often happens in two important ways: time and support. It is not unusual for teachers to assign group tasks, but teachers too often expect groups to come together outside class time and work independently. For groups to work as groups, they must have designated group work time. Otherwise those students who already have skills use them to get the work done, and those students who lack specific skills merely depend on the others. The end result is that little process learning occurs. By making this project a "learning lab" activity where students work in the library media center, teachers can help all group members to be participants, and the appropriate support in resources and technical assistance are available for everyone to succeed.

When adequately motivated, students take responsibility for their own learning. To deliver an effective library media program, it is important to consider the larger context of the students' experiences and background—their prior learning, family and economic advantages or disadvantages, personal traits, and skills.

ACTION STRATEGIES

Learning and Teaching

- Enlist at-risk students with the aptitude for technology as student aides.
- Encourage teachers to allow students to complete assignments using alternative media (such as a computer-based multimedia production or art media) rather than the formal written paper.
- Beyond providing access, teach students how to use electronic resources. For example, offer voluntary "short courses" outside the school day focusing on specific technology applications, or coordinate with teachers to teach electronic resources for specific assignments during class time.
- Support teachers who engage their students in creative work by promoting the center as a "learning laboratory."

Information Access and Delivery

- Provide materials at various levels of difficulty to meet assignment demands, especially in core courses.
- Cooperate with such agencies as neighborhood centers to seek funding for online access to school and public library resources.
- Provide leisure reading, especially magazines, on topics of high interest—if necessary, seek local business funding to support subscriptions.

- Provide access to the World Wide Web with browser bookmarks for topics that match local students' interests. Examples of such special interest sites might be

    Jazz: http://www.acsn.nwu.edu/jazz

    Country and western music: http://www.nol.com/nol/ NOL_Home.html

    Museum: http://www.exploratorium.edu

    Weather: http://wxweb.msu.edu.weather/

    In this way, students begin to explore how to locate and evaluate information about topics of personal interest to them.
- Maintain open hours in the library media center before and after school for students. This schedule may require adjusting work hours or seeking after-school volunteers.
- Market materials at various levels of difficulty to teachers so that students with special learning needs can access information with less frustration.

Program Administration

- In secondary schools with block scheduling, encourage class use of the library media center. Arrange the facility to accommodate multiple activities and groups.

REFERENCES

Abelman, Robert. "Children and TV: The ABCs of TV Literacy," *Childhood Education* 60 (January/February 1984): 200–205.

American Association of School Librarians. "AASL/AECT Information Literacy Standards for Student Learning." Chicago: ALA, 1998.

Ames, Carole. "Children's Achievement Attributions and Self-Reinforcement: Effects of Self-Concept and Competitive Reward Structure," *Journal of Educational Psychology* 70, (June 1978): 345–355.

Baker, Robert and William Turner. "Block Scheduling: Impact on Library Media Programs, *Florida Media Quarterly* 21, no. 2 (1996): 10.

Bal-Tar, Daniel, A. Raviv, and Y. Bal-Tar. "Consistency of Pupils' Attributions Regarding Success and Failure," *Journal of Educational Psychology* 74 (February 1982): 104-110.

Brandt, Ron. "Punished by Rewards? A Conversation with Alfie Kohn," *Educational Leadership* 53 (September 1995): 13–16.

Chance, Paul. "The Rewards of Learning," *Phi Delta Kappan* 73 (November 1992): 200–207.

Chen, Milton. "Six Myths about Television and Children," *Media Studies Journal* 8 (Fall 1994): 105–113.

DeCharms, Richard. "Motivation Changes in Low-Income Black Children" (paper presented to the American Educational Research Association, Minneapolis, Minn., 1970).

———. *Personal Causation: The Internal Effective Determinants of* Behavior (New York: Academic Press, 1968).

Deci, Edward. "Effects of Externally Mediated Rewards on Intrinsic Motivation," *Journal of Personality and Social Psychology* 18 (April 1971): 105–115.

Dickinson, Alyce. "The Detrimental Effects of Extrinsic Reinforcement on 'Intrinsic Motivation,'" *The Behavior Analyst* 12 (Spring 1989): 1–15.

Galt, Joan et al. "Block Scheduling: Comments from Inside the Media Center," *Florida Media Quarterly* 21, no. 2 (1996): 12–13.

Greenberg, Bradley S. et al. "Children's Television Behavior as Perceived by Mother and Child," in George A. Comstock and E. A. Rubenstein, eds., *Television and Social Behavior*, vol. 4 (Washington D.C.: Government Printing Office, 1972).

Heintz, Katharine. "Smarter than We Think—Kids, Passivity, and the Media," *Media Studies Journal* 8 (Fall 1994): 205–219.

Kohn, Alfie. *Punished by Rewards* (Boston: Houghton Mifflin, 1993).

Lepper, M.R., D. Greene, and R.E. Nisbett. "Undermining Children's Intrinsic Interest: A Test of the 'Overjustification' Hypothesis." *Journal of Personality and Social Psychology* 28 (1973): 129–137.

Maslow, Abraham H. *The Farther Reaches of Human Nature* (New York: Viking Press, 1971).

McGill, Larry. "By the Numbers—What Kids Watch," *Media Studies Journal* 8 (Fall 1994): 95–104.

McLeod, J. et al. "Adolescents, Parents and Television Use: Adolescents Self-Report Measures from a Maryland and Wisconsin Sample," in George A. Comstock and E. A. Rubenstein, eds., *Television and Social Behavior*, vol. 3 (Washington D.C.: Government Printing Office, 1972).

National Commission on Children. *Beyond Rhetoric: A New American Agenda for Children and Families* (Washington, D.C.: Government Printing Office, 1991) 31.

Pungente, John. "Getting Started on Media Literacy," *Emergency Librarian* 24 (November–December 1996): 9–11.

Smith, Marilyn. "Television Violence and Behavior: A Research Summary," *Emergency Librarian* 24 (November/December 1996): 34–36.

Smith, Thomas M. "The Condition of Education" (ERIC document ED 371 491, 1994) 136.

Strong, Richard, H. Silver, and A. Robinson."What Do Students Want (and What Really Motivates Them)? *Educational Leadership* 53 (September 1995): 8–12.

Sykes, Charles. *A Nation of Victims; The Decay of the American* Character (New York: St. Martin's Press, 1992).

Times Mirror Center for the People and the Press. *Technology in the American Household: Americans Going Online . . . Explosive Growth, Uncertain Destinations* (Washington, D.C.: Times Mirror Center, 1995).

Chapter 2

Curriculum and Instruction

This chapter

- describes major trends in curriculum and instruction
- identifies how the library media specialist fits into the curriculum development process
- identifies action strategies for working within the context of curriculum

CURRICULUM

Curriculum can be considered as the substance of the experiences teachers intend for students to have in school—the content and the experiences of interacting with that content. Changes in curriculum and instruction are occurring today, gradually in some schools and dramatically in others. Many of these changes offer excellent opportunities to integrate the library media program. Curriculum changes affect both instructional content and processes. Current trends in curriculum that have particular impact on library media programs include emergence of the cognitive theory of constructivism; emphasis on higher-order thinking skills; integrated disciplines; development of graduation standards; acknowledgment of learning's social nature; and recognition of a variety of learning styles.

Constructivism

Guiding students to construct a working knowledge of social studies content is a central idea in "A Vision of Powerful Teaching and Learning in the Social Studies: Building Social Understanding and Civic Efficacy (National Council for Social Studies, 1994). Stoddart (1992) describes the theory of constructivism as follows:

> We believe that learners construct meaning through personal and social experiences; they develop theories about how the world works. We believe they already possess knowledge and beliefs about the content to be learned, so the teaching-learning process involves not simply adding facts or skills but rather developing a new and often very different conceptual perspective through which they understand subject matter. Learning often means changing beliefs, and show-and-tell methods are rarely sufficient to accomplish this (p. 26).

Constructivism pervades other content areas besides social sciences; mathematics and science educators particularly tend to be committed to constructivism where students work with manipulatives and perform hands-on experiments to create their own understanding of numeracy and scientific phenomena.

In a library media center, how do students attack a meaningful information process task? They pose a question, locate information, extract relevant information, and *construct* a meaningful response to the posed question. Information processing is a constructive task, *if* students begin with posing a researchable question. For example, if students are challenged to envision what the major social issues of the twenty-first century will be, they might begin by collecting demographic data such as population projections for the next 50 years. Using these data, they begin to relate population projections to other projections, such as land use trends. Likewise, they might investigate scientific advancements in medicine, transportation, or energy. Once these data are collected and discussed, students can begin to *construct* a picture of the future and envision social problems that may result from these physical, social, and scientific trends. On a much simpler scale, young children can construct their own understanding of community by investigating examples of communities around the world, and developing some generalizations about what those various communities have in common. They then construct for themselves the concept of community. Such constructive tasks are substantially different from writing a report about a country or a historical event. Library media specialists must be creative in designing such learning experiences with teachers so that they challenge students to solve problems or make decisions. They must also teach the necessary skills to locate, analyze, evaluate, and synthesize information.

Higher-Order Thinking Skills

National education associations are creating standards to describe instructional content and processes. For example, in the national social studies standards, exemplary programs are described in various dimensions (National Council for Social Studies, 1994, p. 160). One dimension focuses on encouraging students to apply specific thinking skills:

- acquiring, organizing, interpreting, and communicating information
- processing data in order to investigate questions, develop knowledge, and draw conclusions
- generating and assessing alternative approaches to problems, and making decisions that are both well informed and justified according to democratic principles
- interacting with others in empathetic and responsible ways

Library media specialists want students to apply these processes as they work with information.

Integrated Disciplines

Educators recognize the problem of isolating disciplines. Teachers continue to struggle to relate learning from one discipline to another. Teachers have a certain degree of "tunnel vision" because they tend to be specialized either by discipline or by grade level. The library media specialist is familiar with the content and processes of various disciplines and therefore sits in a strategic position to help facilitate cross-disciplinary work. When a social studies teacher suggests that students do a project involving data analysis, the library media specialist may be the one person aware that those same students are also working at charting and graphing data to recognize and display patterns in mathematics. Bringing these two disciplines together makes the students' work more meaningful in both areas. Or, when a French teacher asks students to prepare a presentation about the culture of a French-speaking country, the library media specialist may be the bridge to the language arts teacher who is teaching public speaking. Learning becomes meaningful when students apply skills and knowledge from one discipline to another. The library media specialist can be a catalyst for integrated learning.

Graduation Standards

Some states have established academic standards for high school graduation. One effect of such mandated standards is that they become the focus for curriculum. One such example is the set of standards issued by the Minnesota Department of Children, Families and Learning (1997). The Minnesota standards include ten "areas of learning":

- Read, view, and listen to complex information in the English language.
- Write and speak effectively in the English language.
- Use and interpret the arts.
- Solve problems by applying mathematics.
- Conduct research and communicate findings.
- Understand and apply scientific concepts.
- Understand interactions between people and cultures.
- Use information to make decisions.
- Manage resources for a household, community, or government.
- Communicate in another language. (optional)

For each area there are descriptions of activities to help students develop the skills and knowledge needed to be successful. Such state mandates come from a societal demand for accountability in schools; business entities are demanding of legislatures that schools graduate people prepared for the work force. Accompanying this demand for accountability is a cynicism about traditional transcripts and a desire to replace the list of courses with demonstration of skills and knowledge attained. These pressures are coming to bear on schools seeking to provide a definition of what a high school diploma represents.

The implications for such graduation standards for the library media program call for both leadership and collaboration. Library media professionals must provide leadership to ensure that information processes are well represented in graduation standards. It is equally important that they collaborate with teachers in the design of instruction based on graduation standards to ensure that information process skills are a part of that instruction. If the intent of graduation standards is to prepare students for the work world, certainly the ability to access, evaluate, and use information will be crucial.

Social Nature of Learning

With the adoption of workplace teams, business and industry have focused the nation's attention on the importance of cooperation among workers. Likewise, educators recognize that students must learn to work together, to accept group roles and responsibilities, and to learn to organize themselves to accomplish tasks as a team. The library media specialist fosters this team approach by making the library media center a workplace for groups. The library media center's physical arrangement, the ambiance, and the tolerance for productive noise are all physical contributors to learning as a social activity. The library media specialist can collaborate with teachers to design tasks that lend themselves to teamwork. This means providing students with open-ended questions, rather than convergent tasks where students are simply seeking a "right" answer. Cooperative work among groups of students improves when teachers facilitate group cohesiveness, provide clear role expectations, and emphasize accountability (Furtwengler, 1992). When both the library media specialist and the teacher work as facilitators, these social processes can be monitored and improved.

Learning Styles

Learning styles fall into five categories:

- environmental (e.g., sound, light, temperature)
- emotional (e.g., persistence, structure)
- sociological (e.g., group, alone)
- physiological (e.g., listening, touching, mobility)
- psychological (Griggs & Dunn, 1996).

While several models describe various learning styles, one that is highly relevant to schools is that of Gregorc (1982). He characterized four psychological learning styles which can be summarized briefly:

- *Concrete Sequential* learners are typically practical and prefer instruction that is ordered, practical, detailed, and exact and that includes clear directions. They prefer an orderly, quiet environment; they like to know the specifications for successful work, and they like to apply ideas in a practical hands-on way.
- *Concrete Random* learners are typically inquisitive and independent and prefer instruction that offers options, is open-ended, and that might include experimentation, problem-solving, and creating products. They are self-directed and have a high degree of curiosity.
- *Abstract Sequential* learners are typically intellectual and prefer the abstract world of thoughts and symbols, reading, working alone, and doing independent research. They think in a structured way, they are analytical, and they work best when they have references and expert sources close at hand.
- *Abstract Random* learners are typically sensitive and subjective and prefer instruction that might include multimedia, thematic approaches, role play, or peer group work. They like personal attention and support and they prefer a noncompetitive atmosphere.

Research indicates that students whose learning styles are accommodated would be expected to achieve 75 percent of a standard deviation higher than students whose learning style has not been accommodated (Dunn et al., 1995). It is impractical, or maybe impossible, to tailor all learning experiences to match each child's learning style. Yet library media specialists can raise awareness of the variations among children and suggest alternatives for teaching and learning so that various styles are accommodated. An obvious example is alternative media for students to use in presenting their work; the library media specialist can offer support and teach students to use video, multimedia, still photography, desktop publishing, and other presentation media. Likewise, the library media specialist can work toward making information resources available in various formats as well.

THE LIBRARY MEDIA SPECIALIST'S EXPERTISE

Uniqueness

The unique perspective of the library media specialist can contribute to curriculum. A library media specialist knows the curriculum content and the teaching strategies in each classroom. The principal and the guidance counselor are also in touch with each teacher. However, their relationships to classrooms usually focus on managerial issues or individual students' personal concerns. The library media specialist's connection with each teacher tends to focus on what is being taught, with what, and how. Such a relationship may place the library media specialist in the position of knowing more than any other professional in the building about the total curriculum. Such knowledge can then be valuable for curriculum articulation.

The library media specialist also has special expertise in both information and instructional technology. Parents and administrators pressure teachers to incorporate technology into their classrooms. For some, this is naturally easy. But for many, technology is intimidating or at least bothersome. Library media specialists guide decisions about meaningful technology use so that children's experiences with technology help them reach high cognitive levels. The library media specialist can also provide teacher in-service training on new technologies, can team-teach in order to reduce teacher anxiety, and can provide facilities and assist students.

Coaching

Library media specialists must apply the questioning skills they learned as reference interviewers to their consulting work with teachers. A reference librarian seeks as much information as necessary in order to provide the client with exactly the needed information. The reference questioning strategy proceeds from identifying the topic to refining the question, analyzing the question to formulate a search strategy, and evaluating the information found to establish that it meets the client's need. A good reference interview accomplishes two objectives. The first "intended" objective is that the librarian understands and subsequently meets the actual information need of the client; the second, perhaps not intentional, is to clarify for the client what he or she is actually seeking. Working with teachers, library media specialists apply similar strategies, with similar results. The questioning strategy of the library media specialist is similar to the strategy, described by Costa, of cognitive coaching (Costa & Garmston, 1994).

In a case study of the library media specialist's consulting role, coaching was identified as one important way for the library media specialist to work with teachers (van Deusen, 1996). In one example from this case, a teacher approached the library media specialist about teaching the *Reader's Guide to Periodical Literature*. Through the reference interview, the library media specialist pursued what the teacher really wanted children to learn. Her questioning revealed that the teacher wanted to improve children's skill in reading nonfiction. The library media specialist offered to locate articles, so that the children spent their time on the reading skills that the teacher wanted to address; she and the teacher team-taught strategies for extracting information from articles. Interaction with the library media specialist caused the teacher to refocus the lesson from using an index to developing strategies for reading nonfiction.

The coaching model emphasizes the importance of reflection on teaching and learning. The coach uses questioning to help the teacher process information that will lead to decisions or future teaching. The model is not that of an expert providing direction to the teacher, but rather of a colleague encouraging another's thought and reflection. Although in this case the library media specialist had opinions about teaching the *Reader's Guide,* rather than declare her position, she raised relevant questions so that the decision was collaborative. Those questions followed a pattern that proceeded from "What is your lesson about?" (describing) to "What exactly will the students be doing?" (translating) to "What will be the order of activities in the unit?" (sequencing) to "How will you know that students have been successful?" (operationalizing criteria). These are similar to the questions identified in Costa's coaching model. By posing such questions, the library media specialist encourages teachers to think through plans, clarify them for themselves, and communicate them to the library media specialist who can then assist in their implementation.

CONCLUSION

Participation in curriculum involves not only being a part of the planning process, but also being part of the implementation. The examples described in this chapter have some common features. Most important, in each case the library media specialist is working with teachers—not working in isolation. Also, in each case the expertise that the library media specialist offers is different from the classroom teacher's—it is the expertise of a specialist. Finally, in each case the library media specialist is taking initiative—not merely responding to a specific request by providing materials.

The worst-case scenario is for the library media specialist to be included in curriculum planning meetings, but to fail to contribute in unique and useful ways. Being on committees is not enough—the challenge is to improve instruction. The question for every library media specialist after every curriculum planning meeting—and after every interchange about curriculum—must be, "In what ways did my contribution improve the content and delivery of the curriculum?"

ACTION STRATEGIES

Learning and Teaching

- Demonstrate interest in what teachers are teaching.
    1. Share interesting curriculum-oriented articles with staff, either one-on-one or at staff meetings.
    2. Join, encourage, or initiate study groups on cross-disciplinary study topics, such as multiage grouping, authentic assessment, block scheduling, or instructional technology.
    3. Attend parent information meetings in your school when teachers are describing curriculum or discussing curricular issues.

- Maintain current awareness of new software and hardware.
    1. Help teachers set criteria for selecting appropriate ways to use technology, so that technology is used as a tool for higher-order thinking—analysis, synthesis, and evaluation—rather than for simple recall.
    2. Offer in-service sessions for teachers on instructional technology uses.
    3. Encourage software preview; do "buddy" software previews with teachers.
    4. Offer to team-teach with new technologies the first time a teacher tries something new, to reduce the anxiety about the technology.

- Develop a written information skills process curriculum.
    1. Share the curriculum with all teachers.
    2. Together with teachers identify the units into which the information skills process curriculum will be infused.

3. Ensure that no part of the curriculum is addressed only once; students need many opportunities to practice applying information strategies.

Information Access and Delivery

- Participate in curriculum development projects. Expect the principal to make you a part of the team, and say so.
    1. Provide literature searches in the topics of interest.
    2. Locate instructional materials to consider.
    3. Design activities for students.
    4. Exploit your knowledge of children's literature to help teachers identify specific titles to develop truly thematic, not topical, literature units.
    5. Design student projects to be used in assessment.
    6. Design lessons to infuse information skills into the content.
    7. Provide information about what is taught at other grade levels or in other disciplines.

Program Administration

- Maintain current awareness of trends in the content areas.
    1. Read (or at least skim) articles (that is, not just materials reviews) in journals from curriculum areas, such as:
        Social Education
        Social Studies and the Young Learner
        English Journal
        Language Arts
        The Reading Teacher
        Science and Children
        Teaching Children Mathematics
        Mathematics Teaching in the Middle School
        Educational Leadership
    2. Attend a professional conference outside the library media area.
    3. Purchase and become familiar with national standards and guidelines from various disciplines.

- Participate in long-range curriculum planning and evaluation.

REFERENCES

Costa, Arthur and Robert Garmston. *Cognitive Coaching: A Foundation for Renaissance Schools* (Norwood, Mass.: Christopher-Gordon, 1994).

Dunn, Rita et al. "A Meta-Analytical Validation of the Dunn and Dunn Learning Style Model," *Journal of Educational Research* 88 (July/August 1995): 353–361.

Furtwengler, Carol B. "How to Observe Cooperative Learning Classrooms," *Educational Leadership* 49 (April 1992): 59–62.

Gregorc, Anthony F. *An Adult's Guide to Style* (Maynard, Mass.: Gabriel Systems, 1982).

Griggs, Shirley and Rita Dunn. "Learning Styles of Asian American Adolescents," *Emergency Librarian* 24 (September/October 1996): 8–13.

Minnesota Department of Children, Families and Learning. "Minnesota Children: Graduation Standards." Available: http://children.state.mn.us/grad/rule.htm [June 2, 1997] .

National Council for Social Studies Task Force on Standards for Teaching and Learning in the Social Studies. "A Vision of Powerful Teaching and Learning in the Social Studies: Building Social Understanding and Civic Efficacy," in *Expectations of Excellence; Curriculum Standards for Social Studies* (Washington, D.C.: National Council for the Social Studies, 1994), 157–177.

Stoddart, T. "Commentary: Fostering Coherence Between Constructivism on Campus and Conventional Practice in Schools," *The Holmes Group Forum* 6, no. 2 (1992): 26–28.

van Deusen, Jean Donham. "The School Library Media Specialist as a Member of the Teaching Team: 'Insider' and 'Outsider,'" *Journal of Curriculum and Supervision* 11 (Spring 1996): 229–248.

Chapter 3

The Principal

This chapter

- describes the role of the principal as leader and manager
- relates the principal's role to the library media specialist's roles
- describes the impact of the principal on the library media program
- describes the effect of shared decision making
- identifies action strategies for working with the principal

PRINCIPAL AS LEADER AND MANAGER

The school principal experiences a constant tension between two distinct expectations: to be a leader and to be a manager. One of these roles might be characterized as an initiating role and the other as a responsive role. A considerable body of research confirms this role ambiguity (Manasse, 1985). This research suggests that principals are often uncertain why they were hired. Furthermore, there is often a lack of agreement among their staff members, the parents, and their superintendents about role expectations. The principal as instructional leader calls for a principal to set a vision for the school and to be engaged in the design of the instructional program. As school manager, the principal attends to the organization, climate, schedule, and administration so that the organization will run smoothly. While these two roles are not necessarily in conflict with one another, each role takes substantial time, knowledge, and skill. It is unlikely that a principal can choose to be only a manager or only a leader; rather, these roles might be seen as opposite ends of a continuum and each principal will function at some point along that continuum.

Leithwood (1994) describes behaviors of principals as leaders. Guiding the school in developing and communicating a vision is perhaps the most prominent activity of a leading principal. By helping teachers, parents, and students perceive and maintain that vision, the principal provides a backdrop for decision making. Setting expectations is another aspect of leadership. School leadership also involves providing intellectual stimulation by encouraging staff to try new practices and to share ideas with colleagues, and by modeling good professional practice.

What does the principal do as manager? Establishing a climate conducive to learning is a crucial responsibility of the principal. Creating clear and consistent school rules and policies tends to improve the general disciplinary climate of the school and contributes to improved staff and student morale (Bryk, Lee, & Smith, 1989). The managerial role also includes the administration of resources: budget, time, and staff. Both leadership and management responsibilities are important for an effective school. The difficulty that principals face is ensuring that the appropriate responsibilities are addressed at the appropriate times.

Library media specialists face a similar dilemma in determining how best to use time. There is a tension between the operational demands and the educational demands of the library media center. And, just as the balance between leader and manager is a key to success for the principal, so is the balance between two competing sets of priorities for the library media specialist. Parallel lists of leader and manager tasks for both the principal and library media specialist are shown in Figure 3.1.

By acknowledging that the principal and the library media specialist struggle with the same tension between roles, the library media specialist can empathize with that situation and can enter into dialogue with the principal, conscious of whether the topic at hand deals with management or leadership.

The principal is a decision maker, whether the decisions are related to instructional leadership or to school management. The decisions principals make as managers are influenced by their activity as leaders. The vision for the school can lead the principal to commit resources to further that vision. If a principal envisions a school characterized by teamwork, then such a vision will undoubtedly influence decisions about hiring; it might also influence decisions about scheduling or purchasing materials. In other words, principals make decisions within a framework that is created out of their leadership.

FIGURE 3.1
Comparison of Dual Roles

Principal	Library Media Specialist
Leader	**Leader**
Goal setting	Goal setting
Modeling	Teaching
Decision making	Collaborating with teachers
Coaching	Providing staff development
Interacting with parents about school vision	Communicating with teachers, administrators, and parents about the library media program
Monitoring programs	Monitoring programs
Manager	**Manager**
Scheduling	Scheduling
Supervising	Supervising
Purchasing	Purchasing
Maintaining the physical plant	Maintaining the facility
Writing policies	Writing policies
Responding to parental concerns	Troubleshooting

Leithwood (1994) describes a problem-solving model that characterizes the influences on decision making in leaders. The model identifies mental activity that can be classified as follows:

- *problem interpretation*: What is the nature of the problem?
- *goals*: What relatively immediate purposes need to be met in response to the problem?
- *constraints*: What barriers or obstacles must be overcome?
- *solution processes*: What does the leader do to solve the problem?
- *principles/values:* What long-term purposes, operating principles, values, and assumptions guide the leader's thinking?
- *affect*: What are the leader's feelings, mood, and sense of self-confidence?

Awareness of this problem-solving model provides an important perspective for the library media specialist. By anticipating each aspect of the problem-solving process, the library media specialist can be prepared to bring to the principal not only problems, but also potential solutions. In addition, the library media specialist can anticipate what information will help the principal progress through the problem-solving process more efficiently. For example, realizing that constraints will enter into the solution, the library media specialist needs to be ready with solutions for overcoming them.

Manasse (1985) summarizes several portrayals of the principal's work day as fragmented days composed of many short, unplanned verbal interactions consisting of 50 to over 100 separate events, and as many as 400 separate interactions. Consider a stream of events that includes dealing with a potential child-abuse situation, a clogged toilet, a teacher in need of more mathematics textbooks, a parent seeking advice about home-schooling his child, a student sent in with chewing tobacco in his pocket . . . all unrelated events requiring prompt attention. This is the school principal's day. Manasse also alludes to studies indicating that secondary school principals have been found to spend relatively more of their time in scheduled meetings than elementary school principals. Still, the bombardment of unrelated problems is a reality for all principals.

**AN EXAMPLE OF ENHANCEMENT IN ACTION:
FURTHERING THE PRINCIPAL'S VISION**

Assume that a principal has a vision for the school to be perceived as a central feature of the community it serves. Likely
goals would be involving parents in the school, increasing communication about the goals of the school, making the community feel at home in the school. The library media specialist wants
students to increase their use of information technologies. By
fitting the library media goal into the community vision of the
principal, an alliance occurs that helps to further both goals.
The library media specialist suggests offering evening classes
for parents to teach them about CD-ROM products (encyclopedias and other resources). It may be that parents will be afraid
to attend and display their naïveté about technology. To address that potential constraint, the library media specialist proposes to make the promotion as nonthreatening as possible to
appeal to persons who are intimidated or unfamiliar with electronic resources. A variety of "community nights" in the school's
library media center target various populations (such as senior
citizens, parents of young children, persons considering purchase of a new computer, and persons who have never used a
computer) depending on local demographics.

RELATING THE PRINCIPAL'S ROLE TO THE SCHOOL LIBRARY MEDIA PROGRAM

In a study by Yetter (1994), one finding was that crucial to the success of
a library media program is the library media specialist's leadership ability, including the capacity to envision a resource-based process and connect it to the principal's agenda for restructuring. By recognizing the
nature of the principal's work, the library media specialist can learn to
interact with the principal to marry their goals. Consider first the principal as leader. What is the principal's vision for the school and how does
the library media program facilitate bringing that vision into reality?

In the example related in the "Enhancement in Action" box, the library media specialist has used the vision of the principal to engender
community support for a component of the library media program. By
fitting the library media program's agenda to that of the principal, the

library media specialist communicates important messages and indicates an alliance with the principal. In the school library media profession it is common to read of the loneliness of the library media specialist as one-of-a-kind in the school. This same aloneness characterizes the principal. The two are a natural team since both must be concerned with all teachers and students in the school. Both share an across-grade-levels and across-disciplines view of the school. But to make the alliance work, it is important for the library media specialist to see the principal's vision as the guiding light for the school. While language such as "The library media center is the hub of the school" is common in advocacy literature, the reality is that the library media center is a comprehensive support system but it is not the driving force of the school's program. That driving force is the mission statement, which grows out of a vision for the school. The library media specialist thus does well to align his or her program explicitly with the school's mission.

Another message sent when the library media specialist aligns the library media program with the principal's vision is that the library media program itself is part of the implementation of the vision. Making the role of the library media program explicit and highly visible is crucial to gaining support for successful library media programming. In the example, opening up the library media center to the community for this specific purpose may garner support from the community for technology expenditures. More important, however, it can engender parental support for the instructional work that the library media program represents in teaching students to be effective users of electronic information resources. When the home supports the school's instructional efforts, the ultimate winners are the students.

The principal also makes decisions as a manager, and the library media specialist hopes that these decisions will benefit the library media program. Again, it is important to consider how the concerns for the library media program can align with the management concerns of the principal. Emphasizing these common concerns can help the library media specialist to take a more active role in the decision-making process.

Why are budget talks often problematic? The principal's perception of budget allocation is likely to be different from that of the library media specialist. The principal perceives budgeting as addressing many competing demands and one of apportioning limited resources. It is again likely that the vision the principal has for the school will influence budget allocation. So, identifying the place of the library media program in the school vision is important in addressing budget issues. If a part of

**AN EXAMPLE OF ENHANCEMENT IN ACTION:
TALKING ABOUT THE BUDGET**

Budget is often a point of contention for the library media specialist and the principal. A conventional approach to budget by library media specialists is to examine the collection, determine what the needs are, and approach the principal for dollars to meet those needs. The needs analysis may be done via a collection map in which the library media specialist assesses the age and quality of materials by category or topic, compares those findings to the demands made on the collection via a curriculum map, and then determines a dollar amount needed to resolve the discrepancy between an existing and ideal collection of materials. The development of collection maps is indeed important; however, these data must be related to the principal so as to fall within his/her context for decision making. Consider the context of the decision making by looking at Leithwood's (1994) problem-solving model.

the principal's vision for the school is an integrated curriculum, then the presentation of library media collection needs should be aligned with that vision. The collection map should highlight the relationship between the status of the collection and the demands of curriculum priorities in the school. How will the enhancement of the collection help teachers move along toward integrating mathematics and science instruction, for example? What specific types of materials will we purchase to further this goal? Who will participate in the decision about what to buy? Will teachers who are adopting integrated curriculum participate in decision making? Can the library media program be a catalyst for integration? The principal will likely be concerned with constraints as well. Often, money is allocated to teachers on a classroom-by-classroom or departmental basis so that individual teachers can buy items exclusively for their classrooms or departments. If the library media specialist wants the principal to increase the collection budget, the money has to be taken from some other source; classroom and departmental allocations might be a possible source, if the library media specialist and the principal can work together to assure teachers of their continued participation in purchasing, but purchasing for a central collection rather than an exclusive collection.

Strategizing how to overcome the obstacles is part of the decision-making process; the library media specialist must be ready to cooperate with the principal in overcoming obstacles. The principal follows some internal assumptions, principles, and values in making decisions. By careful observation, the library media specialist can learn what those values are and can consider them in requests. And, finally, the affective concerns of mood and assuredness on the part of the principal are important concerns of the library media specialist seeking decisions.

Besides considering the decision-making process of the principal, the library media specialist must also keep in mind the nature of the principal's day. The characterization of the day as a bombardment of as many as 400 separate interactions stands as a reminder that getting the undivided attention of the principal for extended development of ideas requires some advance notice and planning. Sensitivity to the nature of the principal's work can help the library media specialist work as a teammate rather than as one more interruption.

Considering the time constraints of the principal, the library media specialist does well to provide critical information efficiently. Monthly reporting on the use of the library media center and its resources is one solution. Good management calls for data-based decisions, and only the library media specialist has the data to portray what the activity of the library media center is. Conventional statistical data—for example, circulation statistics, or facilities usage counts as shown in Figure 3.2—are useful.

Even more helpful, however, are reports that succinctly describe the activity of the library media program to demonstrate its relationship to classroom teaching. The report in Figure 3.3 is an example of such a descriptive report. It shows what classes in the library media center required direct teaching by the library media specialist. A brief description of the activity shows the curriculum connection. The information skills column lists the skill areas taught. The levels of instructional support provide a taxonomy of collaboration between the teacher and the library media specialist. This single page conveys considerable information about the nature, as well as the amount, of teaching and learning activity occurring in the library media center.

While principals may simply file this document away, if the library media specialist then meets even annually with the principal to review the needs for resources or staffing or space, the data are available and can be used effectively and efficiently to help characterize the nature of the needs. Also, in the face of any question from parent, central office

FIGURE 3.2
Monthly Statistics Report to Principal

High School Library Media Center
February Statistics

Books and Print Materials Circulated	3,189	
Nonprint materials circulated	75	
Total Circulation	3,264	

Students using computer lab

268	classes scheduled
3,210	from classes
1,560	study hall/open hours
4,770	total
251	**students per day average**

Students using library media center

204	classes scheduled
3,710	from classes
6,575	study hall/open hours
10,285	total
541.5	**students per day average**

Daily Use of LMC and Computer Lab

Total classes scheduled	472
Average classes per day in 7 available periods per day	24.8

FIGURE 3.3
Instructional Support Monthly Data Summary

This report summarizes support to teachers in preparation for classes. It stresses those areas where the media program enables resource-based teaching, and the areas of the information skills curriculum addressed.

Key to levels of instructional support:
1. Gathering materials in response to teacher requests
2. Working with students on a small-group or individual basis during a teacher-planned activity
3. Teaching classes in support of a teacher-planned activity
4. Sharing equal responsibility with the teacher for planning and delivering instruction

Keys to areas of information skills curriculum:
1. Task definition
2. Information-seeking strategies
3. Location and access
4. Use of information
5. Creation and communication
6. Evaluation and self-assessment

Date	Teacher	Periods	Level	Activities	Info. Skills
April 1,2	Cochran	1,2	2	English 11 Research papers	3,4
April 1,3,5	Smith	4,5	4	English 9 Shakespeare and his times	2,3,4,5
April 1	Garden	5,6,7	2	Adv. Biology Honors Research	3
April 1,4	Roshek	1,2,3,5,6	2	European History Research	3
April 2,3,4,5, 8, 9, 10, 11, 12, 15	Warner	7	3	Futures Careers research	3,4,5
April 4,5,8	Cooper	3	3	Environmental Analysis Research	3,4
April 4,5,8	Phipps	1,3,6	3	US Lit Biographies	2,3

FIGURE 3.3 (Cont.)

Date	Name			Description	
April 5,10,12,15,17	Brown	3,4,6,7	2	Humanities Decades research	3
April 15	Brack	1,5,7	4	US Lit Decades research	3,4,5
April 15	Finken	1,3,4	3	China/Japan Fiction book selection	3
April 16,17, 18,19	Finken	6,7	3	Global Studies Change agent research	2,3,4
April 17,18	Brothers	5	3	Personal history collages	3
April 18,19, 22	Phipps	1,3,6	2	US Lit research	3
April 19	Castor	1,3,6,7	3	English 10 Research	3
April 22,23	Brown	3,4,6,7	2	Humanities	3
April 23,24, 25,26	Brown	2	3	English 10 Honors Research	3,4,5
April 24	Roshek	1,2,3,5,6	2	European History Research post WW II	3,4
April 24,25	Mitchell	4	2	English 10 Research	3
April 24,25,26	Becker	7	2	Panel discussion research	3,4
April 24,25	Finken	6,7	3	Global Studies Change agent research	3,4
April 26,29,30	Cohn	6	2	Panel discussion research	3,4
April 29, 30	Phipps	1,3,6	2	US Lit research	3,4

administrator, or teacher, the principal has available documentation to characterize the library media program.

IMPACT OF THE PRINCIPAL ON THE SCHOOL LIBRARY MEDIA PROGRAM

Both the leadership and management roles of the principal govern the potential for the success of the library media program. At the leadership end of the continuum, it is important for the principal to understand the library media program's potential to advance the vision and mission of the school. Yet studies suggest that principals frequently have little knowledge of that potential. Wilson and colleagues (1993) surveyed 1,000 principals and 1,000 library media specialists to measure their level of expertise about library media programming. In that study, over 68 percent of the principals responding felt that they were not adequately trained in the area of school library media programming and over 78 percent indicated that they should have more training. This naïveté is cause for concern. It seems difficult to imagine that a principal can effectively hire personnel for a library media program without an understanding of the program's role and relationship to the overall school program. Likewise, performance evaluation of library media specialists cannot be effective without fundamental knowledge about library media programming. The intent of evaluation is improvement of professional practice, yet such guidance cannot occur without awareness of what constitutes effective practice. Allocation of funds is the principal's decision. Knowledge of the potential impact the library media program offers can improve principal support for its essential materials and equipment.

Perhaps the greatest impact the principal can have is on integrating the library media program into the school program. A study of the occurrence of consulting between library media specialists and classroom teachers revealed the influence of the principal's expectations (van Deusen & Tallman, 1994). In that study library media specialists reported whether they perceived that their principals held expectations for them to collaborate with teachers. Library media specialists who perceived that their principals expected them to collaborate with classroom teachers reported significantly more instances of consultative work with teachers than those whose principals were not perceived as holding that expectation. In the same study, library media specialists reported the occurrences of their teaching information skills *in association with* classroom instruction. Again, the principal's expectation that such collaboration occur made a significant positive difference in the amount of consultation done by the library media specialist. Likewise, Campbell (1994) found that support from the principal is essential for library media programs to succeed regardless of the professional level of the library media specialist.

SHARED DECISION MAKING

While principals play a major role in shaping school decisions, the movement toward shared decision making is affecting the ways in which principals lead. The shared-decision-making movement is founded on certain assumptions. One assumption is that when those who are affected by a decision share ownership of the decision, their commitment is greater. Another assumption is that better decisions result from the collaboration—a benefit of diverse interests and perspectives. Another expectation is that shared decision making will serve to unify the participants so that they cooperate.

This decision-making culture demands special skills on the part of the principal. Team building, conflict identification and resolution, consensus building, communication, persuasion, and diplomacy are important skill areas for a principal in a shared-decision-making environment. Principals are still expected to have a vision for the school, but the implementation of that vision depends on the principal's ability to promote ownership of the vision among all the stakeholders of the school. Reconciling the principal's authority with staff participation poses a leadership challenge to principals (Broadwell, 1996). The principal becomes a participant in decision making, functioning not as the decision maker, but as facilitator, advisor, and executive officer (Heath & Vik, 1996). The principal must work as a facilitator and a guide; actively listen to the ideas of others and incorporate those new ideas into the assumptions, principles, and values already ingrained; and keep "all eyes on the prize," that is, maintain the vision for the school.

Shared decision making increases the complexity for the library media specialist as well. Whereas in a hierarchical setting the library media specialist must work to align the library media program with the intentions of one person, the principal, in the shared-decision-making environment, that alignment must be evident to many more participants.

AN EXAMPLE OF ENHANCEMENT IN ACTION:
SHARED DECISION MAKING

Consider a setting in which a library media specialist perceives that students are not reading enough and that one possible solution is to establish a sustained silent reading time throughout the school. The library media specialist takes this idea to the decision-making team which includes various teachers, other specialists and the principal. One approach is for the principal to state the problem (too little reading among students) and then state the potential solution (give students reading time every day for the last 15 minutes of the school day). A second approach is to state the problem and offer alternative solutions such as, "We could agree to a silent reading time for the whole school or we could agree that students would all get 15 minutes of sustained silent reading during their language arts class each day." Another approach is to state the problem and ask for potential solutions, allowing the group to propose possible solutions. Which approach will engender the most ownership? Which approach will most likely result in implementation? Will the problem—too little independent reading—be solved?

Clear, concise communication, active listening, and big-picture thinking are important not only for the principal but also for the library media specialist. Taking into account the points of view of the various stakeholders is an important initial step in a shared-decision-making environment.

CONCLUSION

Some topics will be more difficult than others in a shared-decision-making environment, depending on the stakes. Budget allocations will require clear communication of the benefits to be accrued by all when dollars are allocated to any one program. Likewise, scheduling issues can carry high stakes since these decisions affect the nature of the workday for teachers and have student-management implications as well. However, working in this kind of decision-making environment has many of the same requirements as alignment with the principal; consider the perspective of others and determine how the library media program can be aligned with the needs and wants of other programs within the school. The critical issue is to keep the mission and vision clearly in view—an important responsibility of the principal and the library media specialist.

ACTION STRATEGIES

Information Access and Delivery

- Help the principal maintain current awareness of innovations, such as new technologies for instruction or management. E-mail can be useful.
- Arrange with the principal for opportunities to appear as a "regular" on staff meeting agendas and use the time well—to share briefly information that relates directly to concerns of teachers.

Program Administration

- Educate the principal to the role of the library media specialist. Remember what the workday of the principal is; providing the principal with an unsolicited deluge of articles and books to read is not the best approach. Instead, explain your work to the principal in terms of your profession; use terms from the American Association of School Librarians/Association for Educational Communications and Technologies (AASL/AECT) guidelines (1988, 1998) (such as "instructional partner" and "teacher") to identify your roles; make reference to collection maps as a professional tool for describing the state of the collection and show how your professional skills relate to those of the teacher and the principal. Consider the principal's style when deciding whether to encourage drop-in visits or make formal invitations.
- Make opportunities for meaningful communication with the principal. Given the nature of the principal's day, it makes sense to schedule a weekly or monthly 30-minute session with the principal to review issues related to the library media program. These sessions must not be complaint sessions, but productive meetings of give-and-take, advice seeking, brainstorming, and activity reporting. Provide documentation that shows what is occurring in the library media center. Use e-mail for updates, but don't overload the principal's mailbox.

- Be attuned to the vision the principal holds for the school and seek ways to communicate the relationship of the library media program to that vision.
- Help make the principal and the school "look good" by showcasing the library media center to constituents—parents, community members, school board members, and school district officials.

REFERENCES

American Association of School Librarians/Association for Educational Communications and Technology. *Information Power: Building Partnerships for Learning* (Chicago, Washington: AASL/AECT, 1998).

Broadwell, Don. "Situational Leadership and the Educator of the '90s," *Emergency Librarian* 23 (January/February 1996): 21–27.

Bryk, A. S., V. Lee, and J. Smith. "High School Organization and Its Effects on Teachers and Students: An Interpretative Summary of the Research" (paper presented at the conference "Choice and Control in American Education," University of Wisconsin–Madison, May 1989).

Campbell, Barbara. "High School Principal Roles and Implementation Themes for Mainstreaming Information Literacy Instruction" (Ph. D. diss., University of Connecticut, 1994).

Heath, Jay and Phil Vik. "School Site Councils: Building Communities of Leaders," *Principal* 75 (January 1996): 25, 28.

Leithwood, Kenneth. "Leadership for School Restructuring," *Educational Administration Quarterly* 30 (November 1994): 498–518.

Manasse, A. Lorri. "Improving Conditions for Principal Effectiveness: Policy Implications of Research," *The Elementary School Journal* 85 (January 1985): 439–463.

van Deusen, Jean Donham and J. Tallman. "The Impact of Scheduling on Curriculum Consultation and Information Skills Instruction," *School Library Media Quarterly* 23 (Fall 1994): 17–25.

Wilson, Patricia, M. Blake, and J. Lyders. "A Study and a Plan for Partnership," *Emergency Librarian* 21 (September/October 1993): 19–24.

Yetter, Cathleen. "Resource-Based Learning in the Information Age School: The Intersection of Roles and Relationships of the School Library Media Specialist, Teachers, and Principals" (Ed. D. diss., Seattle University, 1994).

Chapter 4

The School District

This chapter

- describes the school district's influence on the school library media program
- considers site-based decision making and centralized decision making
- identifies specific contributions that a library media specialist can make to district planning and policy
- identifies action strategies for working within the school district context

School districts vary in size, number of schools, and number of students. Some districts cover expansive countywide areas, and others govern a single K–12 school. Some districts have an extensive hierarchy of central-office administrators, specialists, and support staff, while others have a single chief officer and a small support staff. Some districts have a library media coordinator or director responsible for library media leadership, while others assign a central office administrator oversight for the library media program (for example, a curriculum director or an assistant superintendent), and many have no central office representative for the library media program at all. In each setting, the position responsible for relating the library media program to the district's direction and policy varies, and in many small districts, it is the building-level library media specialist. Whoever acts as liaison between the central decision-making authority of the district and the school library media program must contend with four major organizational issues: funding, personnel, curriculum, and technology.

FUNDING

Funding is allocated in different ways in different school districts. Wohlstetter and Buffett (1992) studied five major decentralized districts. In those districts, allocation to the schools was based on enrollment. Each school had a total FTE (full-time equivalency) staffing allotment to be "spent" based on building-level decisions and a total dollar amount for each of several budget categories to be spent again based on building decisions.

Centralized districts allocate a per pupil amount earmarked specifically for library media resources. Many library media specialists appreciate this automatic allocation to their program for its reliability and equity across the district. However, where site-based decision making has brought spending decisions to the building level, staff members and principals work together to make decisions about resource spending.

While site-based decision making has caused anxiety among many library media specialists, it may benefit the library media program to have funding decisions made "closer to home." In site-based management, some would say that what the principal considers important is often what happens (Beasley, 1996). In surveying Indiana library media specialists, Callison found a strong relationship between how frequently the library media specialist and principal conversed about budget and the number of dollars per pupil invested in library media materials (Callison, 1994). The differences are summarized in Figure 4.1.

FIGURE 4.1
Per Pupil Allocations for Books Based on Frequency of Media Specialist and Principal Interaction (Callison, 1994)

	State Average	Interaction with Principal			
		None	Annual	Monthly	Weekly
Elementary	$5.91	$5.53	$5.92	$6.79	$9.45
Junior High	$5.85	$5.60	$5.94	$6.21	$6.75
Senior High	$5.43	$4.65	$6.03	$6.57	$6.51

The more frequent the conversations, the higher the dollars. Thus placing responsibility for allocations at the building level may be an opportunity to increase resources, if the library media specialist communicates with colleagues, including the principal.

To learn how well the library media collection responds to teachers' needs, a simple chart can be given to each teacher listing the major units taught for which the library media program should be a resource. Teachers can then complete the chart and return it to provide the library media specialist with indications of their perceived needs. This information starts the conversation with the teacher about how the library media program can improve its support. Next the library media specialist needs to take action based on the teachers' responses and communicate with the teacher about actions taken because of his or her input. An example of such a chart appears in Figure 4.2.

FIGURE 4.2
Teacher Input for Collection Development

To: Mr. Holmes
From: Your library media specialist

How well is our collection working for you? How can we improve?

Please fill in the chart below and return to me by March 1.

Unit	Rating (Excellent Good Fair Poor)	Suggestions for improvement in our library media center	Outside sources I use to supplement
The Short Story			
Romeo and Juliet			
To Kill a Mockingbird			
Expository Writing			
Quests			
Castles			

Site-based decision making calls for increased responsiveness and accountability to the library media program's clients. It calls for justifying the library media center's budget based on program outcomes. Such built-in accountability holds great promise for library media programs because many curriculum innovations depend on strong collections (for example, whole language), and the people most aware of that dependence are classroom teachers who will be participants in budgeting decisions. In a school where resource-based teaching and learning is occurring, the library media specialist does well to provide justification for the program's budget proposal to the entire staff. Figure 4.3 shows an example of a proposal presented at a staff meeting where the building's budget for the coming year is under discussion.

Providing direct information to teachers helps them make decisions based on information; when they can see how library media allocations have been spent, how they will be spent, and the benefit to them and their students, they are much more likely to be supportive. In an environment of shared decision making, sharing data is crucial if decisions are to be rational.

Any teacher who has embraced resource-based teaching, or who uses multiple resources to supplement a textbook, can readily appreciate having locally available the resources he or she needs. Only when teachers feel disenfranchised or underserved by the library media program will they question supporting library media resources. Library media specialists must take the initiative to reach out to teachers to increase their use of the library media center and its resources, and make the resources as accessible as possible. Often teachers want to create their own classroom libraries because they consider the library media center too remote or inaccessible. The benefits of centralizing resources need to be publicized:

- Circulation and inventory control systems already exist there; it will not be necessary for teachers to create a record-keeping system.
- Cataloging reduces duplicate purchases so that more resources can be available.
- Pooling dollars for a central collection rather than dividing them among classrooms makes it possible to buy expensive items when the need arises.
- Access to all materials is improved for both teachers and students.

FIGURE 4.3
Budget Proposal
Elementary School Library Media Center

Expenditures This Year

Item	Comment	Spent
Books	Reading themes, grades 5–6	$1,369
	Reading themes, grades 3–4	$1,211
	Children's Choice Award Books	$235
	Books to support author residency	$116
	Books to support Social studies, 5–6	$118
	Books to support Social studies, 3–4	$165
	Books to support Social studies, 1–2	$50
	MC/NS collection building	$178
	Professional books	$55
	Reference books (almanac, author biography)	$125
	Award winners, student interest	$191
	Pattern books (Kindergarten)	$425
Total Books		**$4,238**

Note that there was very little purchasing for books for student self-selection; most purchases were curriculum-related.

Item	Comment	Spent
Supplies	Laminating film, transparencies, transparency pens, printer cartridges, computer paper	$574
Subscriptions		$395
AV Software	Audio and video tapes	$120
Computer Software	PAWS, Word, Replacements	$375
Total		**$1,464**

Proposal for Next Year
Books

Books for reading themes, Grades 3–6	$1,600
Books for reading themes, Grades K–2 (Includes some science and social studies literature)	$2,000
Science trade books	$1,800
Social Studies trade books	$600
Books for student self-selection	$1,000
Total Request for Books	**$7,000**

Computer Software

Claris Works (Grades 3–6)	$450
Kid Works (Grades 1–2)	$140
Virus Protection	$240
New CD-ROM titles	$300
Total Software Request	**$1,130**

Supplies

Computer paper, printer cartridges, laminating film, videotapes	$750
AV Software (video, audio)	$200
Subscriptions	$400
Total Supplies Request	**$1,350**
Grand Total Request	**$9,480**

While the trend is toward decentralizing budgets for materials, budgets for capital investments often remain centralized. These are larger, long-term expenditures and concern for equity among schools is perhaps one justification for retaining these decisions at the central office. These expenditures affect library media specialists because they typically include equipment (such as projectors, computers, furniture, and peripherals). Which computer platform to use, how many computers should be purchased, what capacity is really needed at each level, what peripherals do schools need, how frequently do overhead projectors need to be replaced, and when is it time to move to the next video format are all complex questions and are often determined centrally. Yet the decisions all have impact on the school library media program.

To influence capital expenditure, either the district library media coordinator, or, if there is not one, a school library media specialist, must develop and nurture a working relationship with the district's financial officer responsible for capital purchases. Finance officers want to spend money wisely, and so do library media specialists. With expertise on equipment specifications and reasonable replacement cycles, library media specialists can improve the value the district gets for its money. It is important to accept some assumptions in working with finance officers; their charge is to conserve, to spread the funding over the many demands from groups throughout the district; unreasonable demands are detrimental. This situation calls for the library media specialist to accept the spending parameters, and then work within those parameters to acquire the best equipment possible. The advantage of quantity purchase is substantial, so working to amass orders is worthwhile; this one simple strategy will be appreciated by the finance officer, and the library media specialist can quickly be seen as a valuable colleague at the district level. Finance officers are also concerned about equity; because they are accountable to a governing board, fairness across the district is important to them. By maintaining awareness of the biases at work at the district level, the library media specialist can increase library media program resources.

PERSONNEL

Of the three major district level functions, the library media specialist may have the least involvement in personnel matters.

However, some aspects of district-level personnel practice do affect the library media program. Two particularly significant ones are staffing allocations for library media professional and support staff and district policies on personnel evaluation. In highly centralized districts, staffing allocations for teachers are determined for each building at the district level. This practice seems to persist even as districts move to site-based management; it is a reasonable practice since staffing accounts for a large percentage of the district's budget—often approaching, or exceeding 80 percent (Wohlstetter & Buffett, 1992). Such a large investment demands close governance and accountability to the governing board. However, the building principal, who may or may not ask staff to participate, usually determines exactly how the allocation is spent (for example, how many teachers will be assigned to each grade level, how many paraprofessionals there will be, and where those paraprofessionals will work).

Specialized staff positions such as guidance counselors, principals, and library media specialists often continue to be district-determined, even in districts with a high commitment to site-based decision making. The district value for equity across schools accounts for this, at least in part. District-level policy thus directly affects the library media program in setting its staffing level. Often districts assign one certified library media specialist per school, regardless of size, or they determine staffing by ranges of student enrollment, so that, for example, schools enrolling up to 700 have one library media specialist; schools from 700 to 1,200 have 1.5; schools over 1,200 have two, and so on. When staffing allocations depend on district policy, the library media program needs high visibility of its effect on teaching and learning so that district policy supports (or increases) those allocations. Without such visibility, the line item for library media personnel in the district budget can be vulnerable whenever administrators need to respond with dollars to a new demand.

CURRICULUM

Consistency, stability, innovation, and equity are values that drive district-level curriculum decisions throughout the district, vertically and horizontally. Consistency calls for curriculum articulation so that common beliefs about such topics as literacy or hands-on science or using calculators in mathematics guide all teachers' practice, and so that the sequence of learning experiences is appropriate. Likewise, stability is a value; while change is a common topic among schools, long-term and effective change in schools tends to be evolutionary. Innovations, while sometimes initiated by teachers or principals, tend to concern the district bureaucracy because they require coordination and resources for implementation. Equity is the fourth value that district-level curriculum specialists strive to maintain. It is important to recognize the difference between equality and equity. Equality suggests that each entity has the same, whereas equity connotes fairness, taking all factors into account. Sometimes, schools in lower socioeconomic neighborhoods need more resources, or different kinds of support to balance disadvantages they might have. Often, district-level curriculum directors become the arbiters of fairness. School library media specialists often base decisions on the same considerations within the school context. Acknowledging the similarities between the perspective of the district-level curriculum specialist and the school library media specialist improves the likelihood that these two professionals can work together toward common ends.

Whatever happens with curriculum at the district level has important influence on the library media program. If new science units are being developed and promoted, if new foreign languages are being taught, or new courses are being added to the social studies program, library media resources may need to change dramatically to support these new developments. Likewise, if new strategies are being considered (such as using manipulative materials in mathematics, or replacing the formal research paper with an I-Search paper, or moving toward performance assessment requiring student production in various media), then library media programs need to change dramatically to provide appropriate materials and develop requisite skills.

While a traditional curriculum development model may be a top-down design, in fact, research suggests that truly effective school systems simultaneously provide opportunities for top-down and bottom-up influence (Cuban, 1984). Still, in larger districts, leadership in curriculum often comes from district curriculum generalists and specialists. They maintain awareness of new trends and directions in their specialties, following the literature and attending conferences and workshops to keep up to date. Often these central office specialists provide staff development to share new ideas with teachers.

Implementing district-level curriculum development and change typically begins through committees led by district-level curriculum specialists. Committees tend to be a primary vehicle for increasing the ownership of new ideas and for disseminating ideas throughout a district. District-level curriculum directors and specialists are initiators and facilitators, and committees are useful for both roles. Curriculum cycles tend to focus on a different content area each year; in districts with a more integrated curriculum, multiple areas, such as mathematics and science together or language arts and social studies, are reviewed simultaneously. Or the focus may be cross-disciplinary and emphasize a strategy such as assessment or technology integration.

However it is organized, most districts have a schedule for curriculum review. Participation in such reviews is crucial for library media specialists. These committees offer opportunities to learn what and how teachers will be teaching. The library media specialist can be the information specialist for the committee (for example, searching professional literature about the topics under discussion, locating relevant teaching resource material, and searching for new trade books or electronic resources to support curriculum innovations). By actively participating when curriculum change is being planned, the library media specialist can help teachers anticipate topics or strategies for which there will be a wealth of materials or for which material will be scarce. This level of participation is clearly preferable to waiting until all curriculum decisions have been made, and then responding by saying, "It will take three months to get what you need," or "What you are asking for doesn't seem to exist!" Simply put, proactive is better than reactive, and participation from the beginning allows the library media specialist to be proactive. In some settings, being appointed to such curriculum committees will require some initiative from the library media specialist. If central office curriculum specialists are unfamiliar with curriculum-involved school library media programs, they may not even think of including a library media specialist on such a committee; initiating contact and articulating why library media specialists should participate in curriculum at the district level may be necessary.

Central office instruction or curriculum supervisors perceive their positions as invisible (Pajak, 1989). They see their role as working to make those in more visible positions—superintendent, principals, and teachers—look good. That invisibility may be something that library media specialists share with curriculum specialists. Both roles involve facilitating the work of others—working behind the scenes. Having this role characteristic in common can bring the library media specialist and curriculum specialist together, since both focus on supporting the work of the "front line." It can also generate competition as each seeks to be a helper. Making the distinction between the content specialist and the resource and instruction specialist is important to foster working relationships.

TECHNOLOGY

Technical support from the district level is an essential ingredient in school districts of all sizes. Networking increases the technical knowledge needed to maintain and upgrade equipment, telecommunication systems, and software. For student production in multimedia, technical knowledge is needed to help building-level library media specialists buy appropriate equipment and learn to use it effectively. Increasingly, districts are employing network specialists and technicians to assist in these specialized needs. Library media specialists can help these technical support people; often technicians are naive about teaching and learning, but highly skilled in the technology itself. Library media specialists can be important intermediaries to help technical support people understand how various technologies will be used so that they can select and deploy equipment in ways that will work most effectively for educational applications.

For district-level planning to be implemented, there must be effective links between district and building. On many matters, the principal provides that link, particularly in areas of staffing, facilities, personnel management, grade reporting practices, and other managerial topics. The library media specialist can also serve as liaison between district and school by serving on district committees for policy, curriculum, or planning issues. One topic that particularly warrants involving the library media specialist as a liaison is technology.

A WORD ABOUT SMALLER DISTRICTS

This chapter has focused on the impact of the district on the school library media program and the influence the library media program can have at the district level. While there are many very small school districts with skeletal central offices, nevertheless, there is an organizational unit known as the school district. That entity, however small, has its own mission and goals, its own beliefs about teaching and learning, and its own relationship to its community. Where districts are very small,

**AN EXAMPLE OF ENHANCEMENT IN ACTION:
THE LIBRARY MEDIA SPECIALIST AND TECHNOLOGY
PLANNING**

Planning for instructional and information technologies is complex. District-level planning encourages equity among schools
and consistency in vision, program, and platform. The district
plan provides the parameters for technology uses. Components
of the district plan usually include a mission statement for technology, recommended applications, software guidelines or criteria, hardware, and staff development plans (Langhorne et al.,
1989). Then each building develops its implementation plan,
using the district technology plan as its framework. For example,
it is likely that a district would determine technology-related
competencies for students. At the building level a technology
planning team must take those competencies and determine
how, when, and by whom they will be taught. The library media
specialist is a natural participant on the district's technology
planning team; after all, this is the person who uses technology
for information seeking. This person is accustomed to tracking
reviews of new titles, previewing materials, and determining their
fit in the school's program. This person has the bird's eye view
of teaching and learning. The ideal is for the district technology
planning committee to include people who work in school buildings and continually learn more by observing technology-related activities, by reading professional literature, and by attending technology-rich conferences and institutes. Such activities constitute a substantial part of the library media
specialist's work.

At the building level, the library media specialist again is an
ideal person to lead in translating the district technology plan
into an action plan for the school. The building plan includes
identifying specific applications and software and correlating
with specific units or courses of study at the building level; de-
ploying and scheduling hardware, either in labs, mini-labs, clus-
ters, or individual classrooms; and providing staff development
opportunities on the applications and software to be used in
the school. The library media specialist has much to contribute

to each of these issues, and can be particularly helpful if he or she has been a member of the district's planning committee, so that the building implementation accurately reflects the district committee's intentions. Besides planning, the library media specialist is responsible for acquiring and managing software and hardware, for providing building-level staff development opportunities, for seeking ways to integrate technology into instruction, and for advocating appropriate technology uses. By performing these roles at the building level, the library media specialist gains experiences and insights that result in his or her increasing importance as a member of the ongoing district planning process. Active participation by the library media specialist at the district level brings important visibility to the library media program.

perhaps a regional agency provides leadership, particularly in areas such as curriculum or technical support or staff development. Regardless of district size, each library media specialist has an overarching organization where visibility and advocacy for the library media program is an important responsibility.

ADVOCACY

While it may seem intuitively obvious to those in the library media profession that library media specialists belong on district committees; have contributions to make to district-level work in finance, curriculum, personnel or technology; and can be key players in implementing district programs, these ideas are rarely obvious to key decision makers at the district level. The importance of taking initiative thus cannot be overemphasized. Library media specialists must make the case for what their specialization can offer, and then must act on their promises. When we say we can provide information, we must provide it in a timely fashion. When we say we can contribute to the conversation about curriculum articulation, we must produce. When we say we have ideas about using technology, we must articulate them. When we suggest that we can save the district money, we must come up with purchasing recommendations that accomplish that. The "say-do ratio" must be high.

WORKING WITHIN THE SYSTEM

More than 30 years ago, Robert Presthus (1962) published an interesting analysis of how people work within organizations. His theory is particularly relevant for the school library media specialist working within the school district context. The responses Presthus described are those of the upward mobile, the organizational indifferent, and the organizational ambivalent. An upward mobile is optimistic about the organization and plays roles within the organization to advance. Upward mobiles identify closely with the organization—the success of the organization is their success. An upward mobile is able to overlook inconsistencies in the system. Accepting the organization's goals commits the upward mobile to conform to whatever the powerful influences in the organization want. The organizational indifferent is a disenfranchised person who does not identify with the organization. An indifferent focuses on his or her own job and remains aloof from the larger system. The organizational ambivalent speculates what the organization ought to be rather than what it is. This type is ambivalent toward his or her status in the organization—a factor of great concern to the upward mobile. The ambivalent wants success but does not want to pay the organizational price—that price is often compromise. Often the ambivalent is characterized as something of an outsider who may lack the political finesse needed to work within the system. Each of these is a pure type, but rarely do people fit into only one category. Indeed, the behavior is often situational. Deciding how to respond to organizational demands requires reflection about stakes and potential consequences. The following two scenarios illustrate the range of responses within an organization.

An Example: R-Rated Movies

In our first scenario, assume that a district-wide decision has been made that no R-rated movies are to be shown in schools. This decision will eliminate showing several films that have been used in high school classes for several years, for example, *The Killing Fields* used in a social studies course on war. How the high school library media specialist accommodates this decision can be classified by Presthus's theory. The upward mobile will support the decision unquestioningly, or this type might diplomatically point out, via a carefully developed and annotated list, those videos for which exceptions might be made. The organizational indifferent will have no opinion. The organizational ambivalent may question the decision, based on principles of intellectual freedom, maintaining that a class of materials ought not to be censored and that such a ruling violates teachers' and students' rights. An organizational ambivalent would probably openly state concerns about the ruling and would be likely to contact the American Library Association Office for Intellectual Freedom for an opinion.

Another Example: Technology for Kindergarten

In our second scenario, a district technology committee is determining where to allocate computers and decides to place computers in kindergarten rooms for the first time. Parents of young children, early childhood teachers, and members of the school board have expressed their desire to increase the young children's access to technology. The library media specialist on the committee believes that it would be more developmentally appropriate for computer use and instruction to begin at third grade when children can begin to take advantage of the computer's capabilities for more sophisticated uses, seeing the computer as a tool rather than a reward. The upward mobile will recognize that the influential forces in the organization want young children to access computers and will accept this allocation, despite needs in upper grades. The organizational indifferent will have no opinion, and probably would not participate on the committee in the first place. The organizational ambivalent might oppose the idea and express concerns about developmental appropriateness or the needs at other grade levels, and might refer to literature from early childhood education to support his or her position.

Deciding how to respond to district-level issues challenges the library media specialist. Each response must be weighed in terms of what is at stake, what are the consequences of agreeing or not agreeing with the district, what will benefit students and teachers most in the long run. There will be times when performing as the upward mobile may seem to be the long-run best choice, and there will be times when, despite the consequences, the organizational ambivalent's posture is called for. Assessing the situation each time challenges the library media specialist to consider repeatedly his or her position within the district context.

The library media specialist contributes to the work at the district level and is affected by district-level policy and planning. As districts adopt more site-based decision making, the district's role shifts toward providing a vision and parameters within which building decisions are made. When decision making moves to the building level, the potential for the library media specialist to influence decisions may increase, if other participants in the process have benefited from the library media program and see its value in improving teaching and learning. Responsiveness to the local clientele increases in consequence as decision making gets closer to the action.

ACTION STRATEGIES

Program Administration

- Participate in district-level policy and planning when you have special expertise. Examples include

  materials selection policy
  copyright policy
  acceptable use policy
  privacy issues
  networking for access to information.

- Develop a positive professional relationship with the district's chief financial officer; demonstrate to him or her your insight into the budgeting process, the importance of differentiating between *needs* and *wants*, the necessity of compromise, and the importance of fiscal accountability.
- Work to ensure that administrators place you on district committees related to curriculum development and revision; emphasize your knowledge of resources and technologies as a potential contribution to the process.
- Develop a network among educators across the district; present yourself as a problem solver.
- Be a friend to the district's physical plant; it is easier to get electrical connections where they are needed, move furniture to accommodate new technologies, and make other physical plant improvements when workers know they are appreciated and respected.
- Periodically provide the superintendent with "good news" to share with the board; choose substantive items to share, but such news as major increases in circulation or visiting authors or mini-grants received by the library media center or participation in library

media events by local "celebrities" might also be examples because they are items that show increased use, community involvement, and initiative.

REFERENCES

Beasley, Augie. "Becoming a Proactive Library Leader: Leadership 101," *School Library Media Activities Monthly* 13 (November 1996): 20–22+.

Callison, Daniel. "The AIME Statewide Survey of School Library Media Centers: Relationships and Associations from the Data," *Indiana Media Journal* 17 (1994): 103–162.

Cuban, L. "Transforming the Frog into a Prince: Effective Schools Research, Policy and Practice at the District Level." *Harvard Educational Review* 54 (1984): 129–151.

Langhorne, Mary Jo et al. *Teaching with Computers: A New Menu for the '90s* (Phoenix, Ariz.: Oryx Press, 1989).

Pajak, Edward. *The Central Office Supervisor of Curriculum and Instruction; Setting the Stage for Success* (Boston: Allyn and Bacon, 1989).

Presthus, Robert. *The Organizational Society; An Analysis and a Theory* (New York: Random House, 1962).

Wohlstetter, Priscilla and Thomas Buffett. "Decentralizing Dollars Under School-Based Management: Have Policies Changed?" *Educational Policy* 6 (March 1992): 35–54.

Chapter 5

The Community

This chapter

- describes the purposes of community involvement
- identifies ways for the library media program to communicate and cooperate with community entities
- identifies action strategies for cooperative community activities

While the school plays a central role in children's development, children benefit when there is interaction between the school and its community. As the saying goes, "It takes a village to raise a child." Parent organizations, school boards, and parent-teacher conferences represent typical school-to-home connections, but these relationships are limited primarily to parents of school-age children or to select community members. The greater community can also share in raising its youth. Businesses, social agencies, museums, and libraries have human, physical, and fiscal resources that can complement the school's resources.

PURPOSES OF INVOLVEMENT

Community involvement in the school library media center can meet several purposes (Gorton & Schneider, 1991). Through involvement, parents and other citizens become informed about how the library media center helps students. Understanding the program helps people support it verbally and fiscally. Perhaps more important, when parents are involved, they are able to help their children academically and socially.

Community participation also provides the school library media program with new ideas and expertise.

FAMILY INVOLVEMENT

On March 31, 1994, the *Goals 2000: Educate America Act* was signed, setting into law eight National Education Goals for the year 2000. Among these goals is one related to family involvement:

> Every school will promote partnerships that will increase parental involvement and participation in promoting children's social, emotional and academic growth.

The family is the core of the school's community. Teachers and the school principal communicate directly with families through parent-teacher conferences, parent organizations, and newsletters. The library media center lacks the direct visibility of the classroom or the football field. Making presentations to parent and community groups is one way to share information about the library media program and gain support from people who have influence on either the school or the district.

For example, a library media specialist can make presentations to parents about choosing materials for the library media center. Often, parents are rather naive about the materials selection process. That naïveté can lead to challenges or concerns about materials in the school library media center, particularly at the elementary school level. Worse can be a sentiment that if the library shelves are full there is no need to spend money on more materials. Topics covered could be the selection policy, including criteria for selection; reviewing sources and selection tools; or procedures for parents, teachers, and students to suggest items for the collection. Naive parents may think that purchasing for a library is akin to a shopping spree, but a presentation like this can help them understand the complexity of collection building. Another area that may interest parents is Internet use. Since the mass media have raised public concern about inappropriate Internet activities, the library media specialist can alleviate this concern with a session in which parents access the Internet and experience appropriate use. During such a session the library media specialist could explain local policies for responsible Internet use. To leave these topics unaddressed opens the door for criticism from parents who have too little information from less reliable sources than the library media specialist. Such informative meetings are likely to increase knowledge, confidence, and communication.

Another possible topic would be computer software used in the school. By sitting down at computers and, with guidance, trying out some software that students use, parents may find it easier to support expenditures for technology. A similar program may be of interest to local service clubs or other groups that include both parents and non-parents.

A library media specialist can also offer parents programs about homework and study skills, particularly at the middle school level. Strategies for note taking, examples of ready-reference materials appropriate for the home, and school library media resources available to help students with their homework can all be topics for such a presentation.

Literacy programs are a natural family-school library media center connection. Such programs can target special populations. For example, if a school has English-as-a-second-language students, then a program might include sharing books that will help children build their English vocabulary, such as picture dictionaries and pattern picture books. It might include demonstrating books on tape or computer-based programs, and encouraging parents to join their children during a designated after-school time to use these materials in the library media center. It might be a program offered cooperatively with the public library to raise awareness of materials and services available there.

Another target audience might be families with preschoolers. A report by Morisset (1993) cites research findings that an effective way to promote language skills and develop strong social interactions among young children is through storybook sharing. She reports that the frequency of listening to stories in the home was found to be directly related to literacy and teacher ratings of students' oral language skills at ages five to seven. Families may benefit from the school library media specialist sharing tips on reading aloud to young children, suggesting books appropriate for the very young (such as books with repetition, pattern books, rhymes, and concept books), or sharing strategies for reading to and with children (for example, paired reading where parent and child take turns reading or chanting refrains together). Programs like this are an investment in future students who will benefit from listening to literature and will gain language experience.

The need for communication between the school library media center and the family extends beyond special presentations. No school newsletter should go home without at least one meaningful item from the school library media center. Brief, readable articles can include suggesting good books to read as a family, describing student activities in the library media center, promoting events in the community, or advising about computers or software for the home. Library media center visibility is key, and the message must be that the library media program is fundamental to learning. It is more important that the communications contain "meat" than that they be clever or cute.

Another way to involve parents is through advisory committees; for example, if the school is developing its technology plan, the committee should include a parent. Periodically, the library media program needs to be evaluated. Districts often have a review cycle, where each program or curricular area has a major evaluative review every five or seven years. Usually, the review process begins with naming a committee or team. When such a team includes parents, they gain important insight into the program, and, as a result, they often become advocates. Moreover, they provide an important perspective on whether the program is really reaching students as it is intended.

A typical review process includes these steps:

- reviewing the current literature to determine "the state of the art"
- assessing the existing program to determine its status (this assessment is often accomplished by means of surveys to several groups: students, teachers, administrators, and parents)
- comparing the results of the literature review and assessment
- developing a vision statement, goals, and an action plan

Surveys should be tailored for each audience in order to get the clearest responses. A sample parent survey for a library media program review appears in Figure 5.1. Parental involvement through the survey and in the review process helps give parents information about the program and offers them a way to express their viewpoints on its effectiveness. Imagine that communicating with parents is communication with the boss—the person paying the bills—because in some ways, it is!

BUSINESS INVOLVEMENT

Local businesses have a real interest in the quality of local education. First, their future employees may come from the local schools. Besides, good schools can be a "selling point" for chambers of commerce in at-

FIGURE 5.1
Parent Survey
School Library Media Program

Item	Strongly Agree	Agree	Disagree	Strongly Disagree	No Knowledge
Students are taught how to use information resources available in the school library media center.					
Students receive assistance in using the library media center.					
Our library media center has enough appropriate materials to meet students' needs.					
My son or daughter can use the library media center whenever he or she has a need.					
The library media center appears well organized.					
The library media center is inviting.					
I receive information about the activities in the library media center.					
I understand the role of the library media center in the school program.					
I would feel comfortable coming to the library media center.					

Additional comments or suggestions:

TWO EXAMPLES OF ENHANCEMENT IN ACTION: PARTNERSHIPS WITH BUSINESS

The following two examples illustrate the power of business partnerships in enhancing teaching and learning. These partnerships could not have begun without a solid foundation built over many years by a strong school library media program.

Example One. In 1993 a school district of 20 schools had no in-district network to provide communication among schools. In the community was the home office of a large corporation whose CEO and the school district superintendent met at a chamber of commerce meeting. In conversation, the topic of e-mail arose, and the superintendent admitted that the district had no capability for e-mail. She emphasized that technology funds were spent on instructional applications, based on a belief that students' needs came first. The CEO was taken aback since he considered e-mail "the way of doing business." He committed himself and his company to network the school district. He led a fund-raising campaign among businesses within the district to collect pledges to wire all schools—today all schools have interschool connections and Internet access.

This business will continue its involvement in the schools, but its focus is targeted toward this project. The library media specialists in the schools will continue to be primary contacts for this partnership since the networks are administered through the library media program. This is a partnership focused on telecommunications. In this example, the business partner offered technical expertise, but all decisions on where networked work stations should be placed, what software should be placed on servers, and what levels of security would be needed were made by school district staff. The business partner remained advisory and primarily supported the project's resources, while the decision making remained with the school district staff.

Example Two. A school district was trying to train its staff to become confident computer users, with the belief that, as they developed confidence themselves, they would be enthusiastic about their students using computers in their classrooms. Teachers complained that they had too little access to computers. While the district was spending substantial sums on computers, they were deployed primarily for student use, leaving teachers poorly equipped. A local bank was approached to provide special low-interest rates for loans that teachers could use to purchase computers, payable by payroll deduction. The bank was most enthusiastic to offer such a loan. A local community college then agreed to fund school district trainers to teach evening classes for computer purchasers, and a local computer vendor offered special computer package options at highly competitive prices. The school district trainers determined the training content; the business partners did not interfere with the substance of the project. All business partners benefited from excellent publicity in the local press as good corporate citizens.

tracting new businesses into the community. Community pride helps keep local business thriving; business benefits from a sense of confidence within a community. All these factors mean that business cares about its schools. Every chamber of commerce has an education committee—an indicator of the importance business places on quality local education. Think of real estate brokers marketing homes to families. One common question is whether the schools in the neighborhood are considered "good" schools. Think of bankers in the home mortgage market. They want customers and they want to be able to assure families that the investment in the community is a good one for them and their children; "good" schools are central to that assurance. Business and education are likely partners.

Businesses enter into partnerships with schools for two reasons: to contribute to the public good and improve the quality of the school, and to increase their own standing in the marketplace. Likewise, schools seek business partnerships for two purposes: to increase their resources and to improve the community understanding and respect for their programs.

There are two important principles to guide school-business partnerships: maintaining a focus and maintaining the school's authority over substance. Focus allows any given business to have a niche for its marketplace advantage; for example, a business can become known as the science partner or the fine arts partner or the reading partner, and this association gives the business an identity in marketing. Focus allows the school to have special-interest staff members take on responsibilities for specific partnerships to nurture the relationships; for example, the library media specialist takes care of the reading partners or the networking partners, and the art and music teachers take care of the fine arts partners.

Perhaps even more important is controlling the substance of the project. One concern is whether the business brings its own special interests or biases to a project. The school should decide the *what* of the partnership; the business's participation is in the *how.* Educators, after all, are responsible for what is taught in schools, and they should be protective of their right to determine content lest inappropriate bias influence instruction. If a partnership is related to substance abuse, for example, professional educators should determine the project's content and approach. Library media specialists must set standards for business participation in order to maintain the integrity of the school library media program (Tinnish, 1996).

In both of the examples schools extended their resources by networking and by equipping teachers with personal computers and relevant training respectively. The businesses contributed to the common good of the community. The school library media programs clearly have extended the local understanding of what they are doing with technology. Business partnerships can be highly valuable to both parties, when the principles of focus and control are monitored.

One caution: effective partnerships take time. A business partnership is a new relationship and relationships can be demanding. School library media specialists considering such a partnership need to expect to give it time. Like any relationship, it will not survive without nurturing. That nurturing involves regular contact with a representative of the business; it requires reporting progress to the business, particularly impact on students; it requires public acknowledgment—the business marketplace purpose cannot be met if the public is unaware of the contribution.

COMMUNITY RESOURCES

In Sweden, a public institution known as a *kulturhus,* a house of culture, incorporates the public library, the local recreation center, and a fine arts center for courses in painting, sculpture, photography, and other media. The *kulturhus* is used by the public and by neighboring schools as a resource for exploration. In the United States, we tend to isolate each of these activities in a separate entity; yet cooperation among community resources makes sense. Each community has resources that can expand the vitality of the school library media program—and the school.

While the public library–school connection seems to be a natural partnership, it is not always what it could be. Haycock (1990) paints a rather dismal picture of school and public library cooperation in his summary of dissertation research. He suggests that school and public librarians communicate very little with each other. He also concludes that "self-preservation and protection of territory override the ideal of cooperation." Yet the relationship has much to offer.

Supporting students' assignments and supporting literacy are two functions common to school and public libraries. For the most part, communication is key to these partnerships. One possibility here is a monthly telephone call or visit. The school library media specialist can report to the public librarian topics coming up in the curriculum. In a perfect world, this would be comprehensive, but the world is not perfect and this report will not be a complete summary of every assignment students will have. Still, a good faith effort is a start. The public librarian can report to the school library media specialist on programming planned for the coming month. The school can then relay this information to teachers and families. While a monthly set time to touch base may seem artificial, it is a way to open communication, and it may lead to additional contacts as the relationship develops. If students get better service and if families know more about programs to help children, then the efforts at cooperation have paid off.

Cooperative activity with museums and other local groups is another means of community involvement. Art museums, science museums, natural history museums, and local historical societies have programs, exhibits, and outreach staff available to connect to the school. Library media specialists serve well as contact persons for these organizations because they know the whole curriculum. Besides organizations, every community has individuals with special knowledge, skills, or talents. One possible way to track community resources is to develop a "community talent bank." Such a resource directory could include these items for each entry:

contact person
address
telephone

topics
curriculum area(s) (e.g., science, art)
description (e.g., a speaker, an exhibit, a demonstration)
limitations (e.g., age groups or group size limitations)

Developing such a directory can begin with the chamber of commerce education committee or with parent organizations. A simple form can facilitate collecting information. Then, the library media specialist can assemble it into a database and make it available to teachers. Of critical importance is that the resources are used by teachers, once the information is collected; this may require some marketing until the database becomes a standard resource. Such community involvement generates support and understanding of the school's program. In many communities the majority of voters are not parents; only about 25 percent of the adults in the United States currently have children enrolled in public schools. Majorities in most communities are young people without children or older citizens whose children are grown. Yet, schools depend on the support of these people for taxes and bond referenda. They need to feel some ownership of the schools. Library media specialists can put their program into the spotlight by taking a central role in the management and organization of a community resource directory. This is one way for the public to see the library media program's central role— something not intuitively obvious to those who remember their school library as a closet-sized room with a few books.

ACTION STRATEGIES

Information Access and Delivery

- Provide access to school library media center resources for parents (e.g., the collection and the technology).
- Initiate communication with the local public library to develop such collaborative programs as an after-school homework center, intergenerational reading, or Saturday dramatics.

Program Administration

- Plan and present parent meetings. Topics can include book talks on books for a specific age or topic; a film festival of videos about parenting borrowed from a local public library or other social agency; a "how to help your child study better" session; an introduction to computer software used at the school; a computer literacy session for parents who have never used a computer; an introduction to the World Wide Web with emphasis on sites that have information pertinent to topics students are studying in school.

- Include something in each newsletter that goes home (e.g., book suggestions, World Wide Web addresses of interest to students, brief descriptions of activities in the library media center).
- Encourage parent or community-member volunteers; give options for weekly or monthly tasks as well as one-time projects; seek volunteers from senior citizen ranks and business employees who are not parents, but who have talents or time to offer. Remember to acknowledge parent help in newsletters; treat volunteers to special events periodically to convey appreciation.
- Make personal contacts with local businesses and identify ways they can be supportive; focus the request to any single business so that each has its own niche, if possible.

REFERENCES

Gorton, Richard A. and G. T. Schneider. *School-Based Leadership: Challenges and Opportunities* (Dubuque, Iowa: Wm. C. Brown, 1991), 520–547.

Haycock, Ken. "What Works: School and Public Library Cooperation," *Emergency Librarian* 18 (November/December 1990): 33.

Morisset, Colleen E. *Language and Emotional Milestones on the Road to Readiness.* Report No. 18 (Arlington, Va.: Center on Families, Communities, Schools and Children's Learning, Zero to Three, National Center for Clinical Infant Programs, 1993).

Tinnish, Dianne. "Big Business in the School Library," *Emergency Librarian* 23 (May/June 1996): 8–11.

PART II

The Library Media Program

Chapter 6

Collaborative Planning

This chapter

- describes the process of collaborative planning
- examines the role of the library media specialist as a member of the instructional team
- discusses how collaboration benefits students, teachers, and library media specialists
- identifies action strategies for collaboration

The increased complexity of today's world calls for teamwork. Reich observes in *Tales of a New America:*

> Rarely do Big Ideas emerge any longer from the solitary labor of genius. Modern science and technology is too complicated for one brain. It requires groups of astronomers, physicists, and computer programmers to discover new dimensions of the universe. . . . With ever more frequency Nobel prizes are awarded to collections of people (Reich, 1987, p. 126).

Increased complexity characterizes the teaching profession as well. De-emphasis on basal textbooks, increased concern for students' learning styles, the explosion of information, advances in instructional and information technologies, advocacy for cooperative learning, and collaborative teaching are factors that increase the complexity in instructional planning. Teams of teachers are more likely to address productively the complex task of planning than individuals working alone.

Not all schools have evolved to team-based work yet. In many settings, long-standing tradition in schools has kept teachers isolated in their self-contained classrooms. Many teachers entered the profession expecting to work alone with their students, having autonomy over their own classroom and students. Yet, that image is out of step today with a society that recognizes that teamwork can increase effectiveness and productivity, and can improve the work environment. Experiments like the General Motors Saturn plant have received considerable attention as teamwork models to improve the product and the process of manufacturing. Underlying much of the discussion about collaboration is the work of Edward Deming whose name is regularly associated with the "quality" movement.

The effectiveness of library media specialists, as well as other specialists, depends on working with other school professionals. Without collaboration, there is little purpose for the collection, the curriculum, or the staff of the library media program. Library media specialists must seek to work collaboratively with classroom teachers in order to improve students' learning experiences.

THE COLLABORATIVE PLANNING PROCESS

Collaboration depends on effective communication and supportive relationships. Next is the need for time. Working together takes more time than working alone. There must be motivation to collaborate. Sometimes that motivation is intrinsic—people trust that the result of collaboration will be better teaching and learning, and it is worth their time. Sometimes the motivation must be external because people lack confidence that collaboration will be beneficial. In these cases, administrators sometimes impose expectations for collaboration, setting team or department meeting times and attending those meetings whenever possible. Sometimes principals build the expectation for collaboration into the personnel evaluation system. In cases where collaboration is an expectation held by the principal, it is particularly important that the benefits be quickly evident to participants.

As members of planning teams, besides working directly with students, library media specialists need to help teachers understand what they have to offer to the planning process. Often, teachers perceive the library media specialist as the person to approach after they finish their planning. It is important for the principal to present the library media specialist in the role of an instructional leader who should be part of curriculum planning from the beginning. The principal is a key element in collaborative planning so that library media specialists and teachers are perceived as equal partners in instruction. When such understanding is lacking at first, the library media specialist may state:

> I will alert you to resources both here at school and elsewhere if I know what you are teaching and expecting your students to do. My concern is to teach students the skills necessary to locate and use information; and if I am here at your planning meetings, then together we can decide how best to give students the practice developing these information skills.

Teamwork requires mutual trust in one another's contributions to the team's work, a no-risk environment for openly sharing ideas, and a shared commitment to the group's decisions. Establishing ground rules from the beginning that recognize these requirements will improve the potential for collaboration. Specific and explicit strategies are useful for helping teamwork proceed:

- *Pose questions using nonthreatening language.* To protect the no-risk atmosphere, phrasing questions so that they do not put others on the defensive is important. No one wants to speak in a group where ideas are at risk of being criticized or attacked, yet open discussion demands that disagreement be voiced. Tact and sensitivity are important. Ask "Might Steinbeck be too difficult for some kids to read?" rather than state, "Steinbeck is too difficult."
- *Ensure that all team members are heard.* Some people tend to be cautious about speaking up, even in small groups. Someone must take responsibility for seeing that all voices are heard. A simple query like, "Mark, we haven't heard from you; what do you think of this idea?" is all that is needed. A round-robin approach asking each person for comments also works well.
- *Clarify terms.* Careful communication is important for teamwork, so think about assumptions and see that they are explicit. For example, a clarification like, "When we say consensus, do we mean agreement by the majority, or do we mean unanimous agreement?" may prevent a serious misunderstanding later on.
- *Keep the discussion focused.* "We began talking about how we would assess students' learning at the end of the Civil War unit, and now we are talking about camcorders. We seem to have gotten off the track."

- *Engage in active listening* (Holcomb, 1996). Elements of active listening are paraphrase what others say, ask probing questions, jot down important points, withhold advice until all information is shared, and listen to advice in full before reacting.

A team meeting must be organized in order to be more than a chat session. Each group needs a facilitator. Meetings should begin with a stated purpose or an agenda, with opportunities for additions from participants. Likewise, meetings should have some kind of outcome—written and distributed minutes, or an oral summary of what was accomplished. These features help all participants know that the time was well spent.

THE INSTRUCTIONAL PLANNING TEAM

A team is a small number of people with complementary skills committed to a common purpose, performance goals, and an approach for which they hold themselves mutually accountable (Katzenbach & Smith, 1993). This definition has several key concepts, each of which deserves exploration.

Common Purpose

For instructional planning teams, the common purpose is to provide effective educational experiences for students. Members of a team collaborate around a common purpose. An important aspect of teamwork is to "keep the eye on the prize." Sometimes team members can become enthusiastic about the activities and events to be planned and lose sight of the purpose. To keep the purpose in focus, team members must ask, "What do we want students to gain from these experiences? What do they need to know or be able to do?"

Performance Goals

Performance goals refer to what each member of the team will do—each teacher, the principal, and the library media specialist. For example, a kindergarten team was observed planning an upcoming unit that would involve several activities, including a field trip. As they talked, each member seemed to have established himself or herself as a specialist:

The *artist* responded to "Will you draw us a pattern?"

The *shopper* responded to "Will you call and bargain for a good deal on the fee for the field trip?"

The *facilitator* asked "Has everyone had a chance to share their ideas now?"

The *challenger* asked "Is that too difficult for our kids?"

The *resource seeker* responded to "Have we got any easy books about the presidents?"

In a follow-up conversation with the observer, the teachers acknowledged that these were typical roles for each of them to play as they planned units. Performance responsibilities will vary with the needs of the group, but clearly each member of the team has performance expectations. Just as members of an athletic team have primary assignments to call the plays, or to cover second base, or to kick the field goal, so in this situation each team member will have unique performance expectations.

Besides substantive responsibilities that help accomplish the work of preparing for instruction, there are affective responsibilities to the team as well. In *Team Players and Teamwork*, Parker (1990) provides a checklist of behaviors for collaboration:

- Help the team establish long-term goals and clarify its current objective or task.
- Help the team see how its work fits into the total organization.
- Regularly remind the team of the need to revisit goals and action plans.
- Encourage the team to establish plans with milestones and appropriate task assignments.
- Pitch in to help other team members who need assistance.
- Work hard to achieve team goals and complete tasks even when you do not agree with them.
- Do not gossip about other team members or share negative comments about the team process with nonmembers.
- Remain flexible and open to new ideas or data that may alter team goals.

These behaviors are appropriate to consider in developing ground rules for formal planning teams. It is unreasonable to expect that people who have been accustomed to working in isolation will automatically know how to perform in a team situation. Explicit discussion of team behavior and team organization provide the groundwork often needed in making the transition to a collaborative planning process.

Accountability

Team members are accountable to one another for meeting their responsibilities. To ensure accountability, some kind of end-of-meeting summary of "who will do what" is necessary. Successful teams set high expectations for team members. Creating a culture of accountability to the team occurs when everyone takes team responsibility seriously.

Complementary Skills

The concept of complementary skills indicates that different team members are good at different aspects of the team's work. In an instructional team, sometimes those complementary skills relate to curriculum knowledge; sometimes they relate to group task skills, like the clarifier, who gives examples or restates problems; the tester, who raises questions to see if the group is ready to decide; or the harmonizer, who mediates differences (see p. 89).

THE LIBRARY MEDIA SPECIALIST AS COLLABORATOR

Loertscher's (1988) taxonomy of involvement in curriculum provides a useful structure for envisioning the roles the library media specialist can play in collaboration with teachers. This taxonomy classifies involvement from minimal participation to central role:

Level 1. No interaction. Some situations require no involvement of the library media specialist.

Level 2. Self-help warehouse. The "warehouse" represents the library media center's resources. Collection development is a collaborative process. Teachers give the library media specialist suggestions of topics, themes, or titles. The library media specialist negotiates with teachers to prioritize needs and determine what will be purchased. This collaborative process is an ongoing one in which information is continually being shared in both directions. Teachers are making requests; library media specialists are alerting teachers to resources that may be of interest; teachers and library media specialists are working together to prioritize; and library media specialists are reporting to teachers what is being purchased or what has been received. Library media specialists are reviewing the existing collection and making decisions for weeding; these decisions, too, are shared with teachers to reduce the chances of withdrawing materials that have value. The "warehouse" extends beyond the physical collection to include resources available online and from other collections. In addition, the organization and access systems of the "warehouse" are communicated clearly to teachers so that they can use it independently.

Level 3. Individual reference assistance. The library media specialist works with the teacher or student to find an answer to a specific question. Reference work is a collaboration between the information seeker and the library media specialist. It often requires careful communication to determine the precise need. For example, a pair of second-graders once approached a library media specialist. Their body language suggested an urgent need as they marched up to the library media specialist. One asserted himself quickly and stated, "I don't suppose you have a Bible in this library!" To that, the library media specialist responded, "Of course," and proceeded to the 200s shelf to retrieve it. As the threesome walked toward the shelf, the second boy asked, "Do you have books about monkeys?" The library media specialist responded, "Yes. Is there something special you would like to know about monkeys?" The boy responded, "Well, I am interested in old monkeys." The library media specialist hesitated thoughtfully, wondering about old monkeys, and then asked, "Are you working on an assignment for Mrs. Adams?" The response came quickly. "No. We are having a disagreement about the beginning of people, and we need to find some information." Immediately the question turned from looking for books about the biology of monkeys to looking for books about evolution. This conversation represents the typical reference interview, and the collaborative process that can occur in individual reference assistance when seeker and specialist communicate and then collaborate to locate the desired information.

Level 4. Spontaneous interaction and gathering. At this level, teacher and library media specialist engage in minimal collaboration. The teacher suddenly discovers a need for something and sends a request, often by way of a student or e-mail, to the library media specialist. "I need a picture that shows the difference between a moth and a butterfly," . . . "I need that videotape about how to deal with strangers, because of an incident reported this morning." However, the confidence that the library media specialist will be able to respond in such an emergency is often the result of more-involved collaboration in the past.

Level 5. Cursory planning. Here, collaboration in the true sense of planning together with teachers begins—but informally. Brief, informal conversations occur where teachers talk about what they are planning to teach, and the library media specialist may interject ideas or resources. Often such conversations are essentially brainstorming; generally they are brief and unstructured. Yet there is communication between the library media specialist and teacher, and often some activity occurs as a result; the library media specialist locates some resource, a lesson is taught in the library media center, a time is set for more in-depth conversation, or an activity is designed.

Level 6. Planned gathering. As a result of communication between teachers and the library media specialist about upcoming instruction, the library media specialist gathers resources. Clear communication between teacher and library media specialist is vital. This interaction cannot be simply a teacher stating a topic and a library media specialist gathering everything available about that topic. That is not collaboration. Collaboration means that the teacher helps the library media specialist know what kinds of resources will be really useful. Several questions need to be answered:

> *How long will you be working on this unit?* The answer to this question will guide the library media specialist regarding how much to collect.
>
> *How will you use the materials?* If the response is that the teacher will be using them as resources for himself or herself, then concern for reading level is not as crucial.
>
> *Is there a particular focus to the unit?* The response will help the library media specialist know, for example, whether to collect materials related to causes of the Civil War or merely to collect information about the battles in the war itself—or both.
>
> *What kinds of activities do you anticipate?* If the response is reading and writing, the kinds of resources considered will be different from those collected if the response is hands-on activities and field trips.

Gathering materials becomes collaborative only when such questions are pursued. If the library media specialist simply pulls all the books about classical mythology or World War II off the shelves, the process is not collaborative. More important, it may not be particularly helpful, since providing teachers with more materials or the wrong materials may actually create unnecessary work for both teacher and library media specialist and may ultimately be counterproductive to the ultimate common purpose of collaboration—improving teaching and learning.

Level 7. Evangelistic outreach. Marketing might be another appropriate image for this level of involvement. Marketing requires clear understanding of the customers' needs and desires. By working closely with teachers, the library media specialist learns what will "sell" in terms of resources and services. In the school setting, one of the most effective approaches is providing in-service teacher education. For in-service training to be successful, teachers must have information about how and why such training will be useful to them. Collaboratively planned in-service training—when the library media specialist and teachers discuss what is possible and what is appropriate for them and their school—may indeed be the most successful. The library media specialist can suggest menus of possible in-service programs and together the group can discuss the local value of each suggestion. Such discussions allow the library media specialist to introduce resources to teachers in the context of their own needs assessment. Marketing activities can also include book talks for teachers, focused on upcoming themes or topics. Again the topic of the in-service training results from collaboration so that all teachers who participate have a sense of purpose about it.

Level 8. Scheduled planning in the support role. Formal collaborative planning occurs when the library media specialist participates in planning sessions with teachers and provides assistance in identifying resources or designing activities. In schools where collaboration is a part of the local school culture, formal team, department, or grade-level meetings occur routinely. Acting in the support role, the library media specialist responds to teacher initiatives, taking away from such sessions a "to-do" list that usually involves fetching resources or designing activities based on the directions of the teachers.

Levels 9 and 10. Instructional design. Here, formal collaboration between the library media specialist moves beyond the support role so that the library media specialist also engages in designing the unit. This team relationship engages teachers and the library media specialist equally in collaborative planning, including determining the goals for the unit, perhaps team-teaching, selecting resources, designing student assessment, and evaluating the unit at its conclusion.

Level 11. Curriculum development. Library media specialists have a legitimate place on curriculum development committees at the school and district levels. Their special expertise makes them important contributors to "big picture" curriculum planning. Library media specialists are, after all, teachers with the same educational qualifications as other teachers. Beyond that, their special expertise about resources, technologies, teaching, and learning strategies makes them valuable participants.

SUBJECT SPECIALIZATION

What is the library media specialist's subject specialization? One specialty is information processing, from articulating the information need through communicating information or applying information to solve a problem. Another is resources; the library media specialist must be able to locate resources of high quality to meet the needs of teachers. Knowing the literature for children and young adults is a particular strength of the library media specialist. Finally, technology, both instructional and informational, can be perceived as the library media specialist's specialization. Library media specialists then must approach teamwork with the confidence that they have something special to contribute. Next, they must make substantive contributions to the work.

GROUP TASK ROLES

The library media specialist has a unique position on a team as both an insider and an outsider (van Deusen, 1996). The library media specialist is a regular member of the team, and a member of the school staff, and as such is an insider. However, as a library media specialist rather than a classroom teacher, he or she is an outsider who brings a different perspective to the planning table—a perspective that incorporates what is being taught throughout the school in different grades or in different departments, a perspective influenced by technology and by a broad variety of resources. This unique insider-outsider view of the planning process creates an opportunity for raising questions that can be at once naive and challenging—questions like, "How does this new fifth-grade unit relate to the existing sixth-grade unit on space exploration?" or, "Should we consider the National Geographic Kids Net project called *Too Much Trash*?" or, "What is it you really want to accomplish in this unit?" Such questions can be posed by this outsider as naive queries that cause the teachers to reflect on their planning, to refocus or to alter their direction.

Variations on the lists of group task roles exist. Drawn from the classic work of Benne and Sheats (1948), these roles can be summarized as:

> The *clarifier* gives relevant examples, offers rationales, restates problems.
>
> The *initiator* suggests new or different ideas.
>
> The *opinion giver* states pertinent beliefs about discussion and others' suggestions.
>
> The *summarizer* reviews discussion, pulls it together.
>
> The *tester* raises questions to test whether the group is ready for a decision.
>
> The *compromiser* yields when necessary for progress.
>
> The *elaborator* builds on the suggestions of others.
>
> The *encourager* praises and supports others.
>
> The *gatekeeper* keeps communication open, encourages participation.
>
> The *harmonizer* mediates differences, reconciles points of view.
>
> The *tension reliever* uses humor or calls for breaks at appropriate times to draw off negative feelings.

Because of their unique insider-outsider status, five of these roles are particularly suited to the library media specialist as a member of the planning team: clarifier, initiator, opinion giver, summarizer, and tester.

As *clarifier*, the library media specialist can pose questions to teachers, "What is it you want children to learn?" or, "Friendship is a very broad topic; what might be the focus of this unit on friendship?" Such questions encourage teachers to reassess their planning and to focus on their goals. As *initiator*, the library media specialist can offer suggestions and alternatives to teachers. Benne and Sheats state that the initiator may suggest a new organizational structure to address a difficult issue. Perhaps a library media specialist might suggest, and subsequently facilitate, a faculty technology study group to examine educational technology issues and to determine in what direction the school should proceed. Similarly, a suggestion for a short course for students on "netiquette" might be in order. These suggestions are behaviors of an initiator. As *opinion giver*, the library media specialist might bring in a different viewpoint or perspective based on the available resources or on the professional literature. For example, the library media specialist might suggest that students should be using a word processor to do their initial drafts—not just their final drafts—to promote use of the computer as a writing process tool rather than a publication tool. The library media specialist might also suggest that dependence on e-mail for communication among teachers may not be appropriate until everyone has in-room access to the network; or the library media specialist might remind teachers to be aware that English-as-a-second-language students cannot depend on text-only resources for information. As *summarizer*, the library media specialist can share the results of listening with teachers, often teachers from various teams. As *tester*, he or she can measure what teachers say or do compared to the mission and philosophy of the school. All of these team task roles involve the library media specialist's ability to step away from the group and become an "outsider" to offer a perspective that could help direct, redirect, or focus the team's efforts. Such a perspective is uniquely valuable to the potential for the team to adhere to its mission and to maintain awareness of its larger context.

The other group task roles may be played by some library media specialists, but their appropriateness is related largely to personal characteristics; some people are natural tension relievers or clowns; others are not. The gatekeeper role may be a role sometimes taken on by library media specialists depending on the issue at hand. Generally these roles are less "mission-critical" for performing the work of the library media specialist on the team, when compared to the first five roles.

Figure 6.1 displays the task assignments adopted by the group in the Enhancement in Action box. This list is an example of the outcome of a planning meeting—a testament to the productive use of time.

AN EXAMPLE OF ENHANCEMENT IN ACTION: TEAM TEACHING

A team of fifth- and sixth-grade teachers is meeting to plan a new unit on oceanography. They are brainstorming subtopics to be covered—ocean animals, sea plants, waves and tides, folk tales and sea chants, navigation and map reading. The library media specialist, as something of an outsider, asks, "What is it you want students to learn in this unit?"

With that one question, the library media specialist begins to bring focus to the unit. Later in the discussion, a teacher suggests that the unit should have a research component, and wonders whether the library media specialist could teach students to look up current literature about environmental concerns for ocean species. The library media specialist responds that the collection does not include enough current periodicals or appropriate indexes for students to look up articles; however, he can provide students with preselected articles from which they could extract information.

The library media specialist has changed the focus of instruction from using indexes to locate information to developing skill in extracting information from resources and using note-taking strategies. Later in the discussion, teachers wonder what they will use to assess learning; after hearing ideas like developing a unit test or requiring an essay, the library media specialist suggests that the class develop a multimedia production about the ocean, with groups responsible for different aspects of the topic. Finally, the group assigns tasks—what will each teacher do and what will the library media specialist do?

FIGURE 6.1
Sample Team Member Assignments

Teacher	Tasks
Library Media Specialist	• locate articles on ocean ecology and environmental issues for exploration • teach lesson on note taking, providing students with two alternative formats • create a template for the class multimedia project • teach students how to use HyperStudio • locate video on whales, including whale songs
Ms. A, Teacher	• design lessons on waves and tides • gather supplies for hands-on waves activities
Mr. B, Teacher	• design lessons on sea mammals • arrange for speaker from local aquarium to discuss dolphins and their communication systems
Ms. C, Teacher	• design lessons on saltwater plant life • set up plant experiments with seaweed
Mr. D, Teacher	• work with library media specialist to design assessment rubric for final project

FORMAL AND INFORMAL COLLABORATION

Collaboration has been described primarily in terms of formal meetings as teams. Less-formal, less-involved activity might be considered cooperation. A teacher stops into a library media center and shares an idea about an upcoming unit, and the library media specialist responds with a suggestion, question, or idea. Collaboration has begun. Where this informal interaction leads depends largely on the kind of response the library media specialist makes. In this situation, the image of Loertscher's taxonomy should appear in the mind's eye of the library media specialist, who then thinks, "How much involvement does this teacher want from me? How much involvement is appropriate for this instance? Do I offer a few books to help the teacher out? Do I suggest that I search for a variety of materials to support this unit? Do I suggest that we sit down and do a little brainstorming about possible activities to engage kids for this unit?" These informal opportunities for collaboration can have the same impact as more formal group meetings; indeed, in many schools where collaborative planning is not a part of the local school culture, this is the only kind of collaborative opportunity.

BENEFITS OF COLLABORATION

Collaboration requires time and energy and it is more complicated than working alone. The benefits of collaboration make it worth the effort in planning for instruction.

Reflective Thought

A number of scholars and educators have written about reflection (for example Feiman, 1979; Tom, 1985; Zeichner & Liston, 1987), based in large part on Dewey's (1993) concept of reflective thinking. Schön's work brought reflective thinking to the forefront. Reflective teachers consistently assess the origins, purposes, and consequences of their work (Nolan & Huber, 1989). Pugach and Johnson (1990) describe reflection as an art of mediated thinking. They propose that reflection among teachers can be mediated and enhanced by collegial dialogue. They suggest that to facilitate reflective thinking one practices restraint and allows teachers to think aloud. Their proposal that a facilitator can promote reflective thinking is relevant to the role that a library media specialist plays in helping teachers plan. The library media specialist can raise questions to generate reflective thought among teachers, whether it is a question of how they would define their thematic unit on friendship, why and when their students should learn keyboarding, or what they want their students to learn about war.

Kottkamp (1990) distinguished between prescriptive and descriptive communication in his discussion of how to facilitate reflection. He emphasized the importance of avoiding prescriptive communication as a facilitator (that is, messages in the form of "you should . . . ") and instead using descriptive language that avoids judgment. The intent of the library media specialist is not to tell teachers what to do, but rather to encourage them to verbalize, to think aloud. Such thinking aloud can lead them to insights of their own and help them communicate with one another. Because of the "outsider" status, the library media specialist can pose naive questions that encourage deliberation among teachers, functioning as a catalyst for reflective thought. Holt (1993) encourages a deliberative climate in schools where teachers consider and determine both what and how to teach. The collegial relationship he describes reflects the exchange of ideas generated in these planning sessions; the library media specialist can facilitate that exchange by being an "insider"(a member of the staff), yet a somewhat naive participant as an "outsider."

Costa and Garmston (1995) state that cognitive coaching provides a safe format for professional dialogue and develops the skills for reflection on practice, both of which are necessary for productive collaboration. The library media specialist acts as a clarifier. By probing for his or her own clarification, the library media specialist encourages the teachers to clarify their thinking and planning for themselves. Poole (1994) describes this phenomenon when she characterizes one teacher as learning not from suggestions of a coach but from the process of reflection that was necessary to articulate her ideas to the colleague. Because the library media specialist is an "outsider," teachers need to articulate quite clearly what they are thinking. As in Poole's case, this process forces clarifying their thinking as well.

Whole-School Coordination

The library media specialist has the advantage of serving the entire school community—all grades, all subjects. By working in collaboration with teachers throughout the school, he or she can share knowledge of the total system with others and help teachers broaden their view of their students' total school experience. The model of self-contained, isolated teaching was based on the assumption that a textbook series would provide the articulation students needed from year to year within a discipline as well as consistency across grade levels. As schools move away from textbook-based learning, the need for coordination is greater. Teachers are designing instruction based on curriculum goals, but the potential is great for gaps and redundancy. Collaboration helps counteract both of those concerns. In his description of the basic school, Boyer (1995) asserts that teachers are leaders who work together. He advocates perceiving the school as a community of learners. The concept of community carries with it the connotation that people are working together in the learning process. Library media specialists can be important community members.

Better Teaching and Learning

It seems intuitive that when more than one mind is put to a task, better ideas, better planning, and ultimately better teaching and learning will occur. Each member of a team brings special kinds of talents, knowledge, experience, and intelligence to the table. It seems difficult to believe that any one of those people can produce better planning than the group working together. Of key importance is the ability of a team's members to behave in ways that take advantage of the synergistic potential of teamwork.

ACTION STRATEGIES

Learning and Teaching

- As a collaborative partner, whether working with an individual teacher or a whole team or department, leave each interaction with a to-do list and complete the tasks promptly, so that teachers gain confidence in collaboration.
- Avoid being merely a "go-fer" for a team; library media specialists have more than "things" to deliver. Ideas for teaching and learning strategies, offers to teach or team-teach, particularly when information processes are a part of the learning, are ways to contribute substantively to the quality of learning.

- Be sensitive to the requests of teachers. When a teacher asks a question, it may not be the *real* question, and an opportunity for collaboration may be presenting itself. For example:

When a teacher says, "Do we have a copy of *Mr. Popper's Penguins*?" he might really be asking, "Can you suggest a good read-aloud for my class?"

When a teacher asks, "May I bring my class to the library media center on Friday?" she might really be saying, "We are going to do some 'research' and I don't think my students know where to begin to find the information they will need."

When a teacher asks, "Do we have any books on Canada?" the real message is, "I am about to begin a unit on Canada, and I have no materials."

Of course, sometimes the simple question is merely seeking the simple direct answer; effectively tuning in and knowing which kind of response is needed is an important first step toward becoming a partner.

Information Access and Delivery

- Share resources about teamwork, such as:

Edie L. Holcomb, *Asking the Right Questions: Tools and Techniques for Teamwork* (Thousand Oaks, Calif.: Corwin Press, 1996).

Glenn Parker, *Team Players and Teamwork* (San Francisco: Jossey-Bass, 1990).

Limball Fisher, *Leading Self-Directed Work Teams—A Guide to Developing New Team Leadership Skills* (New York: McGraw Hill, 1993).

Carl Larson and Frank LaFasto, *Teamwork: What Must Go Right/ What Can Go Wrong* (Thousand Oaks, Calif: Sage Communications, 1989).

Program Administration

- If collaboration is not already a characteristic of the school culture, initiate conversations with individual teachers, including offers to brainstorm ideas or to search for materials; deliver high-quality information or resources promptly so that the teacher can see the benefit of working together.
- Share with the principal your intentions to collaborate with others in the school, and seek help for ways to become more involved in planning with teachers.

REFERENCES

Benne, Kenneth D. and P. Sheats. "Functional Roles of Group Members," *Journal of Social Issues* 4 (Spring 1948): 42–47.

Boyer, Ernest. *The Basic School: A Community for Learning* (Princeton, N.J.: Carnegie Foundation for the Advancement of Teaching, 1995), 46.

Costa, Arthur and R. Garmston. *Cognitive Coaching* (Norwood, Mass.: Christopher-Gordon, 1995), 8.

Dewey, John. *How We Think* (Boston: Heath, 1993).

Feiman, S. "Technique and Inquiry in Teacher Education: A Curricular Case Study," *Curriculum Inquiry* 9 (Spring 1979): 63–79

Holcomb, Edie L. *Asking the Right Questions: Tools and Techniques for Teamwork* (Thousand Oaks, Calif.: Corwin Press, 1996).

Holt, Maurice. "The High School Curriculum in the United States and the United Kingdom," *Journal of Curriculum and Supervision* 8 (Winter 1993): 157–173.

Katzenbach, Jon R. and D. K. Smith. *The Wisdom of Teams* (Boston: Harvard Business School Press, 1993).

Kottkamp, Robert B. "Means for Facilitating Reflection," *Education and Urban Society* 22 (February 1990): 182–203.

Loertscher, David V. *Taxonomies of the School Library Media Program* (Littleton, Colo.: Libraries Unlimited, 1988).

Nolan, James F. and T. Huber. "Nurturing the Reflective Practitioner Through Institutional Supervision: A Review of the Literature," *Journal of Curriculum and Supervision* 4 (Winter 1989): 126–145.

Parker, Glenn. *Team Players and Teamwork* (San Francisco: Jossey-Bass, 1990), 74–75.

Poole, Wendy. "Removing the 'Super' from Supervision, " *Journal of Curriculum and Supervision* 9 (Spring 1994): 284–309.

Pugach, Marleen and L. J. Johnson. "Developing Reflective Practice Through Structured Dialogue," in R. Clift et al., eds., *Encouraging Reflective Practice in Education; An Analysis of Issues and Programs* (New York: Teachers College Press, 1990), 204.

Reich, Robert. *Tales of a New America* (New York: Time Books, 1987).

Schön, Donald. *The Reflective Practitioner* (New York: Basic Books, 1983).

Tom, A. R. "Inquiring into Inquiry-Oriented Teacher Education," *Journal of Teacher Education* 36 (September/October 1985): 35–44

van Deusen, Jean Donham. "The School Library Media Specialist as a Member of the Teaching Team: 'Insider and Outsider'," *Journal of Curriculum and Supervision* 11 (Spring 1996): 229–248.

Zeichner, K. and D. Liston. "Theory and Practice in the Evolution of an Inquiry-Oriented Student Teaching Program," *Harvard Educational Review* 57 (1987): 34–48.

Chapter 7

Scheduling Library Media Activities

This chapter

- describes alternatives for scheduling instruction and information work in the library media center
- reviews the benefits and liabilities of flexible scheduling
- examines the prerequisites for flexible scheduling
- highlights the potential that block scheduling offers in secondary schools
- identifies action strategies for scheduling

Scheduling students into the library media center can be a challenge for the school library media specialist. In many schools, going to the library media center is no different from going to the art room or the music room. While it is good to consider the library media center a classroom because teaching and learning occur there, it is important to recall that the library media center is *more* than a classroom.

The school context is an important consideration for scheduling students into the library media center. Library media programs exist to meet needs for information or instruction. Therefore, scheduling visits at a point of need seems intuitive. Yet, other factors cause scheduling time for instruction and information work to be somewhat counterintuitive. Thus the weekly visit to the library media center is very common in elementary schools. Sending students to the library media center each week for a 30-minute class on "information skills" or literature meets several other needs: it meets the teachers' need to have added planning time, the need for all students to have frequent access to the library media center, the need for library media specialists to know the students in the school, the need to "cover" the information skills curriculum. However, there are inherent problems in counting on a weekly class schedule to achieve what should be the library media program's goal—making students independently effective information consumers. The work students do in the library media center and the lessons they learn ought to have application to real information problems. Information-processing skills are not analogous to music or art curricula where there is content. In the library media center, students learn about the intellectual tools needed to accomplish work within content areas. Designing schedules so that library media instruction occurs within the context of content area instruction makes the teaching and learning meaningful.

SCHEDULING ALTERNATIVES

Most commonly, the literature describes *fixed scheduling* and *flexible scheduling* as the two classic alternatives; in addition, there are variations. *Fixed scheduling* is arranging classes to meet in the library media center on a regular basis, usually once a week or once a scheduling cycle. Classes meet for perhaps 30 minutes, and activities might include direct teaching by the library media specialist, story times, book talks, book selection and checkout, or work on information-based projects. With fixed scheduling, library media specialists can print up their year's schedule, showing when each class will come to the library media center. Space left in the schedule becomes time for specific library media tasks (cataloging and processing, preparation, meeting with teachers, reference work), or it can be offered to teachers for scheduling other library media center activities.

On the other hand, *flexible scheduling* is a plan by which the library media specialist teaches classes when students have a specific activity driven by a need in their classroom; these classes do not have library media instructional time until they have a need. For example, a class might come to the library media center every day for five days—or two weeks in a row—for instruction or work on an assignment or project, and then they may not have any instruction in the library media center for three weeks until a class activity requires it again.

Concern about retention from one session to the next is one good reason to support flexible scheduling. When a library media specialist sets out to teach a complex process, it may take more than one class period to develop the skill. In weekly scheduled classes, seven days intervene between the first and second lessons. How likely is it that students will retain learning from the first week in order to build on it the second week? Another factor is transfer of learning; weekly scheduled classes where the learning is isolated from classroom experiences create situations where application to real need is less likely. What is the likelihood that students will automatically transfer what they learn about indexes to using the index in their American history textbook, unless there is teaching for transfer and the teaching in the library media center is integrated?

Weekly classes can prolong activities over several weeks; this can decrease students' enthusiasm. If a library media specialist is teaching about keyword searching or the Dewey Decimal System, for example, it may take a month or more of weekly lessons to complete the instruction. By the third or fourth installment, student interest can easily decline. Although they have only spent 50 or 75 minutes on the topic, the spread over several weeks makes it feel much longer.

One critical attribute of flexible scheduling is that some classes come to the library media center several days in a row in order to accomplish a task, whereas in other weeks these classes might not come to the library media center as a class at all. Also, the work that students do during the flexibly scheduled class time grows out of assignments from their classroom teacher. The library media center activity is timely—students have genuine concern about what they will learn because it has immediate relevance. In a flexibly scheduled library media program, no two weeks are alike.

Some people describe what they are doing as flexible scheduling but in fact their variations lack some of flexible scheduling's critical attributes. For example, half a class comes to the library media center each week to work with the library media specialist on classroom-generated topics. While this departs from the fixed schedule plan (because it does not involve the whole class coming for instruction all at once and it does not provide the teacher with release time), it is still a once-a-week time slot filled by a scheduled commitment and that slot is not available for a point-of-need request. This limits the students' instruction in the library media center to once-a-week even when more complex tasks would warrant multiple sessions scheduled closer together.

Another variation reserves each class a time slot at the beginning of the year and assures teachers that whenever they want to schedule their class into the library media center, that time slot time is theirs. While this practice fits the flexible scheduling model in that classes do not come to the library media center every week, it does not provide teachers the same degree of flexibility. For example, when science class is doing information work, they can go to the library media center only during science class, and for social studies, they must go during social studies class, for however many days are needed. In other words, the point of need is not really considered. While these alternatives to flexible scheduling have advantages, they should not be confused with true flexible scheduling, where flexible is a literal term and where the teacher can schedule the class into the library media center for instruction or for guided and independent work at the point of need and until the need is met.

BENEFITS OF FLEXIBLE SCHEDULING

Flexible scheduling is supposed to improve both student and library media specialist performance because it supports students' learning and practicing information processing skills *in context* while it supports flexibility in library media specialists' schedules to work collaboratively with teachers. For students, then, the flexible schedule allows them to work and learn information skills *just in time* (that is, when they need to apply them to class work they are doing), rather than *just in case* they might need them some day. Library media specialists who have a fixed schedule typically meet with students when teachers are free to plan. They are therefore unable to participate, even briefly, with teachers during planning. Flexible scheduling, on the other hand, should allow them to make appointments with teachers for collaborative planning. Flexible scheduling allows library media specialists to teach complex skills by having classes meet daily when needed to build understanding from one day to the next, rather than from one week to the next. Flexible scheduling is not intended to reduce the library media specialists' teaching, nor is it intended to reduce contact with students. In fact, a study of time use among elementary school library media specialists found no significant difference in how much time those with fixed schedules and those with flexible schedules spent teaching (van Deusen, 1996). Flexible scheduling is not a strategy to reduce teaching. If it does reduce teaching, then its implementation should be examined to determine if some prerequisite factors (listed below) have not been met.

PREREQUISITES FOR FLEXIBLE SCHEDULING

While there may be no one guaranteed key to success, some features seem to make flexible scheduling more likely to succeed. Six key elements are (van Deusen, 1995)

- information skills curriculum matched with content area curriculum
- flexible access
- team planning
- principal's expectations
- commitment to resource-based learning
- support staff

If these six conditions are not in place, it may be premature to advance flexible scheduling. Beware of the possibility that a move away from fixed scheduling can become a move toward no scheduling (that is, children having little or no access to the library media center and little or no library media instruction).

Information Skills Curriculum

The library media specialist must have a clear plan for what he or she intends to teach. Several models for information process curricula exist; widely known models include those by Eisenberg (Eisenberg & Berkowitz, 1990), Kuhlthau (1994), Stripling (1988), and Pappas (1995). These models can underpin curriculum design. Classroom teachers must also have a clear curriculum plan for their own teaching. Through collaboration and negotiation, classroom teachers and library media specialists match the information skills agenda to the content area goals so that information skills are learned within the context of the content area curriculum. This planning involves designing appropriate instructional activities to support integration and laying out the timeline for the school year. Such planning can occur between individual teachers and the library media specialist, or between teams (grade-level or discipline-based). The crucial fact is that such collaboration must occur to map the integration. If this process is not comprehensive—every teacher, every grade or team—the information process curriculum is hit or miss. We would probably not allow math to be hit or miss, so how can we in good conscience settle for an information curriculum that is hit or miss?

This preliminary planning and mapping require sustained sessions; one possibility is to set aside workshop time before school. Another possibility is to hire substitute teachers so that teachers and the library media specialist can map the integration. The principal's support for a truly integrated information skills curriculum is important in facilitating the planning phase.

Flexible Access

Flexible scheduling means that children no longer have a guaranteed weekly visit to the library media center for book checkout and reading guidance. While we see an increasing emphasis on information processing and information technology, the elementary library media program aims to encourage children to become readers, to guide them in selecting appropriate reading materials, and to provide access to those materials. When the weekly class period is eliminated, it must be replaced with some way to meet these reading goals. Flexible access to the library media center is perhaps the best solution.

Flexible access is complex; its implementation must be systemic. It is not enough to simply say to everyone, "The library media center is open all day. Children may come whenever they wish." Classroom teachers must enable access *from* the classroom and *into* the library media center. Some teachers establish systems for allowing free flow between the classroom and the library media center. For others, concerns about student accountability demands more formalized systems. Systems as simple as creating laminated passes for use in each classroom can govern how many students arrive at the center at once and how many leave a given classroom at one time. Two, three, or four passes per classroom, depending on school and center size, may meet the needs. One would hope that whenever a student has an information need, there is a way to seek the solution in a timely fashion.

Another way to support access is to assign each classroom a 15-minute period each week to come to the center with the teacher so that each child can explore and check out materials. This arrangement differs from weekly scheduled classes in two important ways: the purpose is not direct instruction, and the teacher accompanies the class to assist.

If possible, the library media specialist may want to try to schedule these browse-and-check-out times during periods when it is unlikely that other teachers would be requesting flexibly scheduled instruction (for example when classes are having mathematics, physical education, or other activities less dependent on library media center use). Whatever the system, access for all must be addressed.

Team Planning

Research suggests that in schools where teachers plan as teams (by grade level or content area), flexible scheduling particularly enhances the consultation role (van Deusen & Tallman, 1994). The relationship was not determined to be causal, but is clearly correlative. This finding suggests that the library media specialist ought to provide some leadership toward teachers forming teams and working together if this structure is not already in place.

Principal's Expectations

Research has found that where some form of flexible scheduling was in place and principals had expectations for the library media specialist to participate in instructional planning with teachers, more such participation occurred (Donham, 1993). The importance of the principal perceiving the library media program as a collaborative partner in classroom instruction cannot be overlooked. The library media specialist must help the principal see the relationship between the library media program and the classroom and must demonstrate that relationship in practice.

Commitment to Resource-Based Learning

One of flexible scheduling's advantages is facilitating the library media specialist to work as an instructional consultant with teachers. In that role, library media specialists identify appropriate electronic and print resources and recommend ways those resources can be used in teaching. Resource-based learning fits a constructivist approach to learning; it facilitates student engagement and active learning. If there is no commitment to resource-based learning, it is difficult to envision flexible scheduling serving much purpose; the library media specialist may have less to offer as a consultant in a textbook-bound approach to teaching.

Support Staff

Support staff will almost inevitably enhance a program with flexible scheduling. Research suggests that library media specialists who have support staff do significantly more consulting (van Deusen, 1995). In that study the operational definition of the consulting role included five tasks: gathering materials for teachers, helping teachers identify instructional objectives, helping teachers plan learning activities, team-teaching, and evaluating the instruction. In a follow-up survey, three groups were analyzed: those with no paid support staff, those with support staff for up to 20 hours per week, and those with support staff for 20 hours or more per week. Those library media specialists who had more than 20 hours of paid support staff in their library media centers reported over 150 percent as many instances of four of the five consulting tasks (all except gathering materials) than those who had no support staff. With support staff available in the library media center, the library media specialist can meet with a teacher or a team, and students can still access the center and locate and use resources there. While flexible scheduling can occur without support staff, there may be no one available to help students when the library media specialist is working with classes or teachers. In the follow-up survey, library media specialists indicated that they gathered materials on request of teachers, regardless of support staff availability (van Deusen, 1995). This task may only require a brief conversation between library media specialist and teachers. However, more extensive collaboration must occur for media specialists to join in designing instructional objectives or activities, whereas gathering materials can occur based on a note or an e-mail message. Of course, building size must be considered in determining an appropriate amount of support staff. No significant differences were found between those with no support staff and those with staff for fewer than 20 hours. These findings suggest that, at a minimum, it may take 20 hours per week to begin to make a difference in consulting.

MIXED SCHEDULING

There is a compromise between fixed and flexible scheduling that bears examination. It incorporates both kinds of scheduling. With totally flexible scheduling, there is the concern that many students will never come to the library media center. Perhaps their teacher is reluctant to schedule the class periodically into the library media center; perhaps a student's class schedule limits the opportunities to visit the library media center; or perhaps a student has no motivation to go to the library media center. These students, then, are missing out on opportunities to learn information access and use skills. They are also missing out on browsing—a particularly important activity for younger children who are less independent library media center users. Another concern is teachers' release time. In many schools, teachers have grown dependent on the release time provided while the library media specialist takes their classes, and teachers are understandably reluctant to give up that time.

In response to these concerns for students and teachers, the library media center can schedule weekly or regular visits to the library media center for classes, and in addition offer flexible scheduling. Creating a mixed schedule is challenging because setting time for the regularly scheduled sessions is affected by several factors. Ideally, they should be scheduled during times when other classes might be less likely to need flexibly scheduled class time (such as during art, music, physical education, foreign language or mathematics instruction). Also, these sessions can be short, say 15 minutes in length, because their purpose is scheduled access, not teaching. During this time, it is likely that the library media specialist will do no formal instruction, beyond a few brief book talks or a brief introduction to some new resource in the center. These visits are single purpose: to ensure that all students have regular and frequent access to the library media center. The majority of the library media schedule remains flexible, so that when a class needs sustained instruction or guided information work, that need can be met. The flexibly scheduled time remains a high priority for the library media specialist and for the center. If space allows, flexibly scheduled classes can be double-booked during weekly check-out visits, once regular visitors establish an appropriate level of independence, or if support staff can monitor these visitors and allow the library media specialist to work with classes who need "the expert" for instruction or assistance. Supervision of regularly scheduled check-out groups can even be a volunteer activity; the times are predictable and the skills needed can be taught to volunteers.

Although many library media specialists feel that it is a stop-gap measure, research suggests that the mixed schedule option is indeed worthy of consideration (van Deuson & Tallman, 1994). In a 1993 national study of scheduling, compared to library media specialists with fixed scheduling, those with mixed schedules participated in significantly more consultation with teachers. Furthermore, in the same study those library media specialists with mixed schedules significantly outperformed those with both fixed and flexible scheduling in how frequently they incorporated information skills instruction with classroom curriculum activities. These research results highlight the potential for combining fixed schedule classes, perhaps at certain grade levels, and flexibly scheduled classes.

An example of a mixed schedule appears in Table 7.1, which requires some explanation. This is a schedule for a three-section K–5 school. Each class has a weekly scheduled check-out time to ensure that all students have regular access to the library media center. These 15-minute periods are shown on the schedule in italics. The teacher may or may not come along with the group, depending on local priorities for teacher release time. Generally, these regular sessions are scheduled at times unlikely to be sought for flexible scheduling—at the beginning or end of the day, around the lunch hour, or during times when special area or mathematics classes meet.

The example shows that the two succeeding weeks are not alike, except for the weekly circulation times. It is of particular importance that some classes come to the library media center daily for extended work on a project. There are some classes that come to the center for a single class meeting. Some classes are scheduled for two 30-minute modules; others are scheduled for only one. Many activities involve the whole class, but some involve small groups. Teachers do not have designated time slots for their flexibly scheduled classes. Instead, they schedule classes to fit their teaching needs; for activities in reading, a given class may come to the media center in the morning, but when that class has a project requiring media center resources in science they may schedule to come in the afternoon. The classroom schedule drives the library media center schedule. All these variations are driven by the students' immediate needs—not by a set schedule.

BLOCK SCHEDULING

Secondary schools are rethinking the daily schedule for classes, to seek a system that provides greater opportunities for greater depth in instruction. Block scheduling is one such structure that may provide a solution. Some schools have created variations on the block schedule concept, but one common arrangement is to offer six periods over two days, with Day A (when three classes meet), and Day B (when three other classes meet). Other options exist, but the commonality among them is

FIGURE 7.1
Sample Mixed Schedule

Week 1

	Monday	Tuesday	Wednesday	Thursday	Friday
8:00 –8:30	Meet with KdgTeam			Meet with Grade 1 Team	
8:30–8:45	*Grade 3 Circ Berger*		*Grade 3 Circ Barr*	*Grade 3 Circ Denison*	
8:45–9:00	*Grade 2 Cir Berger*		*Grade 2 Circ Barr*	*Grade 2 Circ Denison*	
9:00–9:30	*Kdg. Story/Circ Smith*	*Kdg. Story/Circ Jones*	Grade 3 Denison Index Lesson Animals Unit		*Kdg.Story/Circ Johnson*
9:30–10:00			Grade 3 Denison Index Lesson Animals Unit		Grade 5 Roy 6 students to work on magazines
10:00–10:30					Grade 5 Roy 6 students to work on magazines
10:30–11:00	Grade 5 Bell Social Studies Culture Proj.	Grade 5 Bell Social Studies Culture Proj.	Grade 5 Bell Social Studies Culture Proj.	Grade 5 Bell Social Studies Culture Proj.	
11:00–11:30	Grade 5 Bell Social Studies Culture Proj.	Grade 5 Bell Social Studies Culture Proj.	Grade 5 Bell Social Studies Culture Proj.	Grade 5 Bell Social Studies Culture Proj.	
11:30–11:45	*Grade 4 Circ Gorman*	*Grade 4 Circ Flynn*			*Grade 4 Circ Hodge*
11:45–12:00				Lunch	Lunch
12:00–12:15	Lunch	Lunch	Lunch	Lunch	Lunch
12:15–12:30	Lunch	Lunch	Lunch *Goff*	*Grade 5 Circ Hart*	*Grade 5 Circ Roy*
12:30–1:00			Green ESL Project	Green ESL Project	
1:00–1:30	Grade 4 Flynn Science HyperStudio Groups	Grade 4 Flynn Science HyperStudio Groups	Grade 4 Flynn Science HyperStudio Groups	Grade 4 Flynn Science HyperStudio Groups	Grade 4 Flynn Science HyperStudio Groups

FIGURE 7.1
(cont.)

1:30–2:00	Grade 4 Flynn Science HyperStudio	Grade 4 Flynn Science HyperStudio	Grade 4 Flynn Science HyperStudio	Grade 4 Flynn Science HyperStudio	Grade 4 Flynn Science HyperStudio
2:00–2:30	Grade 3 Berger Native Am.	Grade 3 Berger Native Am.		Meet with Grade 2 Team	Meet with Grade 3 Team
2:30–2:45	Grade 1 Circ Burke	Grade 1 Circ Burke			Grade 1 Circ Burke
2:45–3:15			Grade 5 Circ Bell	Grade 5 Circ Roy	Grade 5 Circ Travis

Week 2

	Monday	Tuesday	Wednesday	Thursday	Friday
8:00 –8:30	Meet with Grade 5 Team				
8:30–8:45	Grade 3 Circ Berger		Grade 3 Circ Barr	Grade 3 Circ Denison	
8:45–9:00	Grade2 Circ Berger		Grade 2 Circ Barr	Grade2 Circ Denison	
9:00–9:30	Kdg. Story/Circ Smith	Kdg. Story/Circ Jones			Kdg. Story/Circ Johnson
9:30–10:00	Grade 5 Roy 6 students to work on magazines		Grade 4 Gorman State history Research	Grade 4 Gorman State history Research	Grade 4 Gorman State history Research
10:00–10:30	Grade 5 Roy 6 students to work on magazines		Grade 4 Gorman State history Research	Grade 4 Gorman State history Research	Grade 4 Gorman State history Research
10:30–11:00	Grade 3 Barr Poetry Search	Grade 3 Barr Poetry Search	Grade 3 Barr Poetry Search	Grade 3 Deniss Poetry Search	Grade 3 Deniss Poetry Search
11:00–11:30	Grade 3 Berger Poetry Search	Grade 3 Berger Poetry Search	Grade 3 Berger Poetry Search		
11:30-11:45	Grade 4 Circ Gorman	Grade 4 Circ Flynn			Grade 4 Circ Hodge
11:45–12:00			Grade 5 Circ Adams	Lunch	Lunch
12:00–12:15	Lunch	Lunch	Lunch	Lunch	Lunch

FIGURE 7.1
(cont.)

12:15–12:30	Lunch	Lunch	Lunch	*Grade 5 Circ* *Goff*	*Grade 5 Circ* *Hart*
12:30–1:00	Grade 1 Burke Farm Animals	Grade 1 Burke Farm Animals	Grade 5 Roy Booktalks: Biography		Grade 5 Bell Booktalks: Biography
1:00–1:30	Grade 4 Hodge Science HyperStudio	Grade 4 Hodge Science HyperStudio	Grade 4 Hodge Science HyperStudio	Grade 4 Hodge Science HyperStudio	Grade 4 Hodge Science HyperStudio
1:30–2:00	Grade 4 Hodge Science HyperStudio	Grade 4 Hodge Science HyperStudio	Grade 4 Hodge Science HyperStudio	Grade 4 Hodge Science HyperStudio	Grade 4 Hodge Science HyperStudio
2:00–2:30		Grade 4 Flynn Booktalks: Survival Stories			Grade 4 Gorman Booktalks: Family Fiction
2:30–2:45	*Grade 1* *Burke* *Circ*	*Grade 1* *Barnes* *Circ*	G/T Inventions Researdh	G/T Inventions Research	G/T Inventions Research *Grade 1* *Holland* *Circ*
2:45–3:15			*Grade 5 Circ* *Bell* G/T Inventions Research	*Grade 5 Circ* *Roy* G/T Inventions Research	*Grade 5 Circ* *Travis* G/T Inventions Research

longer class periods and usually the elimination of study halls. Extended class periods allow for more varied teaching/learning strategies to be employed beyond the lecture, a method that has been pervasive in situations where there was not enough class time for cooperative learning, hands-on learning, or project work.

Block scheduling offers an ideal opportunity for increased collaboration between library media specialists and teachers. Teachers in such systems have more class time for students to do significant information work in the library media center. Many will, in fact, be searching for ways to change their teaching behaviors, and the time is ideal for library media specialists to team up with them and initiate projects and activities for classes in the library media center. Often by the time a class arrives in the center and receives brief instrucitons about a task, there may be only a few minutes left to carry out work, or students may just begin to really use the information they have located when it is time to pack up and move on. Block scheduling can alleviate these frustrations.

ACTION STRATEGIES

Perhaps the greatest challenge in a fixed schedule is how to make the transition toward a more flexible schedule. Since every school is different, there is no formula for making that happen, but there are some strategies to consider in light of the local situation.

Learning and Teaching

- Provide in-service teacher training about the information skills curriculum, including information access, use, and production; demonstrate with local examples how these skills can be incorporated into what teachers are teaching; show an example of a class that could come to the library media center every day for, say, five days in a row to complete a project (compared to dragging a project out over weeks because it is done one period per week).
- Take a proactive stance to work closely with teachers who are changing to block scheduling; design lessons that incorporate use of the library media center and that help students develop increasingly sophisticated information skills.
- Serve on study committees in schools that are considering a transition to block scheduling, and initiate thinking about how to use the library media program better within instructional programs.

Information Access and Delivery

- Consider mixed scheduling as an appropriate way to accommodate as many needs as possible.

Program Administration

- Meet with the principal to discuss the concerns about weekly classes. Point out the advantages and disadvantages of fixed scheduling as outlined in Figure 7.2.
- Discuss teacher release time, especially if it is a contractual matter, and look for alternative ways to provide the time without fully booking the library media specialist (for example, enlist a teacher associate or volunteer to supervise weekly visits for browsing; develop a long-range schedule showing that teachers actually will

FIGURE 7.2
Advantages and Disadvantages of Fixed Scheduling

Advantages	Disadvantages
Teachers have release time.	Library media specialist is "tied up" when teachers have planning time and is often unavailable to collaborate with teachers.
All students get to the library media center every week.	Students cannot retain what they learned a week ago; the library media specialist cannot build on that information for complex processes.
All students get exposure to information skills.	Skills taught in isolation are usually not mastered because students see no relevance.
The library media specialist's work day is filled with easily documented activity.	The library media specialist may not be available when teachers need help or when students need instruction.
Weekly classes are predictable.	Once-a-week sessions limit the complexity of activities. For example, producing television commercials as a part of a unit on advertising or creating a historical newspaper based on information collected from various sources requires considerable time; such a project accomplished in weekly 25-minute segments drags on and students lose their enthusiasm.

have as much—or more—release time *on average* if classes come to the library media center on a flexible schedule).

- Explore the idea of other specialists (for example, group guidance sessions) providing some classroom teacher release time.
- Given the opportunity for some flexible scheduling, make a monthly report to the principal, documenting the activity in the library media center. The report should indicate
    — classes regularly scheduled and their activities
    — classes flexibly scheduled and their activities
    — evidence of student access to the library media center
    — services provided to teachers
- Review the list of prerequisites for flexible scheduling with the principal:
    — information skills curriculum matched with content area curriculum
    — flexible access
    — team planning
    — principal's expectations
    — commitment to resource-based learning
    — support staff

Work with the principal to develop an action plan to address each of these requirements.

- Accept some compromises at the beginning. For example, while the ideal is that teachers accompany their classes to the library media center for instruction, it is likely that some teachers will believe they are free to leave if the library media specialist is teaching the students. Indeed, it would be helpful for the teacher to know what students have learned. On the other hand, is the teacher's presence worth losing a scheduling scheme that will make library media instruction meaningful for students? Probably not. The optimist will say that, over time, teachers may begin to believe it is worthwhile to attend when the library media specialist is teaching, as they see what their students learn. Meanwhile, the library media specialist does well to keep the teacher informed about the lesson content, and to encourage teacher attendance. Certainly, many teachers will want to be present, and will enjoy the opportunity to collaborate. Still, it may be necessary to accept the decision of those who do not. It is possible that teachers will see little use for flexible scheduling for some grades; often kindergarten teachers focus on building habits in their children and the once-a-week

class meets their needs. They may see little need for flexibly scheduled classes because their children have not attained the literacy
skills needed for some information work. In response the library
media specialist can accept their position, and yet share the possibilities for production activities that may be highly appropriate
for kindergarten children (such as creating an electronic alphabet
picture "book," using a program like Kid Pix [Brøderbund], or creating finger puppets and performing puppet plays in the library
media center). These are activities not easily accomplished in
weekly classes, but with flexible scheduling they occur in a timely
fashion that maintains children's enthusiasm.

REFERENCES

Donham, Jean. "Effects of Fixed Versus Flexible Scheduling on Curriculum Involvement and Skills Integration in Elementary School Library Media Programs," *School Library Media Quarterly* 21 (Spring 1993): 173–182.

Eisenberg, Michael B. and Robert E. Berkowitz. *Information Problem-Solving: The
Big Six Skills Approach to Library and Information Skills Instruction* (Norwood,
N.J.: Ablex, 1990).

Kuhlthau, Carol Collier. *Teaching the Library Research* Process (Metuchen, N.J.:
Scarecrow Press, 1994).

Pappas, Marjorie. *Teaching Electronic Information Skills Series* (Follett Software
Company, 1995).

Stripling, Barbara K. *Brainstorms and Blueprints: Teaching Library Research as a
Thinking Process* (Englewood, Colo.: Libraries Unlimited, 1988).

van Deusen, Jean Donham. "An Analysis of the Time-use of Elementary School
Library Media Specialists and Factors that Influence It," *School Library Media Quarterly* 24 (Winter 1996): 85–92.

———. "Prerequisites for Flexible Scheduling," *Emergency Librarian* 23 (Septem-
ber/October 1995): 16–19.

——— and Julie I. Tallman."The Impact of Scheduling on Curriculum Consultation and Information Skills Instruction," *School Library Media Quarterly* 23
(Fall 1994), 17–25.

Chapter 8

Collection

This chapter

- discusses selection criteria and policy
- describes trends in collection development that reflect more interaction with the context of the library media program
- discusses the new demands on collection planning that result from the introduction of electronic resources
- describes the process for reconsideration of challenged materials
- discusses collection maintenance
- identifies action strategies related to collection

Although the library media program is far more than a warehouse of materials, still the collection is important. In a time when the mass media predict the demise of print, when people speak of virtual libraries, when funding for resources is challenged by those who suggest that there is no need for a collection because all the information is "out there" on the World Wide Web, it may be more important than ever to discuss the library media collection. Electronic access will certainly continue to change the nature and emphasis in collections. Nevertheless, collecting resources to be locally available continues to be important. Naively, administrators sometimes assume that electronic access to information will justify reducing the budget for materials. For several reasons, this is simply not true. For example, the elementary school's reading program demands print resources for children to read and the mathematics program demands manipulative materials (such as items to count and sort or items with which to measure). Students in science classes will continue to use models to understand scientific principles. Students seeking a quick answer to a fact question will often find it most efficient to look in an almanac or another fact book. Furthermore, not all information is readily accessible online. In many schools, online access is limited to one or a few workstations—hardly enough to meet the needs of everyone in the building. Voluntary reading will most likely continue to occur between covers rather than on a screen. Some nonfiction will continue to be better explored in print rather than in electronic resources. A collection that includes both electronic and print resources is likely to continue to characterize school library media centers, despite the growth of online access.

If the library media program is characterized by close collaboration with teachers, involvement with students and their diverse needs, and communication with principals, parents, and the community, then collection use warrants continued fiscal support. High-use patterns should be documented to show that teaching and learning are dependent on the center's physical collection as well as its access to online information. Each year *School Library Journal* publishes the average book price for that year. In 1998, the average book price was listed there as $15.99. This compares to a 1997 average of $15.29, a 2 percent increase in one year (Gerhardt, 1998). The constant rate of book publishing for children and youth promises no imminent demise in print materials, and the infusion of books into content-area learning signals a continued demand; budgets will thus need to keep pace with the market prices. Budgets for local collections continue to be needed for books, CD-ROMs, videos, and other formats in addition to support for online access.

SELECTION CRITERIA AND POLICIES

Each school district should have a formal, board-approved policy governing materials selection and reconsideration. In research on reconsideration of materials, Hopkins found that in those schools where a formal policy exists, library media specialists felt less pressure to be cautious in their selection practices (Hopkins, 1991). The selection policy should include

1. *Statement of responsibility for selection.* This statement is typically a delegation of authority to staff members. Often the responsibility

is delegated to professionally trained and certified staff or to a selection committee.

2. *Criteria for selection.* General criteria might include

- consistent with the general educational goals of the district and the objectives of specific courses
- high in quality of factual content and presentation
- appropriate for the subject area and for the age, emotional development, ability level, and social development of the students for whom the materials are selected
- of aesthetic, literary, or social value
- authored by competent and qualified authors and producers
- fosters respect for women and minority and ethnic groups
- designed to motivate students and staff to examine their own attitudes and behaviors and to comprehend their own duties, responsibilities, rights, and privileges as participating citizens in a pluralistic, nonsexist society
- selected for strengths rather than rejected for weaknesses
- suitable in physical format and appearance for intended use
- provides ideological balance on controversial issues

3. *Selection procedures.* Procedures should ensure quality by advocating use of reviewing media and professional selection tools. Procedures should be outlined for gathering input from the library media program's constituencies, accepting gifts with the same criteria as are applied to new purchases, weeding, and periodically replacing both materials and hardware.

4. *Reconsideration process.* A written procedure for any community member to request formally that an item be reconsidered for inclusion in the collection. This process should include the steps to be taken to request a reconsideration, the composition and operation of the reconsideration committee, a description of the review process, and a statement of the next course of action in the event of a failure to resolve the concern.

Hopkins's research indicates that "support for retention of challenged materials from persons/organizations within or outside the district was greater for written challenges" and that written rather than oral challenges predominate when there is a selection policy in place (Hopkins, 1993, p. 29). One can expect the due process afforded by a written selection policy is more likely to result in retaining challenged materials. These findings underscore the importance of insisting on a written, board-approved policy in order to protect intellectual freedom.

TRENDS

Collection development in school library media centers is changing as a result of such developments as shared decision making, resource-based learning in place of textbook-based teaching, and demands for electronic formats.

Focus

Librarians have traditionally developed collections, in part, with a "just-in-case" mind-set; that is, they have tried to maintain a balanced collection that covers the breadth of potential information needs. A trend toward more focus and away from balance relates to three factors. First, as online access becomes more widespread and more efficient with faster connectivity and better search engines, more reference questions may be answered online. Online access is providing the balance in the collection in place of locally available physical resources. Second, school library media budgets are not growing in step with the increasing costs of materials. Reduced buying power means that library media specialists must prioritize; they cannot maintain broad-based collections and support curricular topics in depth. Third, school library media collections are becoming more curriculum-driven as programs become more integrated with the school curriculum and as teachers depend more on trade resources and less on textbooks.

Curriculum-driven collections tend to have depth in those topics that the curriculum emphasizes. For example, middle schools where American history is taught are likely to have library media collections with substantial depth in that topic. Those same collections may have very little, if any, specialized resources on Asian history if it is not represented in the curriculum.

Curriculum mapping and collection mapping are two strategies useful for measuring how well the collection fits the curriculum. Curriculum mapping is a strategy of identifying the instructional content for each grade level or course, and summarizing it on a chart to show the spectrum. Charting the curriculum shows the articulation of instructional content from grade to grade and course to course. If there are gaps, they become more obvious, and if there are inappropriate repetitions, they too are evident. A curriculum map is a valuable tool for the library media specialist—it facilitates anticipating topics so that appropriate materials can be selected to support instruction.

Collection mapping is a technique for identifying topics and determining the depth of holdings on those topics. Figure 8.1 shows a small segment of a collection map for an elementary school. In this case, the library media specialist was concerned not only with the number of volumes, but also with the age of the collection. The categories for a collection map should compare to curricular topics so that the map reveals how well the collection supports the curriculum. Areas of curriculum emphasis should be consistent with collection depth; where that is not the case, these areas become purchasing priorities, unless the library media specialist has identified external sources that can reliably support needs.

Focusing collection development on curriculum can create challenges. When the collection does not respond to a query, the library media specialist must go to outside sources to provide assistance. Access to the World Wide Web is often a solution for topics infrequently investigated, and interlibrary loan with neighboring schools or public libraries is a traditional resource.

Curriculum changes from time to time, and when it does, the changes will affect the collection. For example, when teachers who have taught a thematic literature unit on the Middle Ages for several years abandon it

FIGURE 8.1
Collection Data for Curricular Emphases

Category	Average Copyright Date	Number of Volumes
Science 590s (Animals)	1970	160
Science 520s (Space Science)	1970	65
Social Studies 970s (American History)	1974	120
Technology 600s	1972	140

in favor of a thematic unit on heroes and heroines, few of the resources collected for the former theme will apply to the new one, and many items about the Middle Ages will go largely unused, except for the rare independent request. A major curriculum change calls for a supplement to the library media budget to accommodate any new in-depth demands on the collection.

Collaboration

Library media specialists usually have the primary responsibility for selecting resources, yet the importance of teachers and library media specialists collaborating on collection decisions cannot be overlooked. In the past, library media specialists read reviews and based their selections largely on what the reviewers said, with an eye to what they thought their clients wanted. In integrated library media programs, the emphasis may be on what the clients are asking for, and secondarily what the reviewers say. When library media specialists are working with teachers' planning teams, they are in very close communication with what is being taught. That information helps them to prioritize according to curricular demands. As units are discussed, they learn what units were frustrating for teachers and students because of resource deficiencies; they learn where the collection has worked well. Direct involvement with teachers in planning and evaluating instruction is a key factor in ensuring that the library media specialist is making good collection development decisions.

Collection development can be collaborative in another way also. In districts with multiple schools, some collaborative collection development can occur among schools. By comparing collections and demands and identifying common needs, it is quite possible to share resources. This strategy is particularly useful for curriculum-based purchases used only once a year. For example, thematic literature units often call for purchase of multiple copies of some titles for common readings. If more than one school will teach a unit on conflict and will use some of the same titles for common reading, is it necessary for every school to purchase the multiple copies? Could the units be coordinated so that they are not taught at the same time and materials could be shared? The cost of materials and the increasing demands for trade books, coupled with minimal increases in budget—in part because of the increasing demands for hardware and technology infrastructure—makes cooperative purchases particularly attractive where possible.

Quality

Collaborating with teachers and encouraging their involvement in collection decisions does not mean that the library media specialist abdicates overall responsibility for the collection. While teachers may indicate collection areas they perceive to be deficient or strong, the library media specialist has data to confirm what the collection includes. Also, the library media specialist can identify external sources to supplement the local collection, particularly for infrequent requests. Maintaining a high standard of quality is of particular importance for the library media specialist. When teachers suggest specific items, library media specialists need to apply the criteria listed in the selection policy. Reviewing media and selection tools continue to be essential resources for final selection decisions. If a teacher requests an item that lacks quality or has been reviewed unfavorably, the library media specialist has a responsibility to communicate that to the teacher and, if possible, identify a substitute of higher quality. It is essential that teachers receive feedback about the recommendations they make—both positive and negative.

Electronic Resources

Electronic resources are demanding a share of the collection budget. In a national survey, Miller and Shontz (1997) described spending for collections in libraries to be stagnant. For the 1995–96 school year they found mean book budgets from local funds to be $6.73 per pupil, while audiovisual and computer software (including CD-ROM) spending showed a mean of $3.71 per pupil. These figures are not substantially different from their findings for 1993–94.

Funding is finite, so it is unreasonable to expect that substantially more dollars will come to the library media budget. Instead, a change in attitude about collection is in order. The top priority for the collection is curriculum support. Access to information via the World Wide Web needs to be considered in collection decisions. What is available online to meet the need? How readily accessible is it? Topics not frequently studied may be voids in the local collection to be filled by access online.

While the general criteria listed in the selection policy apply to electronic resources as well as to print resources, there is still a call for specialized criteria for electronic resources. Informational CD-ROM products are emerging rapidly as producers like Dorling Kindersley and Microsoft produce titles that offer students options for browsing in a topic or seeking specific answers to questions. These resources often provide students the opportunity to learn by exploration and to have considerable choice in what they investigate. Their organizational structure usually places a great deal of control in the hands of the user. Software evaluation needs to take into account beliefs about learning, design of the product, and technical quality. Figure 8.2 provides an example of criteria to be considered in evaluating CD-ROM products. Criteria related to learning are consistent with those recommended by the National Association for the Education of Young Children (Shade, 1996).

CD-ROM and online databases present certain licensing considerations (Martin & Rose, 1996): Can the product be networked? What restrictions are there on networking? What are the legal and technical limits of concurrent users? Are all the features in the stand-alone product available on the networked version? What are the costs for updates? What effect will this purchase have on continuation of print editions? If we purchase a CD-ROM biographical dictionary, should that lead to discontinuing a print subscription? (If we purchase SIRS on CD-ROM, what might be eliminated from the current or future print reference collection?)

Video continues to be a viable format in school library media collections as well. The pervasiveness of the VCR in homes makes this medium highly useful for students seeking information or entertainment (Mason-Robinson, 1996). Again, this medium calls for specific criteria for its selection. Suggested criteria to consider are shown in Figure 8.3.

Online resources present a special concern for library media specialists. The World Wide Web offers a vast array of information resources, but they vary widely in quality, reliability, and stability. Two strategies are particularly common in library media centers where access to the Web is readily available to students for information browsing or seeking. One strategy is to bookmark useful sites to maintain their addresses for future reference. Another strategy is to use software like Adobe Page Mill or Claris Home Page to create home pages for specific courses or assignments. This approach is particularly useful when a class is researching a topic that is stable in the curriculum and when many students will be seeking information on the topic. Home pages take time to create, but they can help to organize what could be an inefficient, maybe chaotic, search for information. While both organizing bookmarks and creating home pages can take considerable time, these tools will certainly help students in the same way as pathfinders. Questions to consider in

FIGURE 8.2
CD-ROM Evaluation Form

Program: _____

Hardware requirements: _____

Intended audience:_____

Producer: _____

Learning Features

Criteria	Comments
Is active learning emphasized?	
Are the concepts age appropriate?	
Is the child "in control" of the software?	
Are concepts represented concretely?	
Is there room for creative or divergent thinking?	
Is the learning intrinsically (rather than extrinsically) motivated?	
Do the content and design represent a "low entry" and "high ceiling"? Is there expanding complexity?	
Is the software open-ended?	
Does this medium suit the content better than any other medium?	
Is there a focus on process?	
Are "powerful" ideas addressed rather than low-level skills?	
Is there a fit with the library's or school's program needs?	

FIGURE 8.2
(cont.)

Design/Performance Features

Criteria	Comments
Is the reading requirement appropriate to the age?	
Do music, motion, and sound add to the substance or are they gratuitous?	
If speech is used, is it authentic and interesting, or mechanized and monotonous?	
Does it operate without error?	
Is installation straightforward and simple?	
Is navigation intuitive?	
Does the navigtion allow choices for the user (e.g., ability to go back, ability to move from topic to topic)?	
Does the documentation provide additional information that enhances the use of the software?	
Is the wait time for loading graphics or accessing data acceptable?	
Is telephone support available?	
Is there online help?	
Are there printing capabilities when desired?	

FIGURE 8.3
Video Evaluation

Title: _____

Intended audience: _____

Producer/Distributor: _____

Content

Criteria	Comments
Is information accurate and up to date?	
Is there evidence of bias?	
Will the video maintain the viewer's interest?	
Are performance rights available if needed?	
Does the video fit the programming needs of the school or library?	
Does documentation indicate sources of information?	
Is the production of significant educational, social or artistic value?	
Are the language and visual elements appropriate to the intended age group?	

FIGURE 8.3
(cont.)

Design

Criteria	Comments
Is video the most appropriate medium for the content?	
Is pacing appropriate to the content and the audience	
Are visuals well produced and effectively used?	
If there is text, is it readable? Does it stay on the screen long enough to be read?	
Is the sound acceptable, e.g., good fidelity, realistic sound effects, synchronized to the visual?	
Are voices easy to listen to and to understand?	
Are accompanying guides useful?	

FIGURE 8.4
Web Site Evaluation Form

URL: _____

Course/Assignment: _____

Teacher: _____

Content	Comments
Content	
Who is the audience?	
What is the purpose of the page— to inform, persuade, educate, explain?	
Is the scope clear?	
How complete and accurate is the information?	
How does the page compare to other sources of information on this topic?	
How comprehensive is the site?	
Are the links relevant and appropriate for the site?	
Do the links offer information not easily available in other sources?	
Is the site truly informative?	
Is the information current?	
Authority	
Who is the author?	
What is the authority or expertise of the person(s) responsible for the site?	
What corporate entity (organization, government agency, university) supports the information?	
Is there any sort of bias?	

FIGURE 8.4
(cont.)

Are there reference citations to support the information?	
When was the site produced?	
When was it last revised?	
Is the site commercial? Is that a problem?	
Structure	
Does the document follow good graphic design principles?	
Do the graphics serve a function or are they decorative?	
Is the site well organized?	
Is the site searchable?	
Are there links back to the home page from lower level pages?	
Does the home page have a "table of contents"?	
Performance	
How reliable are the links?	
Are there links that do not work?	
Has the URL changed? How frequently?	
How readable is the text?	
Are font choices good?	
Is text too small or too crowded?	
How efficient is the loading of graphics?	
Does it do more than print could do?	
Do the pages fit your screen or do you have to do a lot of scrolling?	
Are icons simple, consistent, and intuitive?	

reviewing sites to bookmark or link to a course home page are listed in Figure 8.4. Another Web site evaluation form is available from the American Association of School Librarians ICONnect Task Force Web site (http://www.ala.org/ICONN/curricu2.html). While it is important for library media professionals to apply specific criteria to Web sites, it is also important that they share their criteria with teachers and students (Symons, 1997).

COLLECTION MAINTENANCE

Materials

Maintaining a collection is as important as developing it. Collection maintenance involves two major processes: inventory and weeding. Inventory assures that the materials included in the catalog are indeed in the collection. Automation has streamlined inventory so that with a bar code reader or scanner, the collection can efficiently be inventoried. High-use collections may deserve annual inventory. At a minimum, sections of the collection should be inventoried each year so that the entire collection is checked over a three-year period. During inventory, beside ensuring that materials are physically present, the library media specialist can check for condition and appearance to see whether items should be withdrawn or replaced.

A few years ago, a library media specialist boxed up her entire collection over the summer so that her center could be repainted and carpeted. After the shelves were back in place, she began to unbox the collection. After two years in the school, she knew that the collection needed serious weeding, and she felt that she now knew the curriculum and clientele well enough to proceed with that task. With *Children's Catalog* and *Elementary School Library Collection* at hand to ensure that she did not remove a classic or a title that authorities suggest is the best available for its purpose, she began unboxing and considering each title. By the time she had finished, she had reduced the collection by more than one-third, ridding it of a 20-year accumulation of books now dusty, dirty, tattered, and dingy. At the opening of the school year, students arrived in the library media center and remarked that, although they knew they would see new carpet and paint, they didn't know they were getting so many new books too. In fact, the new books had not yet arrived; it was only that the existing collection looked so much better now that the newer books were visible and the worn-out ones were gone.

This example highlights some of the reasons why collection maintenance is important. First, a collection needs to contain accurate and current information; it is better to have no answer than to have an inaccurate or incorrect answer to a question. Second, weeding is important in making the collection attract users and in communicating that it is a recent and useful collection. Third, a collection needs to be attractive to its potential clientele, and eye-appeal is particularly important to the young. A collection that goes unweeded simply grows, uses more space, and fails to serve the clientele.

Access to the World Wide Web changes the weeding process. It is no longer necessary to keep outdated resources merely because they are the only items on the shelf on a specific subject (Graf, 1996); there are numerous current sources available on the Web.

A schedule for weeding can coincide with the inventory schedule so that the collection is reviewed periodically for content as well. Weeding can be approached in a relatively objective way:

- Establish a cut-off date for circulation (for example, five years), and identify all titles that have not circulated within that period. If an automated circulation system has been in place for that long, this task should simply be a matter of generating a report from the system.
- Pull from the shelves materials not circulated since the cut-off date.
- Ask teachers to examine materials in their areas and flag those items to be retained.
- Evaluate the remaining items by checking to see whether the titles appear in *Children's Catalog, Junior High School Catalog, Senior High School Catalog*, or *Elementary School Library Collection*—whichever are appropriate for the grade levels served. If the title appears in one of these resources, it is likely to be the best currently available title on the topic and probably should not be weeded. Review it for accuracy and currency. Refer to a weeding timetable for guidance on currency; an example appears in Figure 8.5. Also, van Orden offers a weeding timetable in *The Collection Program in Schools* (Libraries Unlimited, 1995).
- Evaluate for physical condition.
- Withdraw the bibliographic records for those items to be weeded.
- Discard materials according to institutional policy. Generally, items weeded from the library media collection ought not to be distrib-

FIGURE 8.5
Weeding Timetable

Class	Subject/ Format	Age	Last Circ	Comments
000	General	5	NA	
	Computers	2–5	2	
020	Library Science	10	3–5	
030	Encyclopedia	5–10	NA	Not longer than 10 years
100	Philos/Psych	10	3–5	
200	Religion	5–10	3–5	Retain basics; weed or do not accept propaganda.
290	Mythology	10–15	5	Be cautious of classics.
300	Social Science	10–15	5	Retain balance on controversial topics.
310	Almanacs	2–5	NA	Have the latest; may store back issues for class use.
320	Poli. Sci	5–10	3–5	
340	Law	10		
350	Government	5–10	3–5	
360	Welfare	10	5	
370	Education	5	3	
380	Commerce	10	5	
390	Etiquette	5	3	
	Customs/ Folklore	10–15	5	Retain basics; classics.
400	Language	10	3–5	Discard texts; retain basics.
500	General	5	3	Retain classics.
510	Math	10	3–5	
570	Biology/ Nat.History	10	3–5	
580	Botany	10	3–5	
600	General	5	3	

FIGURE 8.5
(cont.)

610	Anatomy/ Physiology		5	
	Other 610	5–10	3–5	
620	Applied Science	5–10	3–5	
630	Agriculture	5–10	3–5	
640	Homemaking	5–10	3	Retain cookbooks.
650	Business	10	5	
660	Chemistry/food	5–10	3–5	
690	Manufacturing	10	3–5	Retain material of historical interest.
700	General			Keep basics, especially art history.
745	Crafts		5	Keep well illustrated.
770	Photography	5	3	Avoid dated techniques or equipment.
800	Literature			Keep basics; check indexes before discarding.
900	General	15	5	Demand accuracy, fairness.
910	Travel/Geog	5–10	3–5	Retain expensive, well illustrated.
920	Biography	3–5		
F/E	Fiction/ Everybody	2–5		Keep high demand, literary merit, well written, well illustrated. Check indexes

Adapted from *Weeding the Library Media Center Collections* by Betty Jo Buckingham, Iowa Department of Education, 1984.

uted to teachers for their classroom. If they are not suitable for the library media collection, they are most likely not suitable for classroom use either. In some districts, weeded titles are sent to a central facility for disposal.

RECONSIDERATION OF CHALLENGED MATERIALS

Earlier in this chapter, the components of a materials selection policy were outlined. One important component of that policy is a set of procedures for reconsideration of challenged materials. Responses to materials challenges must strike a balance between the individual's right to protest the inclusion of a particular item in the collection, the library media specialist's responsibility to select materials based on objective criteria rather than on personal beliefs or biases, and the institution's right to remove material deemed inappropriate *after* reasonable due process. Due process is a critical factor in reconsideration cases, and lack of due process has been the turning point for cases taken to the judicial system. The intent of due process is to avoid arbitrary decisions based on an individual's viewpoint or bias. Challenges represent freedom of expression and should not be labeled as inherently harmful. By providing a procedure for reconsideration of challenged materials, the institution is in effect stating that it will indeed reconsider a decision and give that reconsideration due attention and due process. This is a circumstance that brings the library media program and its various constituencies together, and mutual respect is the intended result. The intent of the principle of intellectual freedom is to ensure the right of any person to hold any belief and to express such beliefs or ideas. Censorship, on the other hand, is a denial of the right of freedom of expression; it is a negative act and a way of imposing one's beliefs on everyone. Library media specialists strive to provide to their users a full range of information and ideas and to protect their free access to information and various perspectives.

In schools, the issue of challenged materials is complicated by the definition of a public forum. A classroom is not a public forum; students are required to attend school and the curriculum is under the purview of the school board. In *Minarcini v. Strongsville City School District* (1976), maintenance of a book on a library shelf and maintenance of a book as material required for a course were considered two distinct issues. This case involved a class-action suit brought against a school board by five high school students when the board refused to adopt certain titles recommended by an English teacher for a course. The boards also ordered removal of the books from the school library. At the appellate level, the two issues of library access and classroom requirement were separated. The court found that the board had oversight responsibility for selecting materials to be required of students, but that the library would continue to provide access to the books. This is an important distinction when addressing reconsideration requests.

Often in schools, issues of age appropriateness are central to reconsideration discussions. Parents, in sincere efforts to protect their children, may raise concerns about materials that are available in school library media collections. Often such concerns can be alleviated by conversations with parents to indicate that what one parent finds too mature for a child another parent finds ideal. The library media collection must be responsive to a larger public; if a parent has concerns about his or her child's selections, that is an issue to be addressed within the family. One effective proactive approach to concerns about materials is for the library media specialist to offer a parent organization program about the process of selecting materials. Parents can learn the criteria identified in the selection policy, the reviewing media the library media specialist relies on, and other sources of information and factors considered in purchasing decisions. Knowing the complexity of selection and the care taken in these decisions may be enough to alleviate many parents' anxiety. Still, complaints will come. The library media specialist has six steps to take when a user raises a complaint about an item in the collection:

- Listen sincerely to the position of the complainant.
- Stress the need to respect diversity of the many people who use this collection.
- Inform complainant of how the material is used and how it was selected.
- Explain the procedure for formal reconsideration.
- Provide the appropriate form for a formal request for reconsideration.
- Inform the principal, because no principal wants to be blindsided by a potential controversy.

Remember two important factors about challenged materials. First, the citizen has the right to complain. Second, if a committee elects to remove an item, it does not represent a failure on the part of the library media specialist, nor does it represent censorship when there is appropriate due process.

EQUIPMENT

Equipment is an important part of the library media collection. Selecting equipment requires attention to details. Comparisons of makes and models is important because equipment is expensive, it will be expected to last a long time, and it will get hard use in schools. When one purchases a new stove or iron for home use, usually one or two people at most will be using it. The fact that school equipment will have many users makes the decision particularly weighty. Ease of use, reliability, durability, safety, and performance are all important criteria. By creating a checklist for these five criteria and examining various makes and models side by side, one can make sound decisions.

A final factor to consider carefully in equipment purchase is the reputation of the vendor. When negotiating for volume discounts, when equipment problems arise, when warranty work must be done, when it would be helpful to have a demonstration of a new piece of equipment, it is the vendor who is the first contact. In most districts, cost is the primary consideration, and sales often go to the lowest bidder, but vendor service must still be considered somehow. It is possible to request that specific desired services be included in vendor bids. For volume purchases, it may be appropriate to include in the proposal a price and turnaround time for repairs or parts. Demonstrations or in-service training sessions could also be written into the proposal. Some of these services may eliminate certain low-cost bidders, but including them in the proposal may lead to better service in the long run. Where hands-on examination of a product is not possible, one can refer to *Library Technology Reports* or *Consumer Reports* for evaluations of equipment performance.

Equipment maintenance and repair are essential to good service. Districts can either contract with an outside agency or employ an in-district repair technician. Periodic maintenance primarily involves cleaning equipment. Clean equipment lasts longer and performs better. Lenses need to be cleaned; fans need to have dust removed; overhead projectors need to be opened up and blown-out to remove dust; heads on video equipment need to be cleaned. In most cases, equipment manuals explain how to clean and maintain the equipment.

Replacement. A plan for equipment replacement helps to maintain a functioning equipment collection (van Deusen, 1995). A replacement cycle is simply a schedule identifying which machines to consider for replacement each year. For example, in Year 1 overhead projectors are considered; in Year 2, videocassette recorders and cameras come up for review; in Year 3, CD players and LCD panels are considered; and so on. A five-year cycle is often workable, with all types of equipment distributed across the five years. The replacement cycle cannot be perceived as taking the place of decision making; however, by having a cycle, the library media specialist can ensure that the status of each type of equipment is reviewed on a routine basis. This precludes, for example, overlooking the overhead projectors for many years until they are all 25 years old and unreliable. Another advantage of a replacement cycle is that equipment purchases can be batched for more competitive prices. Furthermore, multiple machines purchased will be the same make and model; this is an advantage in learning to use equipment; in maintenance, troubleshooting, and repair; and in parts inventory, especially for bulbs and batteries.

Each year, the library media specialist looks at what items are due in the replacement cycle and reviews the performance and condition of machines scheduled for that year. Staff input may indicate how much these machines are used, how well they meet the demands, and what features staff members would like replacements to have. Competitive bids can then be prepared for purchase.

A 1986 survey of directors of campus-wide audiovisual media services lists life expectancy of several basic audiovisual equipment items (Post, 1987):

slide projector	12.0 years
overhead projector	12.0
videocassette recorder	7.5
video camera	8.0
television	10.0

These estimates help to identify which machines should be considered for replacement each time the item cycles up for review. Machines at or beyond their life expectancy are the first to be considered. Additional criteria are frequency of use, demand, and condition based on performance record. Longevity of the machine will vary based on how frequently it is used or moved.

The replacement cycle must have some flexibility, so that funds are not spent to buy equipment simply because it is the year to buy it. Some equipment (such as slide projectors and audiocassette recorders) is used infrequently, and may not need to be replaced when it reaches its life expectancy. Less use and good care can extend equipment life. Other equipment (like the 16mm film projector) may not appear on the replacement cycle at all, but may in some year need to be purchased.

Criteria for replacement will be

- machine scheduled to be reviewed in that year
- machine at or beyond its life expectancy according to standard expectations
- machine that users report as unreliable

Once machines are identified for replacement, professional judgment guides the process to determine exactly which machines will be replaced.

Microcomputers create a special set of problems for replacement. Microcomputers and related devices are likely to need upgrading after three years. After three years, typically, upgraded software requires more RAM; or, the software offers capabilities such as sound, speech, or graphics that require added equipment features; or the speed of operation is no longer acceptable. The three-year point calls for a decision: Should we upgrade the equipment, or should we downgrade its use? In other words, should we invest money in improving this machine, or should we reallocate it to a less demanding activity, and replace it for the function under question with a more powerful machine? What factors enter into this decision? First, what kind of upgrading is needed? If the machine simply needs more RAM, that tends to be an inexpensive upgrade; by increasing RAM, one might expect to get two more years out of the machine at that task—if RAM is the only needed upgrade. If disk space is called for, it is likely that an external disk drive could be added for perhaps three more years of service. If increased processor speed or other features are needed, it may be time to reassign the machine. Consultation with those who use the machine most will indicate how well the machine functions for its intended purpose.

A replacement schedule is also in order for microcomputers; the total number of machines in inventory are placed on a schedule based on year of acquisition. The machines are reviewed at the end of three years for possible upgrade or reassignment. At the end of the subsequent three years, they will be again reviewed for reassignment or withdrawal and replacement. Again, the replacement cycle is a guide, not a rule. The library media specialist must make decisions about whether equipment really needs to be upgraded or replaced; the cycle only serves to encourage equipment review in a proactive manner.

RAM upgrades can be estimated to cost approximately 10 percent of the cost of the machine, and 25 percent of the cost of the machine can be estimated for disk space or processor upgrades. Assuming that all machines will be upgraded in Year 3, the upgrade budget could be estimated at 15 percent of the initial purchase cost. For planning purposes, a microcomputer's initial cost should be added to the replacement budget for six years post-purchase.

Microcomputer peripherals (such as printers, modems, scanners, CD-ROM drives, and optical data storage devices) generally have a functional longevity of approximately five years. That is not to say that new and desirable models don't become available more frequently than that, but the functions for which the devices were purchased can typically be met for about five years. Again, a replacement budget can be estimated by adding their purchase price to the replacement budget for five years hence.

ACTION STRATEGIES

Information Access and Delivery

- Route publications with materials reviews to teachers and encourage them to initial those items that they would like to see in the collection. This process allows them to consider quality from the beginning; for many teachers, catalogs have been their primary source of information about new materials.
- At the end of units, particularly those demanding student research or resources for the teacher, ask teachers how well the collection met their needs.
- Reserve a special amount from the budget, perhaps $500, for student-initiated purchases. One library media specialist brought together a committee of students to review the sports section of the collection one year and to help her spend $500 on titles of interest to students. She met with the committee, gave them reviews to

read, as well as some books to preview, and worked with them to arrive at a list of titles for purchase.

- Involve staff members in decisions about replacement of equipment (for example, solicit information on how the equipment is used and what features it should have).
- For both purchasing and weeding decisions, take into account information accessible via the World Wide Web. Consider whether a request for materials on a topic can be adequately served online or whether it demands local materials.
- Offer parent information programs on the materials selection process, to help parents understand the complexities of this process and to help them respect the need for diversity in point of view and level of difficulty within a collection.

Program Administration

- Create a schedule for cleaning equipment—at least annually.
- Provide teachers and the principal with information about the condition of the collection, so that they have data on which to base decisions about allocating the school's resources.

REFERENCES

Gerhardt, Lillian. "Average Book Prices," *School Library Journal* 44 (March 1998): 79.

Graf, Nancy. "Collection Development in the Information Age," *Technology Connection* 3 (November 1996): 8–10.

Hopkins, Dianne McAfee. "Challenges to Materials in Secondary School Library Media Centers: Results of a National Study," *Journal of Youth Services in Libraries* 4 (Winter 1991): 131–140.

———. "Put It in Writing: What You Should Know About Challenges to School Library Materials," *School Library Journal* 39 (January 1993): 26–30.

Martin, Katherine F. and Robert F. Rose. "Managing the CD-ROM Collection Development Process: Issues and Alternatives," in Maureen Pastine, ed., *Collection Development: Past and Future*. (Binghamton, N.Y.: Haworth Press, 1996).

Mason-Robinson, Sally. *Developing and Managing Video Collections: A How-to-Do-It Manual for Librarians* (New York: Neal-Shuman, 1996).

Miller, Marilyn and Marilyn Shontz. "Small Change: Expenditures for Resources in School Library Media Centers, FY1995–96." *School Library Journal* 43 (October 1997): 28–37.

Minarcini v. Strongsville City School District 541F.2d577 (6th Cir 1976).

Post, Richard. "Longevity and Depreciation of Audiovisual Equipment," *Tech Trends* 12 (November 1987): 12–14.

Shade, Daniel. "Software Evaluation," *Young Children* 51 (September 1996): 17–21.

Symons, Ann. "Sizing Up Sites; How to Judge What You Find on the Web," *School Library Journal* (April 1997): 22–25.

van Deusen, Jean Donham. "Managing Equipment: A Proposed Model for Replacement," *Bottom Line* 8 (Spring 1995): 10–14.

Chapter 9

Literacy

This chapter

- explores three purposes of reading
- discusses the role of the library media program in a whole-language approach to reading and language arts
- reviews research that relates to nurturing readers
- discusses reading incentive programs and their impact on aliteracy
- identifies action strategies for encouraging and supporting reading

Literacy is the ability to gain information or vicarious experience from reading. When a student can not only decode the words in a body of text, but can also exhibit understanding by restating, summarizing, or questioning, then that student can begin to be considered literate. If we think of developing literacy as a continuum, then illiteracy represents a point on that continuum where the reader is not yet making meaning out of what is read. Where one sets the point on this continuum to divide the illiterate from the literate is debatable, but at some point the capability to make meaning from text becomes viable. Although the primary responsibility for addressing the concern for illiteracy in schools tends to lie with the classroom teacher, the library media specialist can play an important role in supporting literacy development. Another dimension of the literacy issue is aliteracy—when one can read, but chooses not to. The mass media raise concerns regularly that Americans are reading less. However, Fowles offers these data to counter those claims:

Contrary to what some might guess, every available statistical measure indicates that the reading of books is an increasingly common
practice for the U.S. public. Americans spent a total of $2.9 billion
on books in 1970 and $9.8 billion in 1988. This is more than a three-
fold increase—far too great to be attributed to population growth or
inflation. There were 1.5 million volumes sold in 1975 and 2.2 million in 1988, representing a 47% increase; calculated on a per-capita
basis, book sales grew 29% during those same 13 years. The twice-a-
decade industry surveys from the U.S. Commerce Department revealed that between 1982 and 1987, bookstore sales rose 64.5% which
was well above the average increase for all retail trade. . . . There
were 987 million volumes circulated by public libraries in 1977 and
1,329 million in 1989, for a healthy 35% increase (Fowles, 1993, p. 727).

These facts suggest that, for many, reading is alive and well. This is clearly
good news, but it does not mean that all Americans are readers. Moreover, it does not mean that all children and youth are readers, and it
does not mean that schools have no need to nurture readers. In fact, a
large-scale national study of more than 18,000 U.S. elementary school
children found that both recreational and academic reading attitudes on
average gradually but steadily declined throughout the elementary
school years, beginning at a relatively positive point and ending in rela-
tive indifference (McKenna, Kear, & Ellsworth, 1995).

Developing, extending and sustaining enthusiasm for reading
among children and youth presents a challenge. Both illiteracy and
aliteracy are legitimate concerns for the library media program.

THE PURPOSES OF READING

Often the word reading brings to mind reading stories or fiction. However, reading serves three major purposes and all three demand consideration in school library media programs—reading for literary experience, reading for information, and reading to perform a task.

Reading for literary experience occurs in free voluntary reading and
the reading that students do in reading and literature classes—reading
novels, short stories, poems, plays, and essays. The reader explores the
human condition and the interaction among events, characters' emotions, and possibilities. Students gain insight into how a given author
creates character and uses language. They experience vicariously.

Reading for information includes reading articles in magazines or newspapers, textbooks, entries in encyclopedias and other sources (both print and electronic), and nonfiction books. It requires that the reader be aware of the features found in informative texts, such as charts, footnotes, diagrams, and tables. Students usually acquire information to meet a specific information need and use such reading strategies as scanning and skimming, note taking, and paraphrasing to extract the needed information.

Reading to perform a task involves reading practical documents like schedules, directions, forms, recipes, warranties, and memos. Students must recognize the purpose and structure of practical documents to gain necessary information from them. The pragmatic approach of looking for information to accomplish a task differs substantively from savoring the style or intent of a text or literary work. The reader intends to apply the information to a task at hand.

Rosenblatt's work (1978) provides insight into how one engages in reading, depending on purpose. She describes a continuum of purposes one establishes as a reader. The continuum spans from *efferent* to *aesthetic*. The efferent reader approaches the text to take away information; the purpose is pragmatic, and the artistry of the writing is secondary to its content. From the efferent stance, the focus is on what will remain as residue after the reading experience. At the other end of the continuum, the aesthetic reader attends to the reading experience itself. The text stimulates sensing, feeling, imagining, and thinking, and these behaviors make the aesthetic experience. Rosenblatt further emphasizes reader control—stance relies on what the reader does, not on what the text is. Many texts can be experienced from different points on the continuum. Historical fiction becomes an interesting case in point. It is common for teachers in social studies to ask children to read historical fiction in the context of study of a historical period. For children reading historical fiction, it is important that the teacher know where along the efferent/aesthetic continuum this reading falls. In reading *Number the Stars*, to what extent is the purpose to learn information about the Danish resistance, and to what extent is it to feel the experience of a young Jewish girl living through the horrors of those times? In reading *A Family Apart*, to what extent is the purpose to learn about the Children's Aid Society of the late nineteenth century and the movement of children to the West, and to what extent is it to feel the experience of siblings being separated from one another and from their birth families? An awareness of the reading purpose from the beginning can influence the reading experience. As trade books find their way into the curriculum, how teachers ask students to respond to their reading will influence the reading purpose, experience, and impact. Awareness of the reading stance continuum can increase the sensitivity in designing reading response activities. If the aesthetic experience will complement students' understanding of the times, then reading responses ought to focus on the aesthetic. Asking students to glean information from historical fiction may not be an appropriate activity when the power of the novel is to generate a "feel" for the times—a substantively different experience from reading a textbook. The question to consider, then, is where along that continuum should the reader be to accomplish the current purpose?

Reading's power lies in its potential to develop in the reader new perspectives on times, people, and places, or to engender empathy for others' experiences and feelings. As students read fiction, they gain confidence in their knowledge because the narrative form complements and humanizes the factual.

THE LIBRARY MEDIA PROGRAM AND WHOLE LANGUAGE

Whole-language instruction is a philosophy more than it is a methodology. Its underlying construct is that learners derive meaning by interacting with text (Pearson, Roehler, Dole, & Duffy, p. 386) and relating the text to prior knowledge. Clarke (1987, p. 386) describes the key to a successful whole-language program as the relationships one finds " . . . between children and their reading/writing (one of enjoyment and ownership), between adults and the children (the former are 'encouragers' as well as teachers, the latter 'initiators') and among children (cooperative rather than competitive)." A goal of the whole-language philosophy is to develop an engaged reader who uses prior knowledge to gain information from new material; uses a variety of skills in a strategic way to gain information; is internally motivated to read for information and for pleasure; and interacts socially to make gains in literacy development.

While many schools describe themselves as whole-language schools, not all literature-based reading programs are alike. In her Arbuthnot Lecture in 1992, Huck characterized three types of literature-based reading programs:

- *literary reader programs*: The text contains selections from authentic literature. Huck responds to these: "I don't believe children become lifetime readers by reading selections of stories. Who ever developed a real love of reading by reading *The Reader's Digest*?" She further complains that these programs come with teacher's guides and workbooks filled with fragmented exercises, or, as she describes it, "mindless busywork."
- *trade book as basal reader program*: The teacher provides copies of a single title to all students and uses commercial or homemade guides to accompany the reading, providing black-line masters in place of workbooks to provide "activities" to accompany the reading. Huck (1992, p. 376–77) comments: " . . . these are used by teachers who do not trust the story to make a reader of the child."
- *comprehensive literature program*: The teacher uses real books but gives children a choice of what to read. In these programs, as Huck describes them, children hear stories and books read aloud to them; they also read books in-depth and discuss them, considering both the artistry and the meaning of the text.

The library media program plays a significant role in the whole-language approach to teaching reading. An important contribution for the library media program is providing access to a wide variety of excellent literature. Both quality and quantity are critical factors—and so is access. The books must be available to students at the point of need. Such access occurs when children can move in and out of the library media center as they need to; it also occurs when teachers can take armloads of books from the library media center to their classrooms for in-room collections and can return periodically to exchange those for fresh titles. Library media specialists have the reference tools, the skills, background knowledge, and experience to identify quality in children's materials. Because the emphasis in this holistic approach to reading is on meaning, and since many units center on literary themes, selecting materials that have substance, style, and rich language is crucial. Not just any old books will do to meet the goals of a whole-language program.

Beyond access to rich resources, the library media specialist offers consultation in developing thematic units. As a literature expert, the library media specialist can offer much to help teachers maintain appropriate levels of sophistication in the development of their thematic units. For example, when the theme is families, the library media specialist can suggest some appropriate ways to focus such a topic into a true thematic unit: "Families is a rather broad topic, so how about focusing on sibling relationships, to say 'Siblings can provide important support for one another in times of stress.'" From that point, the library media specialist can generate lists of possible titles to portray that thematic statement in both humorous and serious tones, and can generate possible open-ended questions to stimulate conversation about the treatment of the theme—questions beginning with "Why do you suppose . . . ? What if . . . ? What would you have done when . . . ?"

In the development of such thematic approaches, the library media specialist and teacher might consider several aspects of literary response. Miall and Kuiken (1995) identify six dimensions of reader response that might help to frame questions for student response to literature. These are summarized briefly as

- *insight*: relating the experiences and feelings portrayed in the text to one's own world experiences
- *empathy*: developing sensitivity to the reasons for the behavior or beliefs of others
- *imagery vividness*: sensing the places, people, and emotions portrayed in the text
- *escape*: using literature as a distraction from the real world
- *concern with the author*: relating the literature to the life and times of the author
- *story-driven reading*: engaging in the story primarily to see what happens next

Different readers approach text with different expectations. By keeping in mind these aspects of response, teachers and library media specialists can encourage each reader to respond to literature from a personally meaningful perspective.

Choosing books to read for oneself is a hallmark of whole-language programs, providing an opportunity for the library media specialist to market books. Presenting a book talk as students select what they will read is an important ingredient for generating enthusiasm among students about their reading. Besides formal book talks, individual reading guidance can keep readers reading. In most whole-language programs, students read independently throughout the year. Teachers encourage children to vary the degree of difficulty of what they are reading. The level depends on the teacher's intent—to increase reading fluency or to

increase reading capacity. Individual schools develop their own categories for levels of difficulty. Often, students learn to identify books at three
levels of difficulty. An example of one local set of labels for difficulty
levels is:

- *vacation books*: easy books in which the reader knows all the words
  and easily understands the meaning; books read for fun and to
  develop reading fluency
- *just-right books*: books in which the reader knows enough words to
  be able to figure out meanings; books read to practice reading strategies
- *dream books*: interesting but challenging books that are difficult
  enough to affect comprehension; books best read with the assistance of another person or a tape recording; books browsed for
  captions and illustrations

Library media specialists would do well to know the local labels for
level of difficulty and to use those labels as they advise children in reading selection. Consistency between the classroom and the library media
center will help children assess their reading choices.

Collecting bibliographic tools and professional materials about teaching reading in the whole-language approach is another important support service library media programs provide. Movement away from basal
texts demands that teachers develop their own units. Library media specialists need to provide professional resources to assist teachers, whether
those resources are bibliographic tools; poetry anthologies, stories, and
songs; or professional books to guide teachers in designing whole-language instruction. Effective whole-language programs thrive when the
library media program supports them with resources and professional
collaboration.

NURTURING READERS

Children arrive at school eager to join the community of readers. The
anticipation of learning to read is part of the joy children feel about going to school. How can we sustain that desire to be a reader? There are a
number of ways in which enthusiasm for reading can be nurtured and a
number of ways that it can be squelched. Berglund (Berglund et al., 1991)
surveyed college students to determine what teacher behaviors had sup-

ported their interest for reading and what behaviors had detracted from interest in reading. The list of detractors is particularly worthy of note:

- "round-robin" reading
- lack of choice
- irrelevant reading assignments
- failure to accommodate for diverse reading abilities
- book reports

Unfortunately, these detractors can be seen in most schools and frequently squelch children's enthusiasm for reading, which should be contagious. Enthusiasm for reading among teachers provides an important model for students. Teachers can exhibit that enthusiasm by reading aloud to students, or by presenting book talks, or by frequently referring to books. Library media specialists, in turn, can engender enthusiasm among teachers in both formal and informal ways. A few well-done book talks at the beginning of faculty, departmental, or team meetings can be a good beginning for the meeting and a step toward creating a community of readers among teachers. Sharing reviews or recently acquired books with specific teachers, based on their personal or professional interests, is another way of generating interest in reading among faculty members. Offering to do book talks in classes is, of course, another way to reach out to teachers as well as students. In the end, creating among the teaching staff a community of readers can be a major contribution to creating a community of readers among students.

Too often, young people perceive reading as a solitary rather than a social activity. Creating the spirit of a reading community transforms the perception of reading from a solitary activity to which only the loner retreats to a social activity that engages participants in conversation. The Iowa City project has been ongoing for ten years. It has gained momentum and become a "rite of autumn" for the community. Students anticipate the author's residency; early in the fall, community members begin asking at the bank for information about the book talks. Attendance at the book talks increases each year. Library circulation and bookstore sales of books featured in book talks and author visits persist beyond the duration of the project.

An important perspective for the library media specialist to maintain is that nurturing readers is a responsibility shared by teachers, parents, children and youth, the greater community, and library media spe-

AN EXAMPLE OF ENHANCEMENT IN ACTION: CREATING A COMMUNITY OF READERS

The idea of a community of readers is characterized in the Community Reading Project, a winner of the John Cotton Dana Award for Public Relations in 1995. This project, supported largely by a local bank in Iowa City, Iowa, has for many years worked to turn an entire small city into a "community of readers" to help young people see that being a member of the community requires being a reader (van Deusen & Langhorne, 1997). There are no prizes and no incentives beyond the opportunity to explore and enjoy reading. The development of that community spirit occurs in part because the event has wide sponsorship; participants, besides the bank, include the area public libraries, local bookstores, other local businesses, the senior center, the university, and the community schools. Activities scheduled during a month in the fall include:

- *book talk lunches*: Each week during the month, the public library hosts a book talk luncheon for a special target audience (such as parents of young children, parents of adolescents, adults, business people). Local librarians and booksellers, as well as general community members, are among those presenting the book talks.
- *visiting author*: The bank supports a children's book author in residence for one week each year. In anticipation of the visit, teachers and library media specialists develop a guide to the author's work and use the guide to prepare children for the visit—by having the children read works of the author, or by reading works of the author to them. Guest authors have included Jerry Spinelli, Chris Crutcher, Ashley Bryan, Pat Cummings, Brian Jacques, Phyllis Reynolds Naylor, and Penny Colman.
- *Read-In Day*: One day is identified each year as the Read-In Day when schools identify a 15-minute period devoted to reading. Organizations such as the local senior center host activities for Read-In Day. Various businesses have identified people to be readers in their lobbies or other ar-

eas for the event. Restaurants and delis encourage customers to read as they dine. Families choose an hour or so in the evening on a given date to turn off the TV and read together.

- *newspaper insert*: Another way to extend the invitation to join the local community of readers is a special insert in the newspaper. The Iowa City *Press Citizen* prepares a special newspaper insert for Community Reading Month. The insert includes information on the visiting authors, articles about reading to children, book lists, and other materials to promote reading. The insert is paid for by ads sold to businesses in the community. The ads often feature a child or someone associated with the business describing a favorite book or reading experience.

Events are advertised widely in newspapers, through service clubs and the chamber of commerce, on radio stations, and in displays in businesses. Each year has its own special events as well, but the intent is to arrive at a number of activities that focus attention on reading, to reach that threshold where a majority of the community feels a part of the reading event, so that it is indeed a community of readers and belonging is its own reward.

cialists. Often, though, it is the library media specialist or the public librarian who must initiate and guide the collaborative effort.

Book Discussion

Several studies cite meaningful book discussion as an important contributor to positive attitudes toward reading (for example, Johnson & Gaskins, 1992; Manning & Manning, 1984). Student discussion is important to learning. Research shows that students' verbal exchanges about content improve their learning and increase their level of thinking (Marzano, 1991). Peer interaction is particularly powerful; small-group and paired discussion about books that readers have chosen offer opportunities for meaningful interaction.

Encouraging students' personal response to literature improves their ability to construct meaning. With experience in reader response, over time, students develop increasingly complex responses to literature that help them become better at constructing meaning (Eeds & Wells, 1989). When children's responses to literature are valued, they develop a sense of ownership, pride, and respect for learning. Out of this shared value of learning comes a sense of community. Reader-response strategies call for a much more open-ended approach to discussion of what has been read than the approach often found in novel unit guides or basal reading texts. The reader-response approach intends for readers' experience with text to be at the center of the discussion.

Langer laments that "literature is usually taught and tested in a non-literary manner, as if there is one right answer arrived at through point-of-reference reading or writing." She goes on to describe strategies for opening up the classroom conversation about literature:

> Overall, teachers conceived of the "lesson" (extending across one or many days) as including three major sections: inviting initial understandings, developing interpretations and taking a critical stance. These replaced traditional lesson segments such as vocabulary review or plot summary and provided overall structural options to include or overlook in any given lesson (Langer, 1994, p. 208).

Inviting initial understandings simply involves asking students to describe what is presently on their minds about the piece. *Developing interpretations* calls for teachers to extend students' perspectives by posing questions to extend their thinking. Finally, *taking a critical stance* is the analysis of students' own understanding of the text and their generalizing to life. Langer endorses a sophisticated conversation about reading where the focus is on meaning. Such conversations about literature—and life—increase the sophistication with which students approach literature, engage in thought, and create memorable experiences from their reading. For teachers to interact with students about literature, they must have significant books. Moreover, opportunities to discuss those books with another reading enthusiast—perhaps a school library media specialist—can be valuable as teachers consider what directions their conversations with students may take.

Library media specialists can support reader-response programs by discussing literary pieces with teachers. By collaborating with teachers in the development of thematic units for reader-response activities, the library media specialist can contribute to students' analysis beyond literal comprehension toward evaluation and synthesis. Teachers new to thematic approaches to literature often confuse topical and thematic approaches. A theme is an idea, a complete thought, often a perspective on an issue (van Deusen & Brandt, 1997). While birthdays might constitute a topic, a theme might be "Celebrations bring families or communities together and provide memories that its members can share forever." The point of a thematic approach is to give meaning and purpose to the reading. Figure 9.1 shows examples of themes that develop around topics. By helping students develop a thematic statement and identify titles that provide examples of the theme applied to various settings, characters or situations, the library media specialist is using his or her expertise in literature to add substance to classroom instruction. Likewise, library media specialists can interact with students and engage them in discussions that emphasize the meaning and significance of what is read.

Another way of supporting reader response is to be a critical consumer of commercial literature guides. The publishing market offers a plethora of materials to assist teachers in the use of trade books. Unfortunately, too many of them reduce the reading experience to read and recall rather than to experience, enjoy, interact, and think. Questions to

FIGURE 9.1
Thematic Units

Topic	Theme	Titles
Mentors	While families have great influence on us, often a pivotal person outside our family can change our lives.	*Eleanor* by Barbara Cooney *Ben's Trumpet* by Rachel Isadora *Jip* by Katherine Paterson *The Bobbin Girl* by Emily Arnold McCully
Family	Family life includes enjoying special traditions.	*Just in Time for Christmas* by Louise Borden *Maria Molina and the Days of the Dead* by Kathleen Krull *Pablo's Tree* by Pat Mora
Generations	Family stories help to bridge generations.	*When Jo Louis Won the Title* by Belinda Rochelle *Aunt Flossie's Hats (and Crab Cakes Later)* by Elizabeth Fitzgerald Howard *Pink and Say* by Patricia Polacco *Grandaddy's Place* by Helen Griffith

ask about materials designed to support teaching literature include

- Are student questions primarily literal comprehension questions?
- Are activities cute or clever or artistic but not relevant to the central theme or meaning of the work?
- Are initiating activities helpful in focusing on the central theme or are they tangential?
- Do activities (like vocabulary lists, games, crossword puzzles, or matching problems) fill time more than they encourage the reader to respond to the text?
- Are the questions focused on higher-order thinking (What do you think about . . . ? Why do you think that? How do you know that?)?
- Is the emphasis on the holistic view of the work rather than on isolated details?

Time to Read

Providing time to read is one more way to nurture readers. Various studies, including the work of Neuman (1986), Greaney (1980), and Greaney and Hegarty (1987) have pointed to the minimal amount of time children spend reading. Yet, in the review of research done by Krashen (1993), he concludes the obvious—the more students read, the better readers they are. Also, in a carefully controlled study of 195 students in grades 5 and 6, Taylor, Frye, and Maruyama (1990) found that the amount of time spent reading during the school day contributed significantly to reading achievement. A study of middle school students found the following:

> Voluntary reading of at least one chapter in a book other than a textbook declined from 61% in sixth grade to 29% in eighth grade. In sixth grade, 32% of students reported reading for their own enjoyment almost every day; however, by eighth grade, only 20% reported doing so (Ley, 1994, p. 31).

There should be little argument against advocacy for time during the school day for reading—time for students to just read. Sustained silent reading (SSR) is a legitimate part of the reading program. It can be even more powerful in the development of the reading community when it extends to the entire school. SSR programs seem to work more easily at elementary schools than at secondary schools. Yet it is often at the middle school level when reading diminishes among students. Identifying some time during the middle school day for sustained reading seems one simple measure to encourage adolescents to continue to be readers. The schedule of the school day may require that this be a special added period, perhaps shorter than the standard class sessions, when all students and all teachers read. If reading is valued, there is a way to incorporate it into every students' daily school experience.

Choice

Choice of what to read is an important consideration for nurturing readers. Johnson and Gaskins (1992) found that the element of choice was very important to the fourth graders they studied. Even when the teacher limits the choices to a menu of titles, still the opportunity to control what one will spend time reading has a positive effect. Providing choice demands that teachers have available alternatives that will meet their goals; those alternatives may need to relate to the same theme or come from the same genre, but they must also offer some variety in tone, protagonist, and level of difficulty. The library media specialist can be instrumental in helping the teacher arrive at such alternatives.

Parental Influence

Neuman (1986) investigated the relationship between the home environment and fifth-grade students' leisure reading and identified parental encouragement as a strong correlate with children's leisure reading. She defined parental encouragement as making reading materials available in the home; providing a place for reading; encouraging the child to read books, magazines, and newspapers; reading aloud to their children; and the parents' own reading behavior. She emphasized the importance of what parents do to encourage reading:

> Encouraging parents were inclined to help children relate their reading of newspapers, magazines and books to everyday events, thus making reading an integral part of daily activities. Dinner conversations offered a time to share school and social activities with other members of the family (Neuman, 1986, p. 339).

The library media specialist can help parents in this role. Parents' needs will vary with the nature of the population. It may be that parents need to become aware of their own importance in their child's potential as a reader. Perhaps they need to learn about good books. Perhaps they need help in reading aloud to their children; for example, they might need strategies for reading aloud or guides to selecting books that are especially suited to reading aloud. Perhaps they need ideas for how to support reading at home. Perhaps they need help in becoming readers themselves. Principals are often seeking topics for parent nights; "helping your child be a reader" may be a very attractive topic. Sending home frequent suggestions of good books for "family reads" or reading suggestions for children can help parents. Designing reading events at school that involve parents can be another way of making them aware of their importance: a read-along-with-parents project might be an example of this. A small collection of books to help parents support their children's reading (housed as a special collection in the library media center and available for parent checkout) may be attractive in some settings. Neuman (1995) describes a community-supported parent tutoring program in Philadelphia where parents volunteered to work as a tutor/ mentor with one or two children at a time. The heart of this program is the training that these parent volunteers receive—it undoubtedly also influences the way they will encourage reading by their own children at home. The library media specialist can find allies among parents to help nurture readers. Clearly, outreach to children from less supportive families is another important concern. Library media specialists may need to take a more active interest in the reading activities of children whom they identify as having little reading support at home. This can take the form of regular formal or informal reading conferences with identified children.

Reading Incentive Programs

Incentive programs that feature rewards or prizes for reading are very common. Rewards range from a simple sticker for reading a book to elaborate accumulations of points that are applied toward grander prizes. The fundamental questions are, "Do these incentive programs work— for the long run?" and "Is there a better way to encourage reading?" Kohn (1993) argues against the use of extrinsic rewards to encourage reading—as well as other desirable behaviors. One of his major arguments is that rewards work as long as the rewards last, but when the rewards end, so does the behavior. He suggests that offering an extrinsic reward for a behavior immediately devalues the desired behavior; in short, if reading is so wonderful, why are prizes necessary to get people to do it?

Kohn further makes the point that rewards may indeed work for the short term. Indeed, many reading incentive programs are judged successful by the number of books the participants read during the event—while rewards are available. Rewards do work! At least they are effective at producing temporary compliance. However, the more important question is whether these participants in reading incentive programs extend their behavior beyond the duration of the incentive, or do they regress to their old behaviors—will those who were readers continue to read, and will those who were not discontinue? Some believe that extrinsically motivated exposure to the enjoyment of reading may jump-start the internal desire to be a reader. "What rewards do, and what they do with devastating effectiveness, is smother people's enthusiasm for activities they might otherwise enjoy (Kohn, 1993, p. 74)." The focus on the reward effectively turns the activity into nothing more than the means to an end. He suggests, in fact, that offering such extrinsic rewards can easily result in students doing less than they might have done without the reward system (for example, choosing easier books or reading fewer pages)—doing just enough to get the reward. To nurture readers, is the purpose temporary compliance or is it a lifelong behavior?

The notion of offering rewards as a means of teaching young people to be readers is counter to what constructivists profess about the way people learn. A reward system places the control of behavior on the person or agency holding the prize until such time as the student is deemed worthy to receive it. The locus of control is external to the student. Consistent with a constructivist view of learning would be developing an intrinsic enjoyment of reading. Ley identifies several research-supported ways to develop in students an intrinsic value for reading: surround students with materials about topics of interest to them; provide a nonthreatening situation for reading; give them opportunities to share with peers their reactions to what they have read; read aloud to students (Ley, 1994). Nowhere in the list is the idea of giving students extrinsic rewards for reading.

Often reading incentive plans that make use of extrinsic rewards are justified on the basis that they improve reading achievement. One study that investigated the effect of an extrinsic reward system on reading achievement scores of sixth graders found no statistically significant differences between students who were offered pizzas as rewards and students who were simply encouraged to read more without extrinsic rewards (Adler, 1989).

The term *token economy* describes a system for assigning value to specific tasks and "paying" students with tokens (prizes or privileges) for performing those tasks. One of the most extensive and expensive token economies intended to encourage reading is a system of computerized tests on trade books, with accumulated points to be applied toward purchase of a wide range of prizes. What are the messages that such programs send? We read books, not to discuss them, not to enjoy them, not to appreciate them, not to see ourselves in others lives, but to pass a literal comprehension quiz, to earn points, and to "buy" trinkets. Enormous increases in library circulation support such programs (Woodard, 1995). However, one must continue to ask whether the long-term effect of such programs will be to instill a love of reading. Will students for whom reading the last page of a story means taking a quiz to collect points embrace reading as a pleasure unto itself? Perhaps not! Donna Pool Miller puts it succinctly:

> Would you really enjoy reading or want to read many books if you had to boot up the computer and answer 20 questions before you were allowed to read another one? Further, how would you like it if someone else totally dictated what you could read (Miller, 1995, p. 22)?

Carter (1996) points out that often rewards act as incentives for performing less-than-desirable tasks. She suggests that computer-based reading incentive programs like The Electronic Bookshelf or The Accelerated Reader devalue reading. She suggests that by offering points for reading, these programs place reading among the ranks of lawn-mowing and taking out the garbage. Carter has monitored children's reading selections and has found that they choose not to read books they would probably enjoy if they are not on the program's list. Carter also contends that reading to take a factual test places children immediately at the efferent end of Rosenblatt's continuum. Yet she states that lifetime readers read aesthetically. Her inference is that computer-based programs detract from aesthetic reading and perhaps from the likelihood of lifetime reading.

There is documentation that book talks also have an impact on circulation. Bodart reports highly significant increases in book circulation after students heard book talks in a high school. The effect of the book talks persisted through the school year as the featured books continued to have high circulation (the book talks occurred in October and circulation was monitored through May) (Bodart, 1986).

One type of reading program that merits consideration is summer reading. Sustaining students' reading during the summer can help maintain their reading skills. The state of Illinois has been particularly strong in supporting summer programs through their public libraries. Studies of public library summer reading programs have demonstrated that children who participated in the summer programs indeed improved their reading skills over the summer, when compared with children who did not participate (Carter, 1988; see also Howes, 1986). Of course, there are other factors to be considered. Those students who participated were likely to have more family support for learning and reading than those who did not, and the importance of family support for reading has been discussed earlier. Still, summer programs can help keep children active in reading. More challenging, yet, is to find ways to support reading among children whose families are less likely to frequent the public library. One step is to provide summer hours in school libraries in neighborhoods where families do not visit the public library. By making the school library accessible to children and providing even a limited level of programming, these children may be less likely to pass the entire summer without books in their lives.

In the end, the library media specialist must strive to engender enthusiasm for reading for the sake of reading—whether for aesthetic purposes, the pleasure of the moment, or the efferent purpose of reading for information. The question to ask is, "Will this activity create an *enduring* enthusiasm for the power of reading?"

ACTION STRATEGIES

Learning and Teaching

- Meet with groups of students for book discussions in cooperation with reading or social studies units taught in the classroom.
- Hold individual reading conferences to discuss books with target students who need support to become readers.
- Collaborate with teachers to develop thematic literature units that go beyond topical organization and feature substantive conversation about the meaning and importance of the work's message.

Information Access and Delivery

- Market books to students by doing book talks. School library media specialists who are constrained by having weekly classes can make use of those weekly times to do book talks. In addition, make book talks a standard part of the beginning of social studies units. Consider the possibilities as history classes begin study of the Civil War, World War II, the westward movement or as area studies of the Middle East or women's studies begin.
- Market books to teachers. Use five minutes of faculty or team meetings to promote some of the latest, best books for youth—or an occasional adult book!

Program Administration

- Bring authors to the school to speak to students. Seek support from local businesses to underwrite the event and then give it—and your sponsor—as much press as possible.
- Support and encourage providing time during the school day for students to read.
- Provide parent programs about reading to engender support for reading at home.
- Encourage read-aloud programs. Some schools have all-school thematic oral literature programs that create a community spirit centered on reading (Boothroy & Donham, 1981).
- Cooperate with the local public library to encourage participation in summer reading programs. Encourage staff from the public library to come to the school to market programs and to sign up students for library cards.
- Collaborate with the public library year-round to design, implement, and publicize programs and events to support reading.

REFERENCES

Adler, Jay et al. *A Middle School Experiment: Can a Token Economy Improve Reading Achievement Scores* (paper presented at the annual meeting of the Midwestern Educational Research Association, October 1989), ERIC document ED 312 620.

Berglund, Roberta et al. *Developing a Love of Reading: What Helps, What Hurts.* Literacy Research Report No. 7 (Dekalb, Ill.: Northern Illinois University Reading Clinic, 1991). ERIC document ED 332 168.

Bodart, Joni. "Booktalks Do Work: The Effects of Booktalking on Attitude and Circulation," *Illinois Libraries* 68 (June 1986): 378–381.

Boothroy, Bonnie and Jean Donham. "Listening to Literature: An All-School Program," *The Reading Teacher* 34 (April 1981): 772–774.

Carter, Betty. "Hold the Applause! Do *Accelerated Reader* and *Electronic Bookshelf* Send the Right Message?" *School Library Journal* 42 (October 1996): 22–25.

Carter, Vivian. "The Effect of Summer Reading Program Participation on the Retention of Reading Skills," *Illinois Libraries* 70 (January 1988): 56–60.

Clarke, Mark. "Don't Blame the System: Constraints on 'Whole-Language' Reform," *Language Arts* 64 (April 1987): 384–396.

Eeds, Maryann and Deborah Wells. "Grand Conversations: An Exploration of Meaning Construction in Literature Study Groups," *Research in the Teaching of English* 23 (February 1989): 4–29.

Fowles, Jib. "Are Americans Reading Less? Or More?" *Phi Delta Kappan* 74 (May 1993): 726–730.

Greaney, Vincent. "Factors Related to Amount and Type of Leisure Reading," *Reading Research Quarterly* 15 (1980): 337–357.

Greaney, Vincent and Mary Hegarty. "Correlates of Leisure-Time Reading," *Journal of Research in Reading* 10 (February 1987): 3–20.

Howes, Mary. "Evaluation of the Effects of a Public Library Summer Reading Program on Children's Reading Scores Between First and Second Grade," *Illinois Libraries* 68 (September 1986): 444–450.

Huck, Charlotte S. "Developing Lifetime Readers," *Journal of Youth Services in Libraries* 5 (Summer 1992): 371–382.

Johnson, Carole and Jan Gaskins. "Reading Attitude: Types of Materials and Specific Strategies," *Journal of Reading Improvement* 29 (Summer 1992): 133–139.

Kohn, Alfie. *Punished by Rewards; The Trouble with Gold Stars, Incentive Plans, A's, Praise and Other Bribes* (New York: Houghton Mifflin, 1993).

Krashen, Stephen. *The Power of Reading* (Littleton, Colo.: Libraries Unlimited, 1993).

Langer, Judith. "A Response-Based Approach to Reading Literature," *Language Arts* 71 (March 1994): 203–211.

Ley, Terry C. "Longitudinal Study of the Reading Attitudes and Behaviors of Middle School Students," *Reading Psychology* 15 (January–March 1994): 11–38.

Manning, Gary and Maryann Manning. "What Models of Recreational Reading Make a Difference?" *Reading World* 23 (May 1984): 375–380.

Marzano, Robert J. "Language, the Language Arts, and Thinking," in J. Flood et al., eds., *Handbook of Research in the English Language Arts* (New York: Macmillan, 1991): 559–586.

McKenna, Michael C., Dennis J. Kear, and Randolph A. Ellsworth. "Children's Attitudes Toward Reading: A National Survey," *Reading Research Quarterly* 30 (October/November/December 1995): 934–956.

Miall, David S. and Don Kuiken. "Aspects of Literary Response: A New Questionnaire," *Research in the Teaching of English* 29 (February 1995): 37–58.

Miller, Donna Pool. "Computerized Carrots—Are They Truly Reading Motivators?" *Technology Connection* 2 (November 1995): 21–22.

Neuman, Susan. "The Home Environment and Fifth-Grade Students' Leisure Reading," *The Elementary School Journal* 86 (January 1986): 335–343.

———. "Reading Together: A Community-Supported Parent Tutoring Program," *The Reading Teacher* 49 (October 1995): 120–129.

Pearson, P. D., L. R. Roehler, J. A. Dole, and G. G. Duffy. *Developing Expertise in Reading Comprehension: What Should Be Taught? How Should It Be Taught?* Technical Report No. 512 (Champaign, Ill.: Center for the Study of Reading, September 1990).

Rosenblatt, Louise. *The Reader, the Text, the Poem; The Transactional Theory of the Literary Work* (Carbondale, Ill.: Southern Illinois Press, 1978).

Taylor, Barbara M., Barbara J. Frye, and Geoffrey M. Maruyama. "Time Spent Reading and Reading Growth," *American Educational Research Journal* 27 (Summer 1990): 351-362.

van Deusen, Jean Donham and Paula Brandt. "Designing Thematic Literature Units," *Emergency Librarian* 21 (September/October 1997) 21–24.

van Deusen, Jean Donham and Mary Jo Langhorne. "Iowa City Reads!" *School Library Journal* (May 1997): 32–34.

Woodard, Mary. "Accelerated Reader on the Network Doubles Circulation Figures," *Technology Connection* 2 (November 1995): 20.

Chapter 10

Technology

This chapter

- examines criteria for determining how technology is used
- identifies three categories of powerful technology uses: information access, productivity, and communication
- explores the school library media specialist's roles as technology advocate, coordinator, manager, trainer, and teacher
- considers software selection in the context of beliefs about teaching and learning
- discusses the impact of the World Wide Web on the school library media program
- examines planning for technology within a school and the school library media program
- identifies action strategies related to technology

Information technologies (such as online catalogs, automated circulation systems, and electronic references), productivity applications, (such as word processing, databases, and multimedia production), and telecommunications (such as World Wide Web access, e-mail, and listservs) are central to the work of the library media specialist in teaching, providing information, and consulting with teachers. Integrating technology into the school context requires leadership and informed decision making. It requires understanding the educational goals and philosophy of the school. It requires knowing how technology can improve teaching and learning. The school library media specialist can facilitate the technology infusion by guiding decision making so that technology extends creative and analytical work.

Because of the cost of technology and the media attention it receives, the public holds high expectations for technology's impact on education. This chapter begins with guidelines for careful decision making and proceeds through technology program planning and implementation to help meet those demands.

TECHNOLOGY APPLICATIONS

The ways schools can use technology are numerous and rapidly changing. Clearly, schools cannot afford to "buy into" every application on the market—nor should they want to. Before investing in any technology application, educators must examine such questions as

- Is this technology consistent with our beliefs about what needs to be learned and how learning occurs?
- Will this technology allow students to do something of significance that is otherwise essentially impossible?
- Will this technology allow students to do something of significance substantially better than they could otherwise?
- Why are we attracted to this technology? For its performance? For its "glitz"? Because everyone is talking about it? Because other districts or schools have it? Because it will empower our students to function at higher cognitive levels? Because it will advance us toward an important educational goal?

Several studies have investigated the differences in technology use based on the socioeconomic status (SES) of schools. Sutton, in a review of research, reports that computer use among low-SES students, largely minorities, was drill and practice for 56 percent of the time they used the computers—meaning that "their experience with a computer was when it was in control, asking questions, expecting a response, and informing the student when he or she was correct," and thus having little positive effect on critical thinking skills (Sutton, 1991, p. 482). Likewise King, quoting from a study of inequities in opportunities by R. E. Anderson et al., summarizes that "affluent students are thus learning to tell the computer what to do, while less affluent students are learning to do what the computer tells them" (King, 1987, p. 12). His own study of 141 schools in North Carolina affirmed differences based on socio-economic status. Looking at students from the perspective of ability, Sayers reports "the more exciting programs are reserved for the students in the upper tracks; when lower track and minority students do get access they are much more likely to be assigned to drill-and-practice than to problem solving activities" (p. 768). Piller summarizes the dramatic inequities he observed in his visits to schools when he says, "In most cases, computers simply perpetuate a two-tier system of education for rich and poor" (Piller, 1992, p. 221). An underlying assumption in these studies is that the number of computers available in schools may be less important than the applications for which they are used. Because resources are limited, because change in schools occurs slowly, and because computers are relatively new on the scene in education (since approximately 1982), sophisticated expectations for computers are only now emerging.

An extensive case study describes successful technology integration at Peakview Elementary School (Wilson, 1994). The report includes a list of technology-related activities that were most common in the school. Students used computers primarily to write stories or reports, to find new information, and to make art. Common among these activities are factors to consider in choosing technology applications for schools:

- Students use the computer as a tool for their own productivity.
- The uses of the technology are aligned with learning goals.
- Students, not the computers, are in charge.
- The computers allow students to do work more efficiently and more thoroughly.
- The skills needed for using the computer applications are likely to have lifelong utility.
- Students are using technology at the higher end of Bloom's Taxonomy (application, analysis, synthesis, and evaluation), rather than at the low end (knowledge and comprehension).

One way to classify technology uses is to consider whether the application is grounded in a behaviorist or a constructivist approach to learning. Behaviorist applications place the locus of control with the computer or the teacher. For example, most drill-and-practice software gives feedback, and often rewards, when students give correct answers. The computer determines what will happen next. Students look for a single right answer, usually a factual response. Their learning is perhaps rote—particularly if speed is a factor. At best, it is at the knowledge or comprehension level. A computer-based test bank like *Accelerated Reader* is another example of a behaviorist use of the computer, where students respond to literal comprehension questions. When students use electronic books, and click on graphic elements on the screen, so that doors open or monkeys squeak, they are at best entertaining themselves, but they are not creating significant meaning. In fact, sometimes the gimmicks may distract them from the story line. Regardless of the software, when the computer is a reward for finishing work or for good behavior, the approach is clearly behaviorist. In this case, the locus of control lies with the teacher who decides when a student has earned the reward. These computer uses support low-level student learning, but they are as expensive as many more empowering ways to use computers.

A constructivist would prefer to see students use a computer to create, whether it is a report, a spreadsheet model, or a multimedia production. Giving students a set of raw data is one way to design constructivist learning. For example, when students take facts about family size, infant mortality rates, level of education, and other demographic data for various countries, and enter the information into a database and sort or select to observe patterns in the data, they begin to create their own understanding of relationships among factors and to draw generalizations. The very process of constructing the database causes them to analyze and synthesize, as they generate their own understanding rather than recall someone else's. Desktop publishing software, the word processor, graphing software, databases and spreadsheets, and well-designed simulations are all examples of genres that students use for constructing meaning.

Integrating technology into a program requires a substantial investment in infrastructure, hardware, software, space, and staff time. Because schools have limited human and fiscal resources resources for technology, it is irresponsible not to set high expectations for its impact on learning. Applying stringent criteria for technology represents accountability to the public trust and to the educational future of students. The National Council of Teachers of Mathematics has been at the forefront in development of its curriculum standards. In describing how calculators and computers can enhance mathematics learning, the standards state:

> With the introduction of technology, it is possible to de-emphasize algorithmic skills . . . Technology—computers and calculators—

saves time and more important, gives students access to powerful new ways to explore concepts at a depth not possible in the past (*Professional Standards for Teaching Mathematics*, p. 134)

The standards recommend, for example, graphing utilities and graphing calculators to extend student productivity.

Likewise, in their standards document, the National Council for the Social Studies describes "powerful" social studies teaching and learning; included in that description are several dimensions of teaching, including the use of technology. Their recommendation includes references to information, productivity, and telecommunications applications:

Integrated social studies teaching and learning include effective use of technology that can add important dimensions to students' learning . . . If students have access to computerized data bases, they can search these for relevant research information. If they can communicate with peers in other states or nations, they can engage in personalized cultural exchanges or compare parallel data collected in geographically or culturally diverse locations (*Expectations of Excellence*, 1994, p. 165).

Essentially, there are three categories of technology applications that offer particular power in schools: information access, productivity, and communication. Each of these has several important characteristics:

- The student is "in control," not the computer.
- The computer is perceived as a tool—an extension of the student's mind.
- The student uses the computer to produce, create, or generate.
- Cognitive levels of students using these applications is beyond recall and comprehension as students engage in application, analysis, synthesis, and evaluation.

Information Access

As school curriculum becomes less textbook-based and trends such as integrated curriculum, authentic assessment, resource-based learning, and constructivism evolve, students have more responsibility for gathering information from which to create their own understandings. Simultaneously, availability of information in electronic resources is in-

creasing. Electronic encyclopedias and periodical indexes are nearly standard reference tools in school library media centers, as are electronic
atlases and other general and specialized reference sources. Electronic
information access offers a powerful way to expand learning. Examples
of information sources are *The Way Things Work* (Dorling Kindersley)
for physical science, *Material World* (Star Press Multimedia) for social
science, *The Ultimate Human Body* (Dorling Kindersley) for studying
human biology, and *Who Built America?* (Voyager Software) for American history. Each of these sources allows the student to search efficiently
for information and to access it not only from text but also from graphics, audio, and video sources that enhance its meaningfulness and intellectual accessibility. Beyond these local resources lies the World Wide
Web and the multitude of information resources available there. Not
long ago, students hoped they could find as many as three sources in
response to a query. Now quantity of information is less of a concern;
instead, students need to know what criteria to apply as they select and
evaluate what they find.

Productivity

Productivity software includes authoring software like HyperStudio
(Roger Wagner) or KidPix (Brøderbund) for developing multimedia productions, Super Paint (Aldus) or PhotoShop (Adobe) for graphic productivity; The Writing Center (The Learning Company) or PageMaker
(Adobe) for desktop publication; word processing software; and database and spreadsheet software for problem solving. Students can report
or document their findings by producing videos. With each of these software programs, students create documents that demonstrate or synthesize their learning, and they then can improve their creations, thereby
meeting a higher performance standard than they might otherwise have
set for themselves.

Telecommunications

With telecommunication technology students reach out to people—often beyond the school—to gather or share information. For example,
with the National Geographic software program Kids Net, students collaborate with one another in collecting and analyzing data as they solve
problems in science. This sort of experience extends the resources of the
school and facilitates "real-world" collaborative study. Telecommunica-

tion can also give students authentic audiences. No longer must they simply write for the teacher; instead, they can write to other student audiences or to online experts. Telecommunication also facilitates collaboration among teachers both within and beyond the school.

PLANNING FOR TECHNOLOGY

> Planning is a set of formal and rational activities that seeks to anticipate conditions, directions and challenges at some future point for the purposes of enhancing the readiness of personnel and the organization to perform more effectively and to attain relevant objectives by optimal means (Knezevitch, 1984, p. 88).

There are several key concepts in this definition. First, planning is *formal* and *rational*. Technology costs are too high for schools and school districts not to take an approach to the planning process. *Rational* emphasizes gathering information and making reasonable and informed decisions. Technology is an area where it is easy to fall prey to the "covet thy neighbor" syndrome, where schools buy hardware or software for no reason except that others are doing so. A rational approach to planning calls for analyzing the school's goals and technology's capabilities and then identifying the intersections where technology can substantively improve goal attainment. Another key concept in this definition is *readiness of the personnel and the organization*, that is, staff involvement and careful consideration of the organizational context. A final key term is *optimal means*. Planning involves looking for the best ways to attain the organization's objectives. Quality is important whenever considering technological innovations; the marketplace is vast and not everything in it represents optimal means.

No school or district should be without a formal technology plan, because of the rapid change, the high costs, the range of enthusiasm from zealous to resistant, the importance of broad-based ownership, and the complexity of integration into the instructional program. For technology planning to be effective, some baseline work must occur. Establishing a mission for technology in teaching and learning is an important first step. Such a mission grows out of underlying assumptions about the nature of technology and learning. One such belief is that technology is a tool that allows people to extend their capabilities by working smarter or faster. Another is that learning results when one creates new meaning by relating new experiences and prior learning. Given these two beliefs, a mission for technology might call for students to use technological tools to access, manipulate, and communicate information. What is important is that the technology mission be closely tied to its larger context—the mission for the school.

Consider this example of a school district mission:

> It is the mission of the Iowa City Community Schools [ICCSD] to ensure that all students will become responsible, independent learners capable of making informed decisions in a democratic society as well as the dynamic global community (ICCSD Home Page).

In that district's technology plan, they state the following purpose:

> This plan proposes that it be the goal of the Iowa City Community School District to provide all members of the school community with the technological competencies necessary to be active participants in the information society through an aggressive program of curriculum infusion, equipment acquisition, staff development, and ongoing assessment of effectiveness.

The consistency of the two statements is no accident. Both emphasize the importance of information in decision making required of members of a democratic society. The technology plan for the district is closely aligned to the district's overall strategic plan; it is not an isolated entity, but is tied to its context.

A technology plan must be the result of a broad-based team. Key players include teachers, administrators, parents, local business people, physical plant workers, and library media professionals. Physical plant workers are likely to know secrets about buildings that can make critical differences in networking decisions. Local business people and parents may be helpful in garnering support when they understand the program; they also bring a perspective that may generate valuable ideas or insights that are different from those of educators. Each stakeholder has something to bring to the discussions about technology, and each can serve as an advocate for ideas when implementation begins.

The technology planning process is never finished. While a long-term view is important for establishing mission and goals, short-term planning is ongoing because of the constant changes in available technologies. This is not a process to occur every five years, or even every three. It is continuous. The long-term view must provide for budgeting. Technology is a capital expenditure; without line items in the budget for technology, planning is futile. That budget must include consideration for several items:

- new hardware
- new software
- hardware upgrades: Three years is about as long as computers are likely to run without upgrading to accommodate software upgrades, new releases, and increased CD-ROM drive speed (van Deusen, 1995; see also Chapter 8 of this book)
- software upgrades
- replacement hardware: After about five years, a computer needs to be reviewed for its capacity to continue in its assigned purpose; often by that time, either the clock speed, the memory limitations, or the storage capacity makes the machine less useful for a given application; at this point, a machine may need to be reassigned to a less-demanding task or retired completely. For each new computer installation, the budget five years ahead needs to include a replacement for it.
- staff development: Release time for teachers to participate in training, pay for trainers, facilities, equipment, software and supplies, as well as costs of technology-related conference attendance are all necessary expenses.
- networking: Costs of wiring installation, upgrades, telecommunications, and service providers are examples of ongoing costs, along with network administration either in-house or contracted.
- technical support: As more machines are acquired, maintenance and repair, either by in-house technical staff or by contractors, becomes essential. Existing employees cannot take this on as additional work because it must be the highest priority of the individual. Besides, the work load will grow.

A sound technology plan should be results-driven with a focus on how the technology will be used and what difference it will make (Jukes, 1996). The test questions are: What worthwhile activity can this technology allow that could not be done before? What worthwhile activity can this technology allow to be done substantially better? Staff development needs to be ongoing and incremental—not a collection of one-shot events; it also cannot be a generic set of lessons, a one-size-fits-all approach.

Instead, a sound staff development plan is directly relevant to what the participants will do. For example, staff development for high school mathematics teachers will focus on using the graphing calculator and relating it to specific units in algebra. Lessons on using the Web will include examples specific to the curriculum of teachers who are participating. Besides relevance, staff development must be thorough; a series of lessons with time for teachers to share ideas and to practice is more appropriate than covering many topics superficially. Before teachers can feel confident to add technology to their teaching repertoire, they must feel ownership; that can occur only when they have time to experiment, collaborate, and create for themselves. Teachers need adequate access to computers to build confidence and skill; providing access, either by lending computers for home use or providing computers to teachers for their classrooms, is essential. Teachers are far less likely to embrace technology when they must share computer lab space with students or when they must borrow a computer for limited times at school. Effective staff development calls for a readily available support system; when teachers forget a step in the use of a program or attempt something altogether new, they need a colleague to call—a convenient, knowledgeable, supportive colleague. Such a person can certainly be the school library media specialist.

THE LIBRARY MEDIA SPECIALIST'S ROLES IN TECHNOLOGY

Several responsibilities exist for effectively integrating technology into a school's program: coordination, advocacy, training, and teaching. These responsibilities the library media specialist is well suited to meet. Too often, administrators have considered it necessary to add a separate position of technology coordinator either at the district or school level, and too often the qualifications for such a position call for a person who understands hardware and networking, but not applications for technology in an educational environment. Library media specialists have several attributes that qualify them well for coordinating technology use in a school or a district. First, coordinating technology is akin to coordinating any other resource—this is already the work of the school library media specialist. What knowledge is required to provide such coordination? Clearly, a technology coordinator must be knowledgeable about what is possible to do with technology and what is worth doing. Maintaining current awareness of what is in the marketplace is a tradi-

tional part of the school library media specialist's work. More important, making judgments about quality based on explicit criteria is also a
typical library media specialist's task. To coordinate technology requires
knowing the curriculum, teachers' instructional styles, and the students;
this knowledge of the instructional context is essential to all effective
library media programming.

Coordinator

Library media specialists supervise a facility accessible to all departments or grades; locating shared technology facilities there adds items
to the scheduling task, but does not require a new system or access point
for teachers and students. Technology demands three kinds of support:
the educational leadership that a library media professional can offer,
technical assistance for maintenance and repair, and networking expertise. Other necessary positions are a network specialist, and technicians
to maintain and repair hardware, maintain file servers, attend to wiring,
and install software and upgrades. These technical tasks are just that—
they do not require an educator's expertise. However, coordinating the
application of technology for the overall school program indeed requires
an educator's expertise, and the most appropriate educator is the library
media specialist.

Manager

As manager, one responsibility is supervising computer labs that are
often located near or in the library media center. Access to the Internet
makes this supervision particularly important in order to assist students
in efficient and effective searching for information and to monitor equipment use. Another management task is inventory of equipment—a task
easily accomplished using the library media center's automated circulation system. Each hardware item can be entered into the database and
then "checked out" to its location in the building. Using this already
existing system for equipment inventory means efficiency for the school.
Managing software requires keeping track of licenses—an information
management problem accomplished with a simple database program
with such fields as title, version, publisher, vendor, purchase order number, date purchased, license terms. Physical storage and organization of
software are tasks familiar to the library media specialist.

Advocate

Building-level library media specialists serve as technology advocates. It is, however, important that their advocacy be spent on those applications that make a positive difference to teaching and learning. It is not responsible to advocate indiscriminate use of technology or to support purchase of anything electronic any more than it is responsible to spend library media dollars on poorly written books. Leadership is an important aspect of the technology advocate role, and sometimes leadership requires challenging technology uses that may not comport with the school's beliefs about learning or that may not play out as particularly sound ideas. An interesting example is the Integrated Learning Systems (ILS), which manage instruction. Most ILSs include instruction and practice in basic school subjects. The instructional design of most systems follows behaviorist programmed instruction (Van Dusen & Worthen, 1995). An essential feature of all ILSs is their ability to track student progress. From the system's central server, specific lessons are automatically sent to each student's computer when the student logs on. Lessons are selected for the student based on the ILS's assessment of prior performance. Students typically progress through the prescribed lesson at their own pace. To advocate installing computer-managed instruction of this sort, one must support a behaviorist approach to learning and recalling information. The software is the primary information provider, and the student's task is to take in that information. A school committed to a holistic, interdisciplinary model of learning based on constructivist principles and inquiry would have substantive philosophical differences with Integrated Learning Systems. Advocating an ILS in such a context would not make sense because the technology use and the educational beliefs don't match. Advocacy must be selective, and that requires analyzing the assumptions that underpin any technology use.

Beyond determining how computers should be used comes selecting software to fit the school's beliefs and goals. Materials selection is a traditional part of the school library media specialist's work, and software selection is a logical extension of that work. In recent years, collection development has tended toward a more collaborative process. There was a time when the librarian chose library books without involvement by teachers. However, as the library media collection has become a central factor in curriculum and instruction, library media specialists have become more collaborative in selecting materials. Selection of software, likewise, needs to be a collaborative process, involving teachers and library media specialists.

Choosing software for a school needs to be based on explicit criteria (see Figures 8.2, 8.3, and 8.4 as well as 10.1); a standardized set of criteria should guide purchase (Langhorne et al., 1989). Such a stringent process suggests that quality and "fit" are critical factors (Donham, 1984). The set of evaluation criteria should be locally generated to match local beliefs about teaching and learning. Figure 10.1 shows an example of criteria for software selection in a district committed to constructivist learning. That commitment is evident in several of the criteria. For example, under the "Media Appropriate" category are questions about the relationship between the software and the use of manipulatives or first-hand experiences. Also, under "21st Century–Aware," criteria call for the program to promote critical thinking and investigative problem solving, not rote memorization. These criteria show a direct correlation between the instructional beliefs of the institution and the decision making regarding what software to use.

When a school purchases a book, there is considerable expense because books are not cheap. There are then the added costs of cataloging and processing the book, so the cost increases. After that, the book is ready to be used. Purchase of software becomes more complex than that—How many licenses are needed for it? What staff development will be necessary for its implementation? Where will it be accessed? Is the hardware available adequate for it? (See Chapter 8 for purchase and maintenance of hardware.) More is involved than an investment in an item. Such complexity calls for careful decision making because the cost goes well beyond the sticker price.

Advocacy for technology also requires understanding the change process and being skilled at helping teachers accept new ideas. For some teachers, integrating technologies into their curricula may require substantial changes in educational philosophy, classroom management, and curricular goals. After observing implementation of technology in public schools as a part of a longitudinal study in 14 states, Foa, Schwab, and Johnson (1996) conclude:

> For technologies to be used effectively, teachers must be comfortable with a constructivist or project-based, problem-solving approach to learning; they must be willing to tolerate students progressing independently at widely varying paces; they must trust students to

FIGURE 10.1
Software Evaluation Criteria

Instructional Design

Quality Content
___ The content is well researched, based on sound learning theory, and up-to-date.
___ The program addresses skills and concepts central to teaching objectives.
___ The program supports and enhances the curriculum.
___ The program offers cross-curricular applications.
___ The program is process-oriented.
___ The program does not involve skill drilling.
___ The program promotes active learning.

Media Appropriate
___ The instructional task is appropriate to the medium.
___ The task could not be accomplished effectively with different media.
___ The program complements and extends the use of manipulatives.
___ The program appropriately provides unavailable firsthand experiences.

21st Century–Aware
___ The software promotes independent thinking, critical thinking, and investigative problem solving rather than stressing skills such as rote thinking and out-of-context memorization.

Instructionally Consistent
___ The software is consistently developmentally appropriate for the target audience (i.e., necessary reading levels do not vary greatly, subject matter is appropriate to the intended age group).

Stimulates Curiosity
___ The software engages student interest.

Challenging
___ The program has a low entry/high ceiling.
___ Students feel a sense of accomplishment.

Student Control
___ Students can use the program independently.
___ The program is open-ended
___ Students can create their own pathways rather than merely respond to prompts.

Adaptive
___ The program suits different learning styles.
___ Students with limited English-speaking abilities can use the program.
___ The program offers special education options.

Software Design

You-Are-Here Design
___ Students can determine where they are in the program without feeling lost.
___ Students can quickly begin to use the program with minimal prompting from an adult.

Transparent Interface
___ Students' efforts are devoted to using the program, not learning how to use the program.

Describe how this program can be appropriately used for learning.

Excerpted from the form used by the Iowa City Community School District, Iowa City, Ia.

know more than they do about certain subjects and techniques, and in fact to take on the role of expert teacher at various times; they must be comfortable about not having complete control over what resources the student accesses or what the student learns and they must be flexible enough to change directions when technical glitches occur. For some teachers these practices are all second nature. . . . More often, however, we are asking teachers to integrate dramatically new philosophies of education, curricular goals, classroom management techniques and new ideas about interdisciplinary and individualized education into their daily practice. No wonder the introduction of technologies is often perceived as threatening (Foa, Schwab, & Johnson, 1996, [online])

Sensitivity to teachers is nothing new to the library media specialist whose very curriculum is dependent on collaboration.

Taking Charge of Change (1987) describes the Concerns-Based Adoption Model (CBAM), a sequence of concerns that innovation raises. The sequence begins with *information concerns*, the need for introductory information about the innovation. As technology advocate, the library media specialist simply makes teachers aware of a new use for technology—either hardware or software—that has potential to enhance or expand the current way of learning. People resist innovation when they perceive that there is no need; technology innovations have to promise a substantial improvement in the learning experience before teachers, beyond the zealots, will have enough interest to adopt it. In short, there must be some incentive to undertake the change, and ideally that incentive needs to be the intrinsic value of the technology. Before advocating for a technology implementation, the library media specialist must have confidence that it is worth doing.

Next come *personal concerns*, where the novice wonders how an innovation will affect him or her—What will I need to learn? How will I have to change to adopt this idea? Fear of failure contributes to resistance to change. This anxiety typically calls for support and encouragement. Once personal concerns are alleviated, *management concerns* emerge—How will I make this work in my classroom or schedule? It is natural to want a sense of control; teachers are accustomed to being in control of the content and flow of events in their classrooms. Innovations perceived as potentially eroding their control of instruction or their students are likely to bring resistance (Hartzell, 1996). Beyond management concerns are *consequence concerns*—What difference will this make for my students? Sharing testimony of successful adopters of a technology can help teachers see the potential benefits for their own students. Next, the CBAM model suggests that needs for *collaborating* and *refocusing* emerge. At this point, teachers need to work with someone else to fit the technology precisely to their situation—an opportunity for the library media specialist and teachers to work together. If library media specialists are aware of these concerns when adopting an innovation, they can more easily appreciate the teacher's viewpoint.

Trainer

Trainer is another role library media specialists play. Experienced teachers and novices alike need to learn about technology applications that can be helpful to them and their students. Examples of basic skills all teachers need include how to

- use an online library catalog
- use a CD-ROM encyclopedia
- operate a video camera and video recorder for recording and playback
- use a computerized student record-keeping system
- use a network to communicate with e-mail
- use a word-processing program
- understand and apply copyright guidelines

Gradually, teachers entering the profession should bring these basic skills and others with them, but for a time, some teachers will require training in these basic skills. Yet, how can technology begin to affect student learning until teachers use and value it? Library media specialists who stay at the forefront of technology in their schools can readily offer in-service teacher training. General staff in-service training in basic technology skills is one component of such staff development. Some school districts have established minimum competencies for all teachers, and ask library media specialists to assist teachers in attaining those competencies. One example is Ankeny (Iowa) Community Schools where the district's technology committee established minimum competencies for all teachers, and called on library media specialists to assist teachers in arriving at those competencies. Their expectations are basic, but call for all teachers to have some fundamental computer skills:

- Basics

  open a file
  save to a floppy diskette and a hard drive
  access appropriate applications on a network
  create a folder and save work into it
  print documents

- Word Processing

  enter, move, copy, replace, and delete text
  change font, font style, and font size in selected text
  use spell check
  set and use margins and tabs

- Electronic Card Catalog

  search by author, title, subject, and keyword
  print selected information

- CD-ROM

  access menu of available CD-ROMs and select appropriate re-
      source
  locate information and print

In a similar way, Mankato (Minn.) Public Schools established competencies for professional staff. In both districts, a staff development plan
helps teachers be successful in gaining these minimum competencies,
and library media specialists are key trainers (Johnson, 1995).

A train-the-trainers model is one way library media specialists can
achieve staff development efficiently. In the Iowa City (Iowa) Community Schools, each library media specialist trains a cadre of teachers within
a school to be trainers and mentors for teachers in using technology. The
cadre in elementary schools may include teacher-trainers from each team
or grade level, and in a secondary school they represent various departments. The train-the-trainer model facilitates tailoring training to the
context where it will be used—an important consideration.

The need for training will continue as software is upgraded and
new applications for technology are identified. The library media specialist will always need to be the "crow's nester," looking for what is on
the horizon and what is worth consideration within the context of the
school and its students.

Teacher

Finally comes the role of teacher. Besides training teachers, library media specialists have a substantial role to play in teaching students about information technology. Specific skills to be taught are discussed in Chapter 11. It is important to keep this role in mind, however, and to consider for new technology application these questions: What implications does this have for teaching? How can this be integrated with the information skills curriculum? What ethical questions arise?

THE WORLD WIDE WEB

"The Web" expands dramatically the information available to students and teachers. Some see this broad-based availability of information as threatening to school library media centers. As schools become networked and access is available throughout the building, what happens to the school library media program? Will there no longer be a need for it? Will the Web eliminate the control library media specialists have had on what resources are available within the school? Will there no longer be a need for teaching students about accessing information?

The Web needs to be recognized as just one more resource—not a replacement resource for all information searching. It is a very useful source for certain kinds of queries. One of its strengths is that it can be extremely current. Whether it is for breaking news or for most current information about the national debt (http://www.brillig.com/debt_clock), the Web can be an efficient source. For some information not readily available in a school library media collection—for example, Supreme Court Decisions (http://www/law.cornell.edu/supct/) or legislation (http://www.thomas)—the Web can provide answers. On the other hand, there are many questions that readily available print resources can handle efficiently. It is not necessary to go online to find the capital of a state or country when an atlas is close at hand. A print version of a style manual is an efficient source to check the punctuation for a bibliographic entry. Teaching students to match the source to the need for the most efficient solution is perhaps more important than ever. Often the information available on the Web is brief, and more in-depth study will require other resources such as periodicals, books, or specialized CD-ROM resources. Since this is an open publishing forum, authority can range from a source like the Centers for Disease Control to anyone who chooses to publish his or her ideas. The importance of students' recognizing the bias and authority of their information sources is amplified.

Networking in schools will increase Web access. The availability of information will become more democratic; the amount of readily available information will continue to increase. In response, the school library media specialist must help students become critical information consumers. They need to learn criteria for selecting information: the bias and authority of the source, recency, accuracy and verifiability, thoroughness. They need to learn to use the information effectively, that is, to determine its relevance and the appropriate scope for their need.

Traditionally, selection policies have provided guidelines for what schools buy. However, access to the Web reduces the control educators have. This more open access to information has generated action to protect students and limit access. The best response is to inform students of what will constitute acceptable use of network resources in the school. Principles of intellectual freedom challenge the notion of schools censoring what will be accessible to students. Establishing that school-related information searching is the purpose for network resources seems an appropriate approach. Many schools have developed "Acceptable Use Policies" to define parameters for using network resources. Figure 10.2 contains the text of one acceptable use policy. The policy commits students to appropriate resource utilization.

Copyright of electronic resources is a complex issue. A primary purpose of copyright is to ensure ongoing creation. Those who create must have some means of having their creation protected and, ideally, gaining some compensation for it. This purpose must be balanced against dissemination of ideas necessary for continuing intellectual and creative progress. The Fair Use Doctrine allows certain uses of copyrighted material (for example, criticism, reporting, teaching, and scholarship) that would otherwise be copyright infringements. Four factors determine fair use:

- *the purpose or character of the use*: Use in the regular course of one's educational activities usually satisfies the requirement that the use be for nonprofit educational purposes rather than for commercial purposes.
- *the nature of the copyrighted work*: The Fair Use Doctrine is more likely to apply to factual works or works intended for the educational market than to fictional or creative expression.

FIGURE 10.2
Student Internet Use Agreement
Iowa City Community School District

Internet access is coordinated through a complex association of agencies, regional and state networks, and commercial organizations. To ensure smooth operation of the network, endusers must adhere to established guidelines regarding proper conduct and efficient, ethical, and legal usage. The signatures at the end of this document are legally binding. Signing this document indicates that you have read and agree to abide by its terms and conditions.

1. **Acceptable Use.** The use of your account must be in support of education and research and consistent with the ICCSD Strategic Plan and educational objectives. Use of other organizations' networks or computing resources must comply with the rules appropriate for those networks. Transmissions that violate any district, state, or U.S. regulations are prohibited. These transmissions include but are not limited to copyrighted material, threatening or obscene material, and material protected by trade secret. Use for commercial activities, product advertisement, or political lobbying is prohibited.

2. **Privileges.** The use of the Internet is a privilege, not a right, and inappropriate use will result in a cancellation of those privileges.

3. **Netiquette.** You are expected to abide by the generally accepted rules of network etiquette. These include but are not limited to the following:
    a. Be polite. Do not be abusive in your messages to others.
    b. Use appropriate language. Do not swear, or use vulgarities or any other inappropriate language.
    c. Do not reveal your own personal address or phone number or those of students or colleagues.
    d. Note that electronic mail is not guaranteed to be private. People who operate the system do have access to all mail. Messages relating to or in support of illegal activities may be reported to authorities.
    e. Do not engage in illegal activities. This includes but is not limited to, threats, harassment, stalking, and fraud.
    f. Do not use the network in such a way that you would disrupt the use of the network by other users.
    g. Assume that all communications and information accessible via the network are private property.

h. Respect intellectual property of others by crediting sources and respecting all copyright laws. Users will accept the responsibility of keeping copyrighted software from entering the local area network.

4. **No warranties.** ICCSD makes no warranties of any kind, expressed or implied, for the information or services provided through the network. ICCSD will not be responsible for any damages. This could include loss of data, or service interruptions.

5. **Security.** Security on any computer system is a high priority, especially when the system involves many users. Do not use another individual's account without written permission from that individual. Attempts to log on as a system operator will result in cancellation of user privileges. Any user identified as a security risk may be denied access to the district's computer resource.

6. **Vandalism.** Vandalism will result in cancellation of privileges. Vandalism is defined as any malicious attempt to harm or destroy hardware, software, or data of another user or any of the above listed agencies or other networks. This includes but is not limited to uploading or creating computer viruses, or breaching security measures.

For students: I understand and will abide by the Internet Use Agreement. I further understand that any violation of the regulations above is unethical and may constitute a criminal offense. Should I commit any violation, my access privileges may be revoked, school disciplinary action may be taken, and/or appropriate legal action may be taken.

For parent or guardian: I have read the Internet Use Agreement. I understand that this access is designed for educational purposes. The ICCSD has taken precautions to eliminate controversial material. However, I recognize it is impossible for the ICCSD to restrict access to all controversial materials and I will not hold the district responsible for materials acquired on the network. Further, I accept full responsibility for supervision when student use is not in a school setting.

- *the amount and substantiality of the portion*: Generally, the Fair Use Doctrine requires the least possible use of an original work. The substantiality test means that the essence of the work (for example, the theme of a musical score) is not used.
- *the effect upon the potential market*: Fair use should not adversely affect the original author's economic opportunities.

New multimedia copyright guidelines were agreed to and released in 1997, the result of lengthy discussion between representatives of copyright holders and educators led by the Consortium of College and University Media Centers (Simpson, 1997). While these guidelines are not law, they represent an agreement on limits of use. The guidelines permit students to create multimedia works and retain them in portfolios for job interviews. Teachers may create and use copyrighted material in their multimedia productions in face-to-face instruction and may assign students to look at them independently. Teachers may also display their productions at conferences, when using copyrighted material under the limits set by the guidelines. Quantitative limits set in the guidelines of how much can be used from a copyrighted work include

- *motion media (film/video)*: up to 10 percent or 3 minutes, whichever is less, of an individual program
- *text*: up to 10 percent or 1,000 words, whichever is less; complete short poems; no more than three poems per poet or five poems per anthology
- *music*: up to 10 percent but not more than 30 seconds
- *illustrations*: no more than five images per artist; not more than 10 percent or 16 images from a single collective work

Library media specialists need to encourage students and teachers to be aware of copyright and its protective purposes. Students must learn that access to works on the Web does not automatically mean that these materials can be reproduced and reused without permission or royalty payment; also, some copyrighted works may have been posted without authorization of the copyright holder. According to Fair Use Guidelines for Educational Multimedia, when creating multimedia projects, students should include a statement on the opening screen that certain materials are included under the fair use exemption of the copyright law (CCUMC Fair Use, 1996). These same guidelines suggest that if student work will be disseminated over the World Wide Web, then it is advisable to obtain permission for all copyrighted portions. Students also need to credit sources for works included in multimedia productions.

Technology has caused dramatic changes in how users deal with copyright. Reproduction has become simpler. Because of personal access to technologies, the locus of infringement has moved from a public activity to private or semi-private contexts, raising enforcement problems. Perhaps most significantly, technology creates an expectation for immediate access to information. Advancements in what is possible technologically increase the difficulty in protecting the interests of creators. The library media specialist needs to instill in students an understanding of why copyright exists. Adherence to copyright legislation should be a provision in the acceptable use policy.

EVALUATION

There is no one simple evaluation tool for examining technology's impact. In Chapter 13 a set of rubrics (a range of performance descriptions) is described for use in evaluating technology planning and implementation. The dimensions include technology applications, integration into the curriculum, the planning process, staff development, budget, hardware, software, and policy. Periodic evaluation of the technology program should consider all of these aspects.

Besides an overall review of the technology program, implementation of each technology application in a school needs to be evaluated. What is the expected impact of the technology? Did it meet the expectation? For example, adding an electronic magazine index should result in students identifying more information sources. An increase in magazine use, or an increase in magazine citations should evidence its success. More important, improved content in the students' projects because of increased periodical literature use would be an even better indicator of its success. For each staff development activity, follow-up on how the staff member has implemented newly acquired skills is appropriate. Data to be collected for evaluation can vary; examples include statistical measures like circulation, anecdotal reports from teachers or students, examples of documents or projects created by students or staff, or time-use analysis. These data need to be collected, analyzed, and shared with decision makers and funders so that technology's impact can be seen. Where results show minimal impact, the reasons need to be investigated.

In response to negative findings, some applications will need to be abandoned, some will need to be improved. Potential problems may be a lack of critical mass of equipment to match the need, inadequate staff development, an inappropriate technology application, or software shortcomings. Where results show positive effects, those results need to be shared so that others can see their benefits and so that decision makers can see the outcome of their investment.

ACTION STRATEGIES

Learning and Teaching

- Teach information technologies as part of the information skills curriculum.

Information Access and Delivery

- Facilitate access to technology for teachers and students by reducing barriers:
    - Consider home checkout.
    - Purchase laptop word processors for circulation (Huber, 1997).
    - Pursue special teacher computer-purchase plans. Some school districts have worked with local vendors to offer special purchase plans, in cooperation with local banks for low-interest loans and with the school district business office for payment by payroll deduction.
    - Find creative ways to staff computer facilities so that they are accessible to students during free periods (such as lunch hours, and before and after school).

Program Administration

- Be a leader in the uses of technology for the entire school.
- Read periodicals that help maintain current awareness in the area of technology.
- Establish criteria for technology applications and software selection to promote a commitment to quality in the use of technology.
- Use the automated circulation system to manage hardware inventory.

- Remind teachers and administrators that technology must be used in the context of the instructional program, not as an add-on.
- Provide leadership in developing policies related to acceptable use of resources, copyright, privacy, and intellectual freedom as these relate to technology.
- Collect data to document the uses of technology and its impact; include statistics on use of equipment, facilities, and software, as well as sample documents and projects created by students to demonstrate the qualitative impact technology has had.

REFERENCES

"CCUMC Fair Use Multimedia Guidelines," Consortium of College and University Media Centers (March 28, 1996); available at http://www.libraries.psu.edu/avs/fairuse/guidelinedoc.html

Donham, Jean. "Selecting Computer Software—We Take It Seriously!" *The Computing Teacher* 12 (October 1984): 63–64.

Expectations of Excellence; Curriculum Standards for Social Studies (Washington, D.C.: National Council for the Social Studies, 1994), 165.

Foa, Lin, Richard Schwab, and Michael Johnson. "Upgrading School Technology," *Educational Week* [online] (May 1, 1996): Available: http://teachermag.org

Hartzell, Gary. "Wrestling with Resistance," *Technology Connection* 3 (May 1996): 10–12.

Huber, Joe. "Laptop Word Processors—A Way to Close the Technology Gap," *Technology Connection* 4 (April 1997): 26–27.

[ICCSD} Iowa City Community School District Home Page. Available: http://www.iowa-city.k12.ia.us/

Johnson, Doug. "The New and Improved School Library; How One District Planned for the Future," *School Library Journal* 41 (June 1995): 36–39.

Jukes, Ian. "The Essential Steps of Technology Planning," *The School Administrator* 53 (April 1996): 8–14.

King, Richard A. "Rethinking Equity in Computer Access and Use," *Educational Technology* 27 (April 1987): 12–18.

Knezevitch, Stephen. *Administration of Public Education* (New York: Harper & Row, 1984), 88.

Langhorne, Mary Jo et al., *Teaching with Computers: A New Menu for the 90s* (Phoenix, Ariz.: Oryx Press, 1989).

Piller, Charles. "Separate Realities," *MacWorld* (September 1992): 218–230.

Professional Standards for Teaching Mathematics (Reston, Va.: National Council of Teachers of Mathematics, 1991).

Sayers, Dennis. "Educational Equity Issues in an Information Age," *Teachers College Record* 96, no. 4 (1995): 767–774.

Simpson, Carol. "How Much, How Many, and When: Copyright and Multimedia," *Technology Connection* 4 (March 1997): 10–12.

Sutton, Rosemary. "Equity and Computers in the Schools: A Decade of Research," *Review of Educational Research* 61 (Winter 1991): 475–503.

Taking Charge of Change (Alexandria, Va.: Association for Supervision and Curriculum Development, 1987).

van Deusen, Jean Donham. "Managing Equipment: A Proposed Model for Replacement," *Bottom Line* 8 (Spring 1995): 10–14.

Van Dusen, Lani M. and B. R. Worthen. "Can Integrated Instructional Technology Transform the Classroom?" *Educational Leadership* 53 (October 1995): 28–32.

Wilson, Brent et al. *Technology Making a Difference: The Peakview Elementary School Study* (ERIC Document Ed 381 149, 1994) Syracuse, NY: ERIC Clearinghouse on Information & Technology.

Chapter 11

Information Literacy

This chapter

- examines information skills to be taught within the categories of information literacy, independent learning, and social responsibility
- considers special demands of information technology for today's information skills curriculum
- describes assignments and activities that challenge students to work at high cognitive levels
- explores mental models of information seeking as they influence students' performance
- identifies action strategies for information skills instruction

"AASL's (American Association of School Librarians/Association for Educational Communications and Technology) Information Literacy Standards for Student Learning" identifies three categories of learning: information literacy, independent learning, and social responsibility (AASL/AECT, 1997). Information literacy consists of the student's ability to access, evaluate, and use information. Independent learning refers to effective behaviors of students to pursue information related to personal interests, to appreciate creative expressions of information, and to strive for excellence by assessing quality and revising appropriately. Social responsibility calls for students to recognize the importance of information in a democratic society, to practice ethical behavior, and to participate effectively in groups as they pursue and generate information. The primary concern of this chapter is with information literacy; however, behaviors of independent learning and social responsibility also emerge in discussing how information literacy is effectively taught.

INFORMATION LITERACY SKILLS

Several models for information literacy exist, including those of Eisenberg and Berkowitz (1990), Pappas and Teppe (1995), Kuhlthau (1994), and Stripling (1988). All have some common threads. All incorporate these basis elements: posing an information question, locating potential sources of information, examining and selecting relevant information, synthesizing the information, and communicating results. All acknowledge that information processing is not a simple linear task, but instead is recursive in nature; as students explore a topic, their research question may change. As they examine information and identify gaps, they return to the task of locating information.

Foremost among researchers who have examined information processes is Carol Kuhlthau, who has closely monitored students working in libraries and has analyzed those observations in an effort to understand the process and appreciate students' needs. Only when the information process is understood can library media specialists know what students need in order to be successful. After extensive research, Kuhlthau (1993) identifies some common patterns in students' information work. She describes that process in six stages (initiation, selection, exploration, formulation, collection, and presentation), each with its own typical tasks as well as feelings. As figure 11.1 demonstrates, Kuhlthau's description of the information search process parallels the three standards outlined as information literacy in the AASL Information Literacy Standards.

Throughout her work, Kuhlthau emphasizes that movement from task to task is not necessarily a sequential process, but rather one of moving forward and backward as the results of one part of the process require the student to clarify or expand a previous task.

Kuhlthau's information process model provides a sound guideline for developing an information skills curriculum. Figure 11.2 lists the strategies that could be taught in an information skills curriculum based on Kuhlthau's model. The library media specialist has several tasks to accomplish in implementing an effective information skills curriculum:

FIGURE 11.1
Kuhlthau Stages Parallel AASL Information Literacy Standards

Kuhlthau Stages	Standards
Initiation • recognize the need for information *Selection* • decide on a topic for study *Exploration* • search for information to become familiar with the topic *Formulation* • focus the perspective on the topic	Accesses information efficiently and effectively • recognizes the need for information • recognizes that accurate and comprehensive information is the basis for intelligent decision making • formulates questions • identifies variety of potential sources of information • develops and uses successful strategies for locating information
Collection • gather information	Evaluates information critically and competently • determines accuracy, relevance, and comprehensiveness • distinguishes among facts, point of view, and opinion • identifies inaccurate or misleading information • selects information appropriate to the problem
Presentation • organize information • communicate results	Uses information effectively and creatively • organizes information for practical application • integrates new information into one's own knowledge • applies information in critical thinking and problem solving • produces and communicates information and ideas in appropriate formats

- Identify the strategies to be taught (Figure 11.2 provides starting point).
- Consult with teachers to determine how to relate the teaching of these strategies to the classroom curriculum.
- Consult with teachers about how students can develop these strategies.
- Plan with teachers for the development of these skills.
- Teach lessons and mini-lessons on specific strategies in the context of students' assignments; provide aids such as pathfinders, Netscape bookmarks, annotated bibliographies, or models of bibliographic format.

FIGURE 11.2
Sample Strategies for Information Processing

- Brainstorming
- Free writing
- KWL (Know, Want, Learn)
- Webbing
- Browsing
- Background reading in encyclopedias or general reference or nonfiction materials (For young children, this may mean the teacher or library media specialist will read a book to students.)
- Watching a video and extracting information from it
- Generating a research question
- Writing a thesis statement
- Using a prepared pathfinder
- Setting and using bookmarks for Web sites
- Using keyword searching, including Boolean logic
- Using truncation
- Using navigational features of print and electronic resources (e.g., headings, *Find* commands, cross references, bookmarks)
- Using tables, charts, maps within articles
- Using headings and typography to locate information efficiently
- Skimming and scanning
- Note taking
- Downloading
- Evaluating resources (e.g., appropriateness, availability, relevance, suitability, currency, authority, reliability)
- Identifying patterns or trends
- Determining relationships (e.g., comparison/contrast, cause/effect)
- Outlining
- Creating a product or presentation

At *initiation*, the student must recognize the need for information; this stage is often characterized by some feeling of anxiety. During *selection*, the student must decide on a topic for study. This is a time of intellectual testing to set a direction for exploration, based on assignment requirements, information available, or other criteria. Commonly, this preliminary work gets too little time or attention. At the initiation and selection stages, if students brainstorm with others about possible topics or tap into their own prior knowledge about a topic, they may develop a more meaningful research question. Too often, because the topic decision is rushed, students pose a rather low-level, fact-based research question.

One activity often overlooked in this pre-search stage is background building. Students need to spend time just gaining background about a topic before they begin to generate their research question. This may involve watching a video, reading in general reference sources, taking a field trip, exploring a CD-ROM resource, or browsing the World Wide Web. Whatever the medium, the task is to become knowledgeable enough about the topic to be able to pose significant questions. In this way, the research question can go beyond simple fact finding, because students will have already accomplished that during their background building work. Giving more time to the pre-search stage may make the difference between a research question that asks, "What is chemical warfare?" and one that asks, "What are the technical, social and political barriers to controlling chemical warfare and can they be overcome?"

In *Exploration*, the KWL strategy (derived from the phrases "What I Know," "What I Want to find out, " and "What I Learned") encourages pre-search thinking. The library media specialist must encourage teachers to allocate adequate time to this stage. Activities like background reading without detailed note taking (a good time for general references like encyclopedias), brainstorming, browsing, and KWL exercises will provide the foundation needed for students to enter into the next stages prepared. Browsing is useful to help students move toward a personally interesting, focused investigation (Pappas, 1995). Students can browse by using an electronic encyclopedia, choosing a broad topic like baseball and examining the article titles that emerge. (One might find a specific personality like George Steinbrenner or Connie Mack of interest; or the National Baseball Hall of Fame, or Gambling in Baseball, or the Negro Baseball Leagues may emerge as potential topics after browsing such a list.) Students can browse topics and subtopics in an online catalog or an electronic magazine index to generate ideas for focusing their topic. Browsing print sources (for example, perusing tables of contents or bookshelves) can help in the exploration stage as well. Remember that initiation, selection and exploration are interwoven and occur recursively as students refine their understanding of the topic.

Sometimes a teacher will focus a research assignment topic for students to meet very narrow curricular objectives when the same assignment could also meet other learning goals. In those cases, the library media specialist must encourage teachers to develop topics that move students beyond simple answer seeking toward higher cognitive levels. For example, the common animal research assignment that calls for students to choose an animal, determine what it eats, where it lives, and who its enemies are offers little challenge beyond copying information from the source. Library media specialists can suggest to teachers that this kind of "research" gives students too little intellectual challenge and instead offer an alternative assignment that meets the teacher's content area objective, yet also extends the cognitive level at which students must work. For example, instead of the traditional fact-finding animal report, in one elementary school the teacher asks children to choose an animal about which they will write a story. The story must show the animal behaving in ways that characterize its true nature and the setting must be the natural habitat of the animal. This assignment creates a very different challenge for students than simply reading and reporting. Another example of a more challenging assignment is for students to design a zoo exhibit for the animal studied; their product might be a diorama of the exhibit, accompanied by detailed building instructions. Whether the teacher provides the focus or the students identify it, the exploration stage is a time of particular uneasiness—and it may sometimes seem confusing or overwhelming—if the topic is too general. At this time, the student may be particularly inarticulate about his or her information needs.

Formulation means that there is a focused perspective on the topic. The student knows what to look for and then needs efficient strategies for searching. Kuhlthau describes this stage as "the turning point of the search process," when the focus of the information quest becomes clear. Increased confidence may characterize this stage. *Collection* involves gathering information; now the student can specify his or her needs more clearly, and can better select relevant information. At the collection stage, students need to know how to access information sources. They will appreciate a pathfinder (see Figure 11.3) from the library media specialist. Pathfinders give students reminders of where to look along with

FIGURE 11.3
Pathfinder Template

Not every pathfinder will have all categories of information; the students' assignment will determine which sources are most appropriate.

Source	Hints
Reference Collection	Briefly identify titles that apply to the topic being investigated; give a brief annotation indicating what kind of information is provided, location and call number.
General Collection	Suggest keywords or combinations of keywords that might be used in searching for the topic; include useful search hints.
Magazines	Suggest keywords or combinations of keywords that might be used in searching for the topic; include useful search hints. Indicate how to get the document itself once the citation has been found.
Specialized CD-ROM Resources	Identify any specialized CD-ROM resources that relate to the topic and suggest keywords or combinations of keywords that might be used in searching for the topic; include useful search hints.
World Wide Web	Give brief instructions on how to approach the topic via an appropriate search engine. See Debbie Abilock's Web page for assistance in choosing an appropriate search engine: http://www.nueva.pvt.k12.ca.us/~debbie/library/research/adviceengine.html
Knowledgeable Individuals	Suggest arranging a time to interview an expert on the topic. Advise students about preparing questions in advance and either taking notes or recording the interview.
Outside Source	Suggest other libraries or resources and give steps for accessing them (modem access, telephone numbers, addresses, hours, etc.)

helpful hints. Besides aids of this sort, students need search strategies. Here library media specialists teach lessons on choosing keywords, using Boolean operators, and truncation, skimming and scanning in either print or electronic formats, downloading, note taking (using "notepad" features of electronic resources as well as paper-based note taking and highlighting), and organizing findings.

Finally, at the *presentation* stage, students begin to synthesize what they have found and apply their findings to the research question. As they work in this stage, it is not uncommon for them to return to earlier stages to collect additional information or even adjust their focus. Here students will need skill in creating a product or presentation to communicate what they have discovered. The specific media they use will determine what presentation skills they need. Library media specialists can offer suggestions of various forms for presentation (for example, debates, letters and journals, multimedia projects, speeches, posters, printed brochures, case studies, or video). Whatever the format, the library media program must be ready to provide the resources and guidance for students to create quality products. Suggesting formats for presentation should occur at the beginning of the process, since it will influence the kinds of material students seek during the collection stage.

Information work takes time. Quality work demands that teachers allocate enough time for students to move methodically through all tasks, to reflect on what they are learning as they collect information, and to create an effective way to present what they have learned. Advocacy for time—particularly time in the library media center—is an important responsibility for the library media specialist. Another critical concern is teaching. The information process grows more complex as more information is available and as search tools expand in number and complexity. It is never appropriate to say that students no longer need direct instruction as well as one-on-one help. At least brief mini-lessons (outlining the idiosyncrasies of a specific search tool, introducing specialized print sources on a relevant topic, or presenting ways to determine a resource's authority) will be appropriate throughout high school. Such lessons, at all grade levels, must be taught at the point of need (that is, when students are engaged in a task that will require use of these sources).

INFORMATION TECHNOLOGY AND INFORMATION SKILLS

Information technologies pose special challenges for teaching in the library media center. At the lowest cognitive level, students learn the specific commands and menus for available resources. Beyond that, they need to know what use each resource has (What kind of information is in *SIRS?* What are the ways that I can search *NewsBank?* How comprehensive is *Magazine Articles Summaries?*) Students also must know how to manage these electronic resources to get the most relevant information efficiently. One common student mistake is to conduct too broad a search and then merely take the first several hits, rather than redefine the search to be more precise. Another common student error is to ignore availability of information (for example, electronic periodical indexes often provide an indication of where a publication is available, but students often ignore that information).

Perhaps the most challenging concern for today's student searches is determining the quality of the information accessed. The AASL Standards call for students to evaluate information critically. To do that, they need to apply criteria as they search for information (*Information Literacy Curriculum Guide*, 1998):

- *appropriateness*: Where should I look for information?

  Sample questions:
  If I want general information, what is the best source?
  If I want the most current information, what is the best source?
  If I want graphic information, what is the best source?

- *availability*: How accessible is the information for me?

  Sample questions:
  Will I make better use of my time by using what is available locally, or searching for what I can get outside the school (e.g., searching the local public library catalog or other external resources)?
  Can I find enough information locally without needing to go beyond?

- *relevance*: Is this source of information directly relevant to my focused topic? If not, how can I change my search strategy to find sources that are more directly relevant?

Sample questions:

Does the abstract relate directly to my focused topic?

As I skim the article, does it appear to be too specific or too general?

- *suitability*: How suitable is this resource for me?

  Sample questions:

  Do I understand the language?

  Can I easily paraphrase what I am reading?

- *currency*: How important is copyright date for my topic?

  Sample questions:

  What is the copyright date of this information source?

  Is it likely that newer information since that date would affect accuracy?

- *authority*: Does the information source represent authoritative background, reputation, and knowledge for this topic?

  Sample questions:

  What is the background of the author providing the information?

  What reputation does the publisher have?

  Is there an authoritative organization supporting this information?

  Is there potential for bias from a commercial enterprise?

- *reliability*: Is the information based on fact or is it simply opinion?

  Sample questions:

  Is the language used objective and free of stereotypes or "loaded" language?

  Are other sources given that can be used to verify information?

Applying these criteria to the information collected will cause students to be critical consumers of information as called for in the national standards. As electronic searching continues to expand the amount of available information, critical consumption of information will become increasingly important.

ASSIGNMENTS FOR TEACHING INFORMATION LITERACY

A key ingredient for students to develop information literacy is the type of assignments teachers give them. Assignments can demand nothing more than fact finding, or they can demand analyzing and applying information. Library media specialists need to consult with teachers about the nature of their expectations and keep at the forefront the cognitive demands of assignments. Consider the Civil War as an example. Middle school students can be assigned to write a report about a specific battle or a specific personality from the Civil War era. Either of these tasks can quickly become an encyclopedia article in style and content. More important, the process for completing the assignment can simply be transfer of information from a print or electronic source to the student's paper or diskette. Alternatives to that assignment can challenge students to do more than rewrite the information they find. Some possibilities include:

- *letters*: Read about the conditions of soldiers during the Civil War. Write a letter as a Civil War soldier describing life in a camp, or a battle, or a prison camp, or as an African American soldier in the Colored Troops. Criteria for evaluation will include how specific and accurate your details are and how authentic the writing is to the personality you created.
- *editorial*: Read about slavery from both the Union and Confederate points of view. Write two newspaper editorials, one for a Southern newspaper and one from the Abolitionist viewpoint. Criteria for evaluation will include how specific and accurate the supporting details are and how effectively you develop the argument for each side.
- *news story*: Read about a specific battle. Write a newspaper article or create a television news report about it as if you were an on-the-scene reporter. Criteria for evaluation will include how specific and accurate the details of your report are, how well you adapt the facts to a news-reporting style, and how well you match your reporting to the target audience (North or South).

What are the attributes that set these assignments apart from simply reporting facts? These students are seeking information to apply to a larger problem—a letter, an editorial, a news story. They will not simply rewrite the facts but rather incorporate them into meaningful communication. The first attribute is that *the assignment goes beyond fact finding*. These assignments demand careful selection of information. Relevance is crucial because they are not merely reporting a list of facts, but must choose information that exactly suits the end product—the news story, the editorial, or the letter. Students will likely reject at least as much information as they will use. Learning to select what really matters makes students critical information consumers. These students have considerable latitude in choosing what they will do, which often results in increased commitment—and ultimately engagement in the task at hand. Not only do students choose among the three options, but within each there is still an opportunity to focus the task. So, the second attribute is *student choice*. Because these options all take a human interest approach to the assignment, students are not writing and thinking in the manner of a textbook writer. That human interest approach makes history become a story of real life, not merely a collection of facts. The third attribute, then, is that these assignments offer students a sense of *personal interest*. Eisner (1994) has observed that affective and cognitive processes are interdependent strands that lead to a unified understanding. By incorporating a personal, affective aspect to the assignments, these two domains interact, creating a more meaningful experience for students. Finally, these options are *open-ended*. There is not one right answer for any of the assignments; rather there are criteria for determining quality. Questions demand analysis, synthesis, and evaluation. This moves the information process well beyond fact finding and incorporates creativity. Students can gather their information in a variety of ways—reading historical fiction, watching a video, or examining primary and secondary sources. The presentation of their findings invites creativity—a likely way to engender interest in the task. Four factors should characterize assignments: assignments should go beyond fact finding, they should offer students choices, they should provide a sense of personal interest, and they should be open-ended (that is, seeking answers should require thinking at higher levels of Bloom's Taxonomy).

Designing challenging and engaging assignments can make it possible to teach an information skills curriculum that ensures that students are effective users of information and ideas. Without intellectually demanding and personally engaging assignments, students will not move beyond the lowest levels of information work (the mechanics of information searching and fact collection). While there are times when locating a single fact solves an information need, it remains important that students develop skills in critically assessing information and in applying them to more complex problems as well.

MENTAL MODELS OF INFORMATION PROCESSING

A mental model is an intellectual framework created by integrating within a given concept or activity what one knows or has experienced. Learning is the process of putting new information into an existing context, framework, or mental model by reorganizing ideas (assimilating) or by reconstructing an old framework until the new ideas or experiences fit (accommodating) and a new mental model emerges (Stripling, 1995). Pitts (1995) investigated the effects of mental models on students' information work. Her findings offer insight into students' library use. She classified learners, based on their mental models of information processing, as either novices or experts. The novice has little prior knowledge in the topic; his or her personal understandings are fragmentary, based on a limited perspective. The expert has more connected understandings and a more global perspective.

Pitts examined the work of a high school class assigned to create a video documentary on a topic related to marine biology. For this project, there was no direct instruction related to either the process or the content of the assignment. Pitts's assessment of the students' information processing is that they used very little information from libraries and that they were often unsuccessful in their search for information. She identifies several reasons for their unsuccessful use of libraries. First, she suggests that students had incomplete subject-matter mental models and that this led to incomplete identification of their information needs. Her analysis of student searching revealed that most searches were very general in nature. In addition, she observes that students had limited mental models for information-seeking and information-use systems, that is, they had no mental framework for the organization of information in libraries. They nearly always looked in only one place, the electronic catalog. If they did go beyond the electronic catalog, they showed little understanding of which other resources would be likely to provide what they sought. A final problem she identifies is the inaccurate mental models that adults had of the students' subject-matter expertise or of their information skills. Adults tended to provide locational advice only, assuming either that the student could identify the most appropriate resource or overestimating the student's expertise in the topic.

Pitts's findings have some powerful implications for schools. First, library media specialists can help students develop a method for information processing by providing a model of the information process and the tasks associated with it, as well as a framework for the organization of information. Models like this enable students to approach information work with an appropriate frame of reference. In addition, teachers can provide students with a structure for the discipline within which they are working. Finally, adult support throughout the information process—not just at the beginning or at the end—will help students maintain a sense of direction about their work. Various strategies are useful in guiding students (Stripling, 1995).

- *encapsulation*: At the end of a work session, students briefly record their understanding of the information they gathered.
- *research log*: Students maintain a research log throughout the process, recording each day what they have learned, what questions they now have, and what they need to do next.
- *conferencing*: Library media specialists and teachers confer with individuals or small groups at the end of a work session to discuss their reflections on their work so far.
- *reflection*: Teachers and library media specialists pose questions for students to ask themselves along the way: Am I really interested in this topic? Do my research questions go beyond collecting information to interpreting or evaluating? Do I have support for all of my conclusions?
- *rubrics*: Library media specialists and teachers develop rubrics for the information-processing tasks and refer students to them during each work session.

Maintaining students' awareness of the whole information process as they work should result in a more systematic and efficient approach to their task. Overall, the instructional goals of the library media program link directly to the work students bring to the library media center from the classroom. Collaboration between the library media specialist and the teacher is essential to achieve library media instructional goals. Library media specialists bring to that collaboration a set of processes and strategies for students to learn while the classroom teacher has instructional goals related to the content area. By creating challenging assignments and providing instruction, support, and adequate time, this team provides students with the tools needed to be critical information consumers.

ACTION STRATEGIES

Learning and Teaching

- Review information processing skills models and identify which one will be the basis for your information skills curriculum.
- Review assignments with teachers to assess what level of Bloom's Taxonomy is necessary to accomplish the tasks.
- Teach specific strategies or skills in information processing when classes come to the library media center. This is appropriate at all grade levels. Often there is an assumption that high school students do not need instruction; however, as their assignments grow more complex, their search skills need to become more sophisticated—strategies they learned in middle school may not help them at this level.

Information Access and Delivery

- Work with classroom teachers to develop a map or matrix of information process skills for each grade level. Skills can be matched to specific classroom assignments. Be certain that specific skills appear more than once, so that students apply them in different contexts and at increasing levels of sophistication.

REFERENCES

American Association of School Librarians. *AASL Information Literacy Standards for Student Learning*. Chicago: ALA, 1998.

Eisenberg, Michael B. and Robert E. Berkowitz. *Information Problem-Solving: The Big Six Skills Approach to Library and Information Skills Instruction*. (Norwood, N.J.: Ablex, 1990.

Eisner, Elliot. *Cognition and Curriculum Reconsidered* (New York: Teachers College Press, 1994).

Kuhlthau, Carol Collier. *Seeking Meaning: A Process Approach to Library and Information Services* (Norwood, N.J.: Ablex, 1993).

———. *Teaching the Library Research Process* (Metuchen, N.J.: Scarecrow Press, 1994).

Langhorne, Mary Jo, ed. *Developing an Information Literacy Curriculum K–12* (New York: Neal-Schuman, 1998).

Pappas, Marjorie. "Information Skills for Electronic Resources," *School Library Media Activities Monthly* 11 (April 1995): 39–40.

────── and Ann Teppe. "Information Skills Model," in *Teaching Electronic Information Skills: A Resource Guide Series* (McHenry, Ill.: Follett Software Company, 1995).

Pitts, Judy M. "Mental Models of Information: The 1993–94 AASL/Highsmith Research Award Study," *School Library Media Quarterly* 23 (Spring 1995): 177–184.

Stripling, Barbara K. *Brainstorms and Blueprints: Teaching Library Research as a Thinking Process* (Englewood, Colo.: Libraries Unlimited, 1988).

──────. "Learning-Centered Libraries: Implications from Research," *School Library Media Quarterly* 23 (Spring 1995): 163–170.

Chapter 12

Assessment of Student Work

This chapter

- defines assessment and clarifies its purposes
- applies performance assessment to information processes
- discusses rubrics and the benefits they offer in defining and assessing the information skills curriculum
- discusses how rubrics help define the information process curriculum
- describes other assesment tools
- discusses self-assessment
- identifies action strategies for assessment

ASSESSMENT DEFINED

Assessment and evaluation are easily confused. Examining their etymologies helps to clarify the critical differences between them. *Assess(us)* is the past participle of the Latin verb *assidere*; the prefix is the preposition *ad* meaning near and the root is the verb *sidere* meaning to sit. The visual image of assessment then is sitting down beside someone. It is a cooperative task. It has come to mean careful examination based on the close observation that comes from sitting together. Evaluation, on the other hand, carries a connotation of judgment, as it means ascribing value to something. Its visual image is of something being done *to*, rather than done *with*, someone. Nothing in the etymology of *evaluation* suggests that it is a collaborative process. Its meaning suggests that its primary purpose is to make a judgment about the value of something.

Assessment serves four purposes, two for teachers and two for students. First, and perhaps most important for the students, assessment is a means of monitoring progress in order to improve their performance. The basic question is, "How is the student progressing on the established criteria?" When students know how their work compares to a standard, they can then set appropriate goals for themselves and they can focus on what needs to be improved. Assessment contributes to student evaluation—its second purpose. Periodically, at conference time, report card time, or the end of a school year, student progress is synthesized into a grade or a narrative. The purpose is to recognize accomplishment; this too informs the student. Assessment provides information for the teacher as well. Assessment contributes to instructional decisions. The basic question is, "How can I use the evidence provided by assessment to improve my teaching so that these students do better?" Finally, the results of assessment can inform the teacher about how well the instructional program is working and what needs to be modified or improved so that future students will perform more successfully. In summary, assessment serves these four purposes:

- to improve student achievement by giving feedback on student progress
- to evaluate student performance
- to improve instruction by giving feedback on its effectiveness
- to redesign instructional programs by monitoring student achievement

Three terms are often encountered in the literature of assessment, and they can sometimes be confused. *Alternative assessment* refers to any assessments that differ from multiple choice, one-shot approaches that characterize most standardized and many classroom tests. The use of the term alternative assumes that most assessment practices are paper-pencil tasks and are one-time events. Assessment is not a single event, but rather a part of the learning experience. Some would say that observers should not be able to distinguish immediately between teaching and assessing because the two processes are so integrated. Assessment as a teaching strategy—not a testing strategy—is the essence of alternative assessment. *Authentic assessment* suggests that assessments should engage students in applying knowledge and skills in the same way they are used in the real world. When a student researches a local solid-waste disposal problem and proposes real solutions by writing a letter or making a presentation to the city council, there is an opportunity for authentic assessment. While there is clearly value in authenticity, it is not crucial to the task of using assessment as a teaching strategy. *Performance assessment* refers to students demonstrating their understanding with a tangible product or observable performance. Performance assessments have been a part of the arts programs for years as the solo festivals, the concerts, the plays; the assessments occur when the judge applies criteria for good performance to review a student's performance. Performance assessments are, of course, a part of athletics when the coach reviews the players' performance in the game. In these situations, what the students *do* demonstrates what the students have learned.

To envision assessment in the library media center is to see the library media specialist moving among students as they work, sitting down beside individual students, and comparing their processes and products to a set of expectations. Sometimes a checklist encapsulates the expectations. If a fourth-grade student is researching an animal for life science, the checklist might be a list of the possible sources:

____ encyclopedia
____ library catalog
____ *The Animals* CD-ROM

Sometimes a simple checklist may not be adequate to help students be successful; in those cases they may need a guide that is more descriptive, that defines for them what excellence looks like, both in process and in product. One form for such a descriptive guide is a rubric.

RUBRICS

Rubric derives from the Latin adjective for red. Rubrics in a liturgical context are directions for conduct of religious services, written in prayer books in red ink. In education, rubrics are also intended to direct students. An assessment rubric is an ordered set of criteria that clearly describes for the student and the teacher what the range of acceptable and unacceptable performance looks like. This definition has several key words, the first of which is *ordered*. A rubric sets out to describe a continuum of performance from expert to novice. Descriptions occur at points along the continuum, and these descriptions are ordered from high to low. Each rubric describes levels or degrees of performance. *Criteria* is the next key word in the definition. A rubric provides criteria for excellence in performance in order to compare a student's performance to criteria, not to the performance of other students. The next key word is *describes,* for a rubric creates a visual image of what excellent performance looks like, as well as a description of the degrees of excellence along the continuum. Descriptive language is a key to the rubric; for example, we can say that a student took notes effectively. This does not describe the note taking; it labels it as effective. In a well-written rubric we might instead say, "A student paraphrased the essential relevant information from the source." Or, to describe delivery in public speaking, one might state, "The rate of speaking and the voice quality varied so that major points were emphasized." Such a description creates a mental model for the student because the performance is described, not merely labeled as "Rate: Excellent."

The *range* of performance portrayed by a rubric is another key idea in the definition. A rubric describes a range of performance descriptions, so that students can gauge themselves along a performance continuum. Most often, students improve their performance incrementally. Descriptions of stages toward excellence guide such incremental growth. Usually rubrics have three or four levels of performance. Sometimes each of these levels of performance is assigned a score (4=highest level, 1=lowest level). Using words, rather than numbers, to identify those levels of performance helps give students a sense of the progressive nature of rubrics. For example:

novice
apprentice
competent
expert

These identifiers suggest that the student can progress toward the expert level, whereas assigning numbers suggests attainment of a score that has permanence. The words *novice* and *apprentice* suggest that the student is on the path toward *expert,* but simply isn't there yet. Such language connotes more confidence in the student's ability to succeed than do the labels of 0 or F. Rubrics should offer a guide so that students know what it takes to be an expert.

Another way to envision a rubric is to consider it a roadmap to success for students. Of course, roadmaps are examined at the beginning of trips, and so with rubrics, it is crucial that they be given to students in advance, and then used throughout the task to gauge where students are and to nudge them up the performance continuum. When students "get lost" in a project spending too much time creating a beautiful cover, the rubric is useful to refocus their efforts. Students can know how to be successful when they know at the outset what success looks like.

Creating Rubrics

Rubrics represent a carefully articulated description of performance across a continuum of quality or sophistication—a continuum from novice to exemplary performance. To create such a description requires careful analysis of the desired performance. One of the best ways to generate rubrics is to begin by observing closely a range of products or performances. If the topic is to generate a thesis statement for a research paper—a part of the task-definition phase of research—then observing products created by a variety of students will yield a range of quality and sophistication. Consider, for example, a high school research paper assignment where students write a thesis statement that represents a position taken on an issue. These examples might emerge from students:

- This paper is about chemical warfare.
- There are many examples of the use of chemical warfare in twentieth-century history.
- Control of chemical warfare is complex.
- It is impossible to control chemical warfare today because of scientific, tactical, and political factors.

By analyzing examples of students' thesis statements, the critical attributes of an exemplary statement become more clear: the thesis statement reveals what the student believes about a topic. The thesis statement includes the topic and a debatable position statement. Three critical attributes are sought: statement of topic, statement of position, and the potential for the position to be argued.

The rubric becomes a description of progress toward a goal like the one displayed in Figure 12.1, where the three critical attributes or dimensions of writing a thesis statement are identified and then levels of performance about each are described.

FIGURE 12.1
Writing the Thesis Statement

	Expert	Apprentice	Novice
Topic statement	The topic is narrowly focused.	The topic is too broad.	The topic is unclear.
Arguable position	The position taken in the statement could have a counter statement written in opposition to it.	The position taken is a statement of opinion but there is little or no argument against it.	The position taken is a statement of fact.
Position statement	The thesis statement includes a statement of opinion about the topic.	The thesis statement describes the topic, but takes no stand.	The thesis statement is too general.

Steps for writing a rubric include

- *identifying attributes or dimensions of good performance*: For example, in writing a rubric about note taking, the first question is, "What are the critical attributes or dimensions of good note taking? What should students be conscious of?" Answers might be use of paraphrasing, organization, and relevance.
- *organizing the attributes into a range of descriptions*:The range most often will have three or four distinct points.
- *describing performances of graduated degrees of quality or sophistication*: One way is to envision good performance and poor performance; another is to observe performance or examine products. In the example above, the attributes of a thesis statement were statement of the topic, statement of a position, and the potential for the position to be argued. In the note-taking example, one asks, "What does exemplary use of paraphrasing look like? What does poor use of paraphrasing look like?"

At the end of such a process, a rubric provides both teacher and student with *descriptions* of what good performances look like—a veritable *roadmap* for students to follow. It describes where they are in their performance toward improved quality. Students then have information to tell them what they need to do to improve and the teacher has information about what students need to learn. A useful rubric contains ordered positions along a continuum. Whether the continuum includes three levels of performance or four, it is important that each level be distinguishable from those on either side of it.

A common error in designing rubrics is to describe performance with adverbs like *frequently, sometimes,* or *always.* Rubrics are more often used to assess a single performance. These modifiers suggest that the assessment relates to multiple performances; as such they are appropriate for summative—but not formative—evaluation. Other adverbs to avoid are words like *effectively, well, poorly.* These words judge, but don't describe. Be aware that rubrics are intended to describe quality, not quantity, in performance. Avoid developing rubrics where better performance is only more, for example, instead of more library resources the description should be more apt resources (Wiggins, 1996). One way to guide development of rubrics is to use one. Figure 12.2 provides a rubric for rubrics. Using it as a guide can help to improve the quality of rubric writing itself.

Types of Rubrics

Rubrics can be written in at least two forms: holistic and analytic. A holistic rubric has only one general descriptor for performance as a whole, whereas an analytic rubric includes multiple rubrics organized according to the dimensions of the performance being assessed. To assess a student's writing by listing the qualities that make it excellent, good, or "not there yet" is to look at it holistically. This type of rubric is most useful at the summative stages of assessment when overall performance is at issue. For a pianist, the feedback at the end of the recital may indeed be a holistic view, interrelating tone, expression, time, posture, and volume into a complex rubric called style. An advantage of analytic rubrics is that they describe the discrete elements or dimensions of the performance separately. In Figure 12.3 the rubric breaks down the criteria for note taking, so that attention focuses on use of paraphrasing, relevance, and organization, three specific qualities of concern in the note-taking process.

Rubrics for Assessing Student Performance in the Library Media Program

Rubrics offer a structure for assessing student performance both at the formative and summative stages. In the formative stages, using rubrics is a teaching strategy.

FIGURE 12.2
Assessment of a Rubric

Content	
Expert	The rubric identifies the critical attributes or dimensions of performance.
Proficient	The rubric addresses a skill or concept, but not that which is crucial to success.
Apprentice	The focus of the rubric is fuzzy.
Novice	The rubric focuses attention on an inappropriate attribute or dimension.
Language	
Expert	The rubric describes in specific language various qualities of performance, including action verbs that help direct a quality performance.
Proficient	The rubric is descriptive, but lacks specificity so that it is difficult to improve performance.
Apprentice	The rubric uses comparative language (e.g., *more, less, sometimes*) to describe levels of quality, shifting the emphasis from quality to quantity.
Novice	The rubric uses evaluative language (e.g., *good, excellent, exemplary*) to rate various qualities of performance with a risk of subjectivity or personal judgment rather than qualitative description.
Range	
Expert	The "cut point" between *acceptable* and *not acceptable* is clear, and the "top point" describes excellence.
Proficient	The "cut point" between *acceptable* and *not acceptable* is clear, but the top point only describes acceptable performance, not excellence.
Apprentice	Marginal performances could arbitrarily land on either side of the "cut point."
Novice	The student cannot tell where the "cut point" is.

FIGURE 12.3
Rubric: Note Taking

Relevance	
Expert	The information in my notes relates directly to my research question(s).
Proficient	My notes have some information related to my topic but not to my research question(s).
Novice	The information in my notes does not answer my research question and doesn't quite fit my topic.
Comprehension	
Expert	I understand everything I have written in my notes; there are no words that I cannot define.
Proficient	There are words or ideas in my notes that I cannot explain myself, but I can get more information so that they make sense to me.
Novice	My notes are copied from my sources and I don't really understand them.
Organization	
Expert	My notes are grouped according to each research question or subtopic.
Proficient	My notes are grouped according to the source where I found the information.
Apprentice	My notes are organized according to when I took them.
Novice	My notes are written as one list of information.

**AN EXAMPLE OF ENHANCEMENT IN ACTION:
EVALUATING AN ASSIGNMENT**

In a U.S. history class, students have this assignment: choose a decade in twentieth-century U.S. history and create a HyperStudio presentation about it. Your production should create an informative portrayal of the decade, including economic, political, and social aspects. You should develop essential questions about each aspect (i.e., questions that lead to the essence of the decade); your questions should help frame your inquiry so that you effectively portray the character of the decade. You may need to do some background reading before you develop your questions. The information included in your product should represent responses to those essential questions. The presentation should exhibit effective use of HyperStudio's capabilities (e.g., graphics, use of color and sound, user-control for access), as well as important textual information.

For the example of a U.S. history assignment, the teacher and library media specialist might work together to develop a rubric-based assessment instrument that would be given to students at the beginning of the project. An important benefit of using rubrics in teaching information processes in the library media program is that rubrics describe processes in ways that are meaningful to classroom teachers as well. They become a way of defining the information skills curriculum not only for the library media specialist and the students, but also for the teachers.

An example of such a rubric is that used in the U.S. history class example (Figure 12.4). Note that this rubric does not address every aspect of work that students will do to accomplish this task. Instead, the focus of the rubric is those aspects that the teacher and library media specialist feel deserve emphasis. This rubric would be used by the student and the teacher or library media specialist as a guide to individual students as they work. Traditionally a library media specialist might approach a table where students are working and ask, "How are you doing?"; if the response is, "OK," he or she would then proceed to the next table. Instead, using a rubric to guide assessment as teaching, the library media specialist would say, "Let's look at how you are doing.

FIGURE 12.4
Rubric: Studying a Decade

Task Definition: Formulating a focus	
Expert	I chose information that answered my essential questions about the decade.
Proficient	I chose information that was relevant to the portrayal of the decade.
Apprentice	I chose information that presented interesting facts about the decade.
Novice	I chose information that was irrelevant, trivial, or unimportant to a portrayal of the decade.

Organizing information from multiple sources	
Expert	I organized information according to topics and subtopics that I created.
Proficient	I based my organization on one source and added some details or examples from other sources.
Apprentice	I summarized information from individual sources but did not relate information from one source to that from another.
Novice	I used a single source for the majority of information.

Producing a multimedia presentation Organization/design of stack	
Expert	I created a logical organization for the stack and the cards.
Proficient	I planned the cards within the stack clearly, but the navigation between cards is sometimes confusing.
Apprentice	I used some elements in ways that distract from the message, e.g., too many different transitions, too many or too few graphics, irrelevant sounds or graphics.
Novice	My screens are too cluttered or too sparse; the user might have difficulty navigating.

Multimedia Elements	
Expert	My stack has text elements that are balanced with relevant visual or sound elements.
Proficient	My stack has text, graphics, and sound, but they are not always directly related to one another.
Apprentice	My stack has too little text or too few graphics.
Novice	My stack is all text or all graphics.

Look at the rubric for note taking and let's look at your notes. Where are you on the continuum?" Assessing where the student is *while the work is in progress* may result in a correction of their information seeking that will save them time and improve the quality of their process and their end product. That is, after all, the intention of assessment. Likewise, as students go through other aspects of the assignment, other dimensions of the rubric can be applied.

To use a rubric, first analyze the assignment to determine what process skills are most important for the task. Generate rubrics for those process skills in language appropriate to the level of the students. Distribute the rubrics when the assignment is given to the students. Depending on the age and the style of interaction, the group can review the rubrics together, or students can be encouraged to review them individually. Most important, as students work on the assignment, they have the rubrics before them. As teachers and library media specialists approach students to monitor progress, the rubrics are the focus of conversation:

> Let's take a look at your notes so far. Our rubric for organization suggests that notes be organized in some way. Which statement from the rubric describes how your notes are organized? What does the description at the next level up say? Can you follow that method and get your notes organized in that way? I think it will make the writing a lot easier.

There are some crucial conditions for using rubrics as a teaching strategy. First, students must have the rubrics before they begin the task. The idea is for these to be guidelines to success, so they are not kept secret until grading time. Students receive the rubrics at the time of the assignment. Second, one-time use of a rubric is unproductive. If the intent is to improve performance, then students need multiple opportunities to continue their progress. If students receive a rubric for note taking along with an assignment, it should reappear with future assignments in order for students to gain from their previous learning and extend their skills.

Besides using rubrics as a guide to student work, rubrics can be useful for end-of-term or end-of-unit assessment of student work. At the summative stage, assessment becomes evaluation, yet the rubric format can still be useful for describing to students the qualities of their work and the qualities of exemplary work, so that they can see how close or far it is. A grade labels the student achievement, but provides no specific information to help the student improve performance; it says, "Good enough" or "Not good enough," when what is needed is a specific description of what "good enough" represents and how to reach that level. In this way, the rubric justifies the grade; while students may argue with a B, it is harder to argue when the B is supported by a rubric that describes the student's performance. Finally, using rubrics in summative assessment can contribute to consistency; the more defined the criteria are, the easier it becomes to apply the criteria evenly among students and across performances.

Rubrics for Defining the Information Process Curriculum

While rubrics are usually considered important for the part they play in student assessment, they also have an important place in helping to define curriculum. Writing a rubric requires examination of the outcome—a performance or a product—to determine what constitutes success. By such examination, one can analyze what students need to learn to be successful. The rubric essentially provides a structure for task analysis. For example, when introducing children to keyword searching, one task is to identify the keywords or key concepts in the research question. Observing students doing keyword searches will quickly reveal what they need to know. How often do children make one attempt in an online catalog, find nothing based on that keyword search, and declare that the library has nothing on their topic? A rubric for keyword searching may help analyze what must be taught and may guide students beyond that first trial-and-fail effort. The task at hand is to examine their question and determine what to enter as a keyword. If the question is, "What are the beliefs about life after death among Confucians?" The novice is likely to look for a word in the question and type that word in as the keyword. However, *Confucians* may not result in any hits. Students should progress from finding a keyword in the research question toward identifying a list of relevant terms. The more sophisticated searcher distinguishes between broader and narrower terms, identifies synonyms, and uses truncation. The rubric format helps clarify what may need explicit teaching—in this case, creating a list of alternative search terms and using truncation.

An information skills curriculum might include the identification of an information process model, the discrete information-processing skills to be taught, and a set of rubrics to accompany the discrete skills.

These rubrics then, would become something of a rubrics warehouse. Whenever students begin an assignment, an assessment instrument is created and rubrics for relevant information-processing skills are incorporated drawing from the curriculum guide. For example, a K–12 information skills curriculum might have a list of information-processing skills and accompanying rubrics for the following aspects of information work:

Defining the task
- selecting a topic
- formulating a focus
- stating a position

Seeking information

- identifying keywords and key concepts in the research question
- filtering sources (e.g., distinguishing fact and fiction, skimming, scanning, applying criteria such as relevancy, authority, accuracy, and currency)

Accessing information

- searching by keyword (e.g., using synonyms, truncation, Boolean logic)
- using an index

Using information

- taking notes
- interviewing
- paraphrasing

Synthesizing information

- organizing information from multiple sources
- determining patterns or trends
- creating comparisons or contrasts
- relating information to the research focus

Presenting information

- presenting information in an appropriate format (e.g., written report, multimedia presentation, speech, exhibit)
- creating a bibliography

To translate this curriculum guide into practice, the rubrics are a reference for the development of specific assessment instruments for student assignments. The rubric in Figure 12.4 derives from rubrics in such a curriculum guide. Activities would include

- *having brief, informal conferences with students as they proceed through an assignment and/or as they complete it*: This is what the library media specialist does when classes are working in the center.
- *communicating with teachers about student progress*: This is probably the brief conversation at the end of the period, or the quick note written on the rubric sheet and sent to the teacher via e-mail or her mail box saying, "Here is where I see students having difficulty, based on specific rubric points."
- *reviewing curriculum and lessons based on student assessment*: This is the evaluation of how things went, ideally carried out with the teacher at the end of the unit, with notes for change for next time.

These activities relate to the purposes of assessment: to give feedback to students to improve their progress and to acknowledge quality; to inform teachers so that necessary teaching occurs to improve student performance; to inform teachers about the instructional program so that it can be revised to meet student needs better.

Some people find rubrics too constraining for the student or the teacher. In some cases it seems that the highest level of performance is not high enough for some students. One solution to that concern is to add a column at the high end of the rubric, label it "Legendary Performance," and ask the student to write the description of what he or she does beyond the highest level (Lockett, 1996). Another concern is that students may work hard at moving to the next level of performance on a rubric, but narrowly fail to make it to the next level. Again, the consultant suggests simply adding "skinny columns," that is, lines drawn between labeled points where a performance falls between levels to indicate to a student that he or she is progressing and is almost there.

A final concern about rubrics is that library media specialists might focus too tightly on details and lose sight of the overall information process. Writing a rubric about finding the index at the back of a book is probably unnecessary. More important is using the index to access the needed information, so the rubrics for index use need to be related to choosing search terms, using pagination information, using cross references and subheadings. The point is that, like task analysis, rubric development can be taken to an unnecessary extreme. Consider the processes that need teaching, reteaching and repeated practice, and consider the processes for which there are levels of sophistication in performance; these are the processes for which rubrics can be helpful. A key question may be: Is this something one either does or does not do, or are there degrees of quality? If there are degrees of quality, then a rubric may help students move to higher and higher levels of performance.

Rubrics for Self-Assessment

Self-assessment is an important skill for lifelong learning. Golfers continue to improve their game by analyzing and monitoring their own performance; when a ball falls short of its intended mark, they review the backswing, the follow-through, the stance, to determine what went wrong and how to improve. This same self-assessment behavior will help students continue to use information resources effectively as adults. When an online search about buying a used car yields too much information, they can consider what they have done wrong and how best to correct it. The key for the golfer or the consumer is to have criteria on which to base their self-assessment. What should the good swing look like? How can the keyword search be modified?

By developing in students the practice of assessing their work, the focus shifts from the task to the process. The use of specific criteria for assessing the process gives students practice at thinking about criteria for high-quality performance. While journaling and other narrative techniques are also useful self-assessment strategies, they lack the structure of criteria-based assessment found in rubrics; without some guidance, students may not focus their assessment on what matters most in a process. Developing skill in applying criteria can help students look at their own work more objectively. When rubrics are provided, students should be encouraged to identify which level best describes their own work, before a teacher identifies for them where they are on the continuum. If the teacher disagrees, then a conversation can begin to justify that position. However, if independence is a goal, then the first attempt at assessment needs to belong to the learner. For rubrics to work effectively for self-assessment, there are three critical attributes:

- *explicit criteria*: The criteria provide enough description that students know what successful performance looks like,
- *structured feedback*: The criteria is ordered so as to show students

how close to excellence they are. Feedback is not hit-or-miss—all
students get feedback.
- *front-end information*: The criteria for success are provided as the
  student *begins* the work, not at the end.

OTHER ASSESSMENT TOOLS

Performance assessment is based on observable activity. Clearly, some
intellectual processes cannot be observed directly. One can only make
assumptions about those processes based on outward actions by the student. This means that some thought processes will be difficult to assess
based on performance or product. Other assessment strategies are available to help students analyze their work. Two examples of narrative
methods are the I-Search process, advocated by Macrorie (1988) and
described by Joyce and Tallman (1996), and student research journaling.
In the I-Search process, students report their research as a personal narrative describing not only what information they have found but also
how they found it. By explicitly describing their process, students reveal their research strategies, and self-assess what worked and what
did not. When their self-assessment is coupled with feedback from teachers, students gain further insight into what works and what does not.

Student journaling is another strategy for self-analysis in the research
process. Here, students periodically step back from their work and make
journal entries about their progress, their frustrations, and their successes.
Careful monitoring of the journal can inform teachers of what students
need to learn. Both the I-Search process and journaling engage students
and teachers in a dialogue about their information work. These strategies are open-ended; therefore, they demand some sophistication about
the information processes in students, or they require some specific
prompting from teachers to focus students' remarks. Prompts like "Write
an entry in your journal today about organizing your notecards," or
"Write an entry in your journal today about the problems with searching in the electronic magazine index," may give students enough of a
cue to reflect on what they know about the process and may reveal
enough about their frustrations to cue the library media specialist about
what they need to learn. Such information becomes a point of departure
for either individual conversation with students or mini-lessons for whole
classes to facilitate their progress. A comprehensive program will use
various assessment strategies over time, based at least in part on the

sophistication of understanding of the students, their propensity for writing, the preferences of the teacher, and the character of the information work.

A checklist may be an appropriate assessment instrument when the question is simply a matter of whether a student did or did not accomplish a step in a process or include a component of a product. For example, in a travel brochure completed for a geography class, the checklist might include

Content
> name of country
> weather
> sightseeing
> transportation

Presentation
> graphics: picture or map
> readable text

End-of-unit interviews are another way to assess students as they complete information work. Brief, structured interviews can provide insight into what the students know about the research process. The teacher and library media specialist can share responsibility for brief interviews with students at the end of a unit involving intensive research. Questions to ask might be

Tell me about your project.
How did you find your information?
Did you ever get stuck? What did you do then?
What was hard about doing research?
How could you tell when you were done with research?
How could you tell if you did a good job?
What did you learn from this research?

Conventional testing is still a viable form of assessment as well. What is crucial in using testing is to ensure that the test measures what matters. Most schools use standardized tests, and most standardized tests have a subtest on using reference sources. Library media specialists do well to examine the items on tests to know what is being asked. Boolean logic, truncation, evaluating sources are all topics emphasized in information literacy curricula; standardized tests currently place heavy emphasis on identifying keywords, alphabetizing, and choosing an appropriate print resource for a given question. Testing services are struggling to update their tests to match existing curricula; however, they tend to be conservative out of concern for equity across the nation—they worry that schools without computerized catalogs and indexes will be at a disadvantage when test items assume familiarity with resources not available to them. These are times to be monitoring test items carefully to observe how well the test items reflect the local resources. Where test items do not match what is being taught, it is important to make teachers, administrators, and parents aware of that discrepancy.

Rubrics, I-Searching, research journals, checklists, conferences, and tests are all assessment strategies that provide information for student evaluation and that will help educators know what needs to be taught in the future. Matching the assessment tool to the needs calls for judgment by the library media specialist and the teacher. It is important to have a variety of assessment techniques in one's repertoire.

ACTION STRATEGIES

Learning and Teaching

- Observe students doing information work. As you observe, think in terms of the range of performance sophistication or quality, and structure your thoughts around a rubric. What do you see when a novice approaches an electronic encyclopedia to develop a search strategy? What do you see when an expert begins the same task?
- Consider a variety of methods for assessment (including checklists, interviews, rubrics, journaling and the I-Search process) in order to focus students' attention on the research process, not just the end-product.
- Examine standardized test items to determine what is being asked of students. Provide information to teachers to help them interpret the match between items on the test and what is being taught.

Program Administration

- Review the information skills curriculum, and identify the major skills to be taught. For those skills, develop rubrics to describe levels of performance. Share rubrics with teachers to extend their vision of information skills and processes.

- To help align what happens in the library media center with classroom practices, discuss with teachers what methods of assessment they use.

REFERENCES

Joyce, Marilyn and Julie Tallman. *Making the Writing and Research Connection with the I-Search Process: A How-To-Do-It Manual for Teachers and School Librarians* (New York: Neal-Schuman, 1996).

Lockett, Nancy. *Rubrics in the Classroom,* Iowa Success Network Workshop (Cedar Rapids, Ia.: January 11–12, 1996) Handout.

Macrorie, Ken. *The I-Search Process* (Portsmouth, N.H.: Heinemann, 1988).

Wiggins, Grant. "Practicing What We Preach in Designing Authentic Assessments," *Educational Leadership* 54 (December 1996/January 1997): 18–25

Chapter 13

Program Evaluation

This chapter
- discusses the importance and purpose of program evaluation
- suggests rubrics for assessment of program components
- identifies action strategies for program evaluation

PURPOSE OF EVALUATION

"What gets measured gets done" is a familiar maxim among educators. It speaks to the importance of program evaluation. Measuring a program against a set of standards has been one typical approach to program evaluation. Accrediting organizations have set and applied standards such as number of volumes in the collection, full-time equivalency of professional staff, number of hours of support staff, seating capacity of facility, and number of computer workstations available. These standards can be classified as inputs, that is, these are resources the program needs to function. Other measures include circulation counts, attendance counts, or number of classes scheduled into the facility; these measures can be classified as outputs, that is, they measure use of the resources. However, while these measures have value, a program is more than simple inputs and outputs. Critical questions about a library media program might be:

- What difference does it make to student learning?
- What contributions does it make toward increasing teacher effectiveness?

- What difference does it make to the intellectual atmosphere of the school?
- In what ways does it improve the coordination across grade levels and disciplines?
- How consistent is the program with its instructional context?

Latrobe and Laughlin developed an instrument for evaluation of library media programs based on *Information Power* (Latrobe, 1992). They used the instrument to evaluate library media programs in the Oklahoma City schools in 1988 and 1991. Latrobe expresses concern that *Information Power* is too abstract in its recommendations and calls for more concrete detail in future editions to aid in effective evaluation.

In many states, mandates for library media programs are either nonexistent or so general that schools within one jurisdiction could have either a minimal program or an exemplary program and meet the guidelines. This open-endedness, especially in times of diminishing resources, can render the library media program vulnerable and calls for careful accountability to decision makers. Another reason for caring about evaluation is the fact that administrators typically have little formal training about school library media programs during their career preparation (Barron, 1987). Consequently, they need to learn about the library media program's potential. Their naïveté calls for an evaluation strategy that provides descriptive information about what to look for in a program.

Evaluation can serve multiple purposes. It can inform the library media specialist about what is working well and what needs improvement. Program evaluation can also inform administrators about what the program should be doing for students and teachers, as well as diagnose what steps may need to be taken to bring the program closer to its potential. In *Operating and Evaluating School Library Media Programs: A Handbook for Administrators and Librarians*, Yesner and Jay (1998) provide a topical approach for looking at positive and negative features of programs and provide strategies for improvement. For parents, students, and teachers, evaluation can provide insight into ways to make better use of the library media program by making them more aware of its services.

Evaluating the library media program presents these challenges:

- confusing evaluation of the library media specialist with evaluation of the program

- finding ways to address the lack of administrators' knowledge about what the program should be or do
- applying performance standards that are primarily inputs (for example, number of volumes, computers, seats, staff members)
- applying performance standards that are primarily numeric outputs (for example, circulation, number of classes met) without connection to the impact they have on student learning

Three strategies are important in the process of evaluating a library media program:

- *Collect data* to indicate what is happening in the library media center.
- *Involve the stakeholders* (administrators, teachers, parents, community members, students) so that they can learn as much as possible about the program's potential.
- *Educate the stakeholders* by giving them descriptive language about the program; one possible tool for this is a rubric.

It is important to collect data that demonstrate not simply that there is use of the library media center and its resources, but also data that indicate the complexity and quality of that use. An example of such data collection is shown in Figure 3.3. This monthly report succinctly communicates what aspects of the information skills curriculum are being emphasized (this report shows an emphasis on *location and access* and *creation and communication*, while little or no evidence of teaching other information skills appears). Such information is a wake-up call to the library media specialist to examine whether this is a consistent pattern and to begin to remedy the situation if it is. Likewise, it is easy to see which departments dominated the month's activities. It is also readily clear that the library media specialist is working beyond merely gathering materials and is in fact involved in significant teaching activity— useful information to be provided to a principal. This summary sheet is completed at the end of each month and shared with the principal during the monthly library media specialist–principal meeting. The data collected here answer several questions, such as:

- Which information skills are *not* being taught?
- Which departments are not making use of the library media center?

- How much collaboration is occurring between teachers and the library media specialist?
- What is the nature of assistance the library media specialist is providing to teachers?

Besides collecting data of this sort, other useful measures might be simply the number of classes scheduled into the library media center for the month, the number of students using the center (for example, in class, from classrooms, from open hour or study hall), and circulation counts.

A brief survey at the end of a resource-based unit can be another indication of how well the library media program is performing. An example of a survey to be completed by teachers is the following list of four questions, which can be used as a survey instrument for older children as well.

- Were your students frustrated in searching for information for their assignment?
- What topics/questions went underserved?
- Did your students have all the necessary information literacy skills to do their assignment?
- Did students have enough time in the library media center to complete their work?

By being involved in the evaluation of the library media program, stakeholders increase their understanding and ownership of the program. Involve teachers, administrators, and parents in designing survey instruments and in analyzing the results of such surveys. As results are analyzed, it is important that the stakeholders participate in identifying accomplishments to be recognized and in setting goals for continued improvement of the program. Participation in the analysis is the part that really provides a feeling of ownership. Finally, when stakeholders help report the results to the constituents (parent organizations, faculty, and staff, for example), they develop a sense of pride in their findings and enthusiasm for the next steps—and readily support allocating the resources needed to continue improvement.

RUBRICS FOR PROGRAM EVALUATION

Program evaluation provides the opportunity to educate stakeholders in what the program is doing to support teaching and learning. Rubrics provide an excellent form for program evaluation because they describe a range of levels of quality in a performance. By providing rubrics on the various dimensions of a library media program, it becomes apparent where the strengths and weaknesses of the program are. More important, because of their descriptive nature, rubrics communicate a program's quality to those outside the library media profession. Far too many teachers, parents, and administrators have not seen the best quality in all aspects of the library media program. Rubrics can help them to extend their vision, so that they can understand more clearly what the goals of the library media professional might be for the program.

In the previous chapter, rubrics are described as an effective way to assess student progress. They offer a description of good and less-than-good performance and a scaled guide that gives a range of performance quality. For program evaluation, the rubric adds structure. Figure 13.1 (p. 233) presents rubrics focused on the program elements described in *Information Power: Building Partnerships for Learning* (American Association of School Librarians, 1998). Within each of those elements are rubrics for specific aspects of the program: Teaching and Learning: Information Skills, Technology, Reading, Collaboration; Information Access and Delivery: Collection, Climate, Technology; and Program Administration: Planning, Staff, Communications, Resources, Scheduling. Perhaps these rubrics will serve as a model for designing a program evaluation process that incorporates the priorities of the local library media program.

ACTION STRATEGIES

Learning and Teaching

- Analyze students' work using Bloom's Taxonomy as a guide, to determine whether they are merely recalling information or instead are analyzing, synthesizing, and evaluating information.
- Maintain a file of units developed collaboratively by teachers and the library media specialist to document contributions to teaching and learning.

Program Administration

- Review a mission statement for the program.
- Review the professional literature to build background for assessing the existing program.
- Involve various constituencies—administrators, teachers, students, parents—in the evaluation process. Provide them with summaries of background information from the literature. Gather input from them using surveys, focus groups, or other input strategies.
- Design and use rubrics that describe the elements of the program in concrete language with emphasis on the program's impact on teaching and learning.
- Use a matrix or curriculum map to monitor teaching of information skills in the context of classroom curriculum.
- Collect data to profile the status of the program based on inputs (e.g., staff, facilities, access, resource collection, equipment) and outputs (e.g., circulation, classes, staff development, teacher consultation, student production).
- Develop new goals for the program based on collected data and on rubric-based assessment.
- Identify needed inputs for accomplishment of new goals.

REFERENCES

American Association of School Librarians. *Information Power: Building Partnerships for Learning* (Chicago: ALA, 1998).

Barron, Daniel D. "Communicating What SLM Specialists Do: The Evaluation Process," *School Library Journal* 33 (March 1987): 95–99.

Latrobe, Kathy Howard. "Evaluating Library Media Programs in Terms of *Information Power*; Implications for Theory and Practice," *School Library Media Quarterly* 21 (Fall 1992): 37–45.

Yesner, Bernice L. and Hilda L. Jay. *Operating and Evaluating School Library Media Programs: A Handbook for Administrators and Librarians* (New York: Neal-Schuman, 1998).

FIGURE 13.1
Rubrics for Program Evaluation

Rubrics for Library Media Program Evaluation

Teaching and Learning

Information Skills

Skills Curriculum	**Comprehensive.** A written curriculum guide, based on an information process model, contains a sequence of information-seeking and using strategies and model lessons.	**In progress.** A written curriculum guide contains a sequence of information-seeking and using strategies.	**Under development.** Plans exist for developing a formal curriculum guide.
Integration	**Integrated.** A matrix or map identifies where all information skills fit into classroom activities for introduction, elaboration, and reinforcement; lessons are taught in coordination with classroom activities.	**Ad hoc.** As teachers make assignments, information-seeking and using strategies are taught in relation to the assignment.	**Isolated.** The library media specialist teaches information skills sequentially without regard to classroom activities.
Assessment	**Proactive.** The library media specialist teaches, in cooperation with the classroom teacher, and ensures that the information-seeking processes are a part of student assessment.	**In-house.** The library media specialist uses assessment strategies as a part of teaching, but there is no classroom follow-up in assessment related to information skills.	**Incidental.** Information literacy skills are a part of the school's standardized testing program.

Inquiry	**Student-generated.** Students generate their own research questions based on information problems originating from classroom activities or their own curiosity.	**Open-ended.** Students seek information to respond to holistic questions.	**Teacher-driven.** Students seek facts to respond to teacher-generated queries.

Technology

Technology Use	**High cognitive level.** Uses of technology cause students to work at Bloom's application level or higher.	**Low cognitive level.** Uses of technology require students to work at the knowledge or comprehension level.	**No cognitive criteria.** No criteria are applied for selection of technology uses based on cognitive level.
Integration	**Full integration.** Uses of technology are chosen to expand existing curriculum goals.	**Aligned.** Uses of technology are connected to the curriculum.	**Isolated.** Technology applications are taught for their own sake.
Planning Process	**Formalized.** Planning for technology integration is ongoing and includes broad-based participation.	**Ad hoc.** When money is available, a planning committee convenes to decide how to spend it.	**Unilateral.** A single individual or a select few make decisions about technology.
Staff Development	**Comprehensive.** All staff members must meet a set of competencies for using technology.	**Adaptable.** Staff development includes use of applications that can be adapted to meet individual needs.	**Elective.** Staff members choose from a menu of technology training based on their own self-assessment or personal interest.

Relevant. Staff development has direct application to the work of the staff members who participate.	**Need-driven.** Staff members seek out technology-related training as they identify a specific need.	**Basic.** Staff development focuses on the basics of how to operate equipment.
Hands-on. Training is hands-on with modeling by instructors.	**Modeled.** Technology skills are taught by modeling.	**Theoretical.** Technology training is theoretical without practical application opportunities.
Ongoing. Support is readily available as staff members integrate new skills into their work.	**Intermittent.** Review sessions are offered periodically.	**One-time.** Training occurs at scheduled times and no ongoing assistance is conveniently available.

Reading

Classroom Support	**Integral.** The library media specialist meets with teachers as they plan units and define the focus for thematic units and provides reading resources.	**Supportive.** The library media specialist identifies resources to support units and delivers them to teachers.	**Supplemental.** The library media specialist responds to specific requests from individual teachers by providing supplementary materials.
Materials Support	**Selective.** The library media specialist provides materials that meet exact specifications for the instructional focus, for appropriate levels of difficulty, and for high-quality standards.	**Expansive.** The library media specialist delivers to teachers whatever materials are available on the general topic of the unit.	**Self-help.** The library media specialist encourages teachers to visit the library media center and explore available materials.

Promotion	**Initiating.** The library media specialist promotes reading by initiating book talks and individualized reading guidance.	**Responsive.** The library media specialist supports students' interest in reading when asked.	**Passive.** The library media specialist sets up displays and provides book lists to support existing interest in reading.
	Continuous. Reading promotion is ongoing.	**Periodic.** Special short-term reading promotion activities occur.	**Intermittent.** Reading promotion primarily occurs as special events.
	Intrinsic. Activities to promote reading are grounded in intrinsic motivation (i.e., reading for the sake of enjoyment or information).	**Neutral.** Effort focuses on students continuing to read.	**Extrinsic.** Special reading promotions feature extrinsic rewards for students who read.

Collaboration

Team Roles	**Defined.** Members of the planning team, including the library media specialist, have clearly defined roles and expectations.	**Informal.** When a task needs to be done, whoever volunteers does it.	**Unassigned.** Conversations do not lead to assignment of tasks.
Level of Professional Complexity	**Professional.** The library media specialist collaborates with teachers to design instructional objectives, activities, and/or assessment and to identify resources.	**Supportive.** The library media specialist recommends and provides resources.	**"Go-fer."** The library media specialist provides resources requested by teachers.

Information Access and Delivery

Collection

Collaboration	**Collaborative.** Decisions about collection priorities are made in collaboration between library media specialist and teachers.	**Consultative.** Teachers offer suggestions for collection development.	**Autocratic.** The library media specialist makes collection decisions independently.
Curriculum Support	**Curriculum-based.** Curriculum support is a high priority for collection additions.	**Curriculum-related.** Curricular topics are considered in collection development, but not as a high priority.	**Balanced.** Balance is the highest priority in collection development.
Levels of Difficulty	**Client-based.** Level of difficulty responds to assessment of the local student clientele.	**Balanced.** A balance among easy and challenging materials is sought.	**Unheeded.** Criteria other than level of difficulty are considered.
Diversity	**Multicultural.** Cultural diversity is considered in collection development.	**Client-based.** Materials are selected to match those cultures represented in the school's population.	**Spontaneous.** Multicultural materials are selected as they are requested, but without specific planning.
Currency	**Current.** Collection is kept current by additions and weeding.	**Mixed.** Some parts of the collection, particularly time-sensitive topics, are maintained by additions and weeding.	**Outdated.** Collection shows evidence of little or no weeding.

Adequacy	**Ample**. Collection has ample materials to meet the needs of its clientele.	**Adequate**. Collection can usually meet the basic needs of clientele.	**Inadequate**. Collection lacks materials for topics commonly investigated.
Quality	**Criteria-based**. Selection of materials is based on explicit criteria defined by quality, learning goals, and beliefs.	**Quality-based**. Selection is based on standards of quality defined by reviewing media.	**Demand-based**. Selection is based on what teachers and/or students request exclusively.

Climate

Friendliness	**Inviting**. Students and staff feel welcome to use the library media center and show no hesitation to ask questions.	**Neutral**. The library media center has no affect—it is neither friendly nor unfriendly.	**Austere**. Student and staff only use the library media center when necessary; they are reluctant to seek assistance.
Productivity	**Productive**. Students are working productively at worthwhile tasks; a buzz of activity is evident as groups converse about their work.	**Silent**. Students work quietly and in isolation.	**Distracting**. Too much social activity distracts from work.
User Orientation	**Assistive**. Students and staff perceive the library media center as a place for assistance. They feel like important "customers" because they get help.	**Passive**. Library media staff will answer questions when asked, but do not initiate assistance.	**Supervisory**. Library media staff supervise behavior rather than provide information assistance.

Physical Facility	**Conducive to work.** Furniture, lighting, and space are attractive and match the needs of the students. Space allows for various simultaneous activities—group and individual, quiet and interactive, electronic and print-based.	**Limited.** Lighting, furniture, or space accommodate some but not all demands.	**Minimal.** Space allows only one kind of activity at a time.
Ethics	**Assertive.** The library media program assertively supports and teaches principles of intellectual freedom, confidentiality, appropriate uses of information and information technology intellectual property, and copyright.	**Responsive.** When relevant situations arise, professional ethical principles are raised.	**Passive.** Ethical principles are not explicitly expressed in written policies or lessons.

Technology

Hardware	**Focused critical mass.** As each technology application is recommended, the necessary critical mass of hardware is purchased.	**Scattered deployment.** Hardware is deployed to spread available resources throughout the school fairly rather than considering what critical mass is needed to meet a specific need effectively.	**Under-equipped.** Too little hardware is available to accomplish an identified goal.
Software	**Criteria-based.** Software selection is based on explicit criteria related to learning goals and beliefs.	**Quality-based.** Software selection is based on standards of quality as defined by reviewing media.	**Demand-based.** Software selection is based on what teachers and/or students request exclusively.

Policy	**Formalized.** Written policy exists for copyright, intellectual freedom in electronic environments, equity, privacy and other technology-related concerns. These policies have school board approval, are reviewed systematically, and are shared with all appropriate constituencies.	**Informal.** Policy decisions about technology-related issues have been discussed and agreed to, but are not formalized.	**In progress.** Policy for technology-related issues is under discussion.

Program Administration

Planning

Vision	**Long- and short-range.** Program planning includes a long-range comprehensive vision for its relationship to the school's goals and mission and includes action steps for attaining the goals.	**Dependent.** Planning for the library media program occurs only as a part of the school's planning; it only responds to school needs as they arise.	**Short-range.** Planning for the library media program is on a year-to-year basis, often focusing on budget and resources.

Staff

Qualifications	**Differentiated.** Library media staff includes both professional and support staff positions whose responsibilities are delineated to indicate specific responsibilities corresponding to expertise.	**Adequate.** Both professional and support staff positions are assigned to the library media program, but they may have inappropriate responsibilities limited by time allocations.	**Singular.** The only or primary staff member must compensate for limited staff by meeting demands not consistent with his/her training.

Quantity	**Data-driven.** The number of positions in the library media program is based on data (e.g., analysis of time use, professional literature, state recommendations).	**Adequate.** The library media center is staffed by a full-time professional and by support staff to provide technical and clerical services.	**Minimal.** Even in the smallest center, to accommodate open access, there must be one full-time qualified staff member.
Evaluation	**Position-specific.** Each library media staff position has a formal written job description, accompanied by a performance appraisal system that addresses the specific job expectations	**Criteria-based.** Each library media staff person's performance is formally evaluated based on stated criteria, but criteria are not position-specific.	**Informal.** Some, or all, library media staff experience only informal feedback on job performance.
Staff Development	**Continuous and position-specific.** All library media staff members participate in frequent, formal staff development directly related to their positions within the school and at the district, community, regional, or national level.	**Periodic.** Each library media staff member participates in occasional staff development experiences that have at least tangential relevance to their work.	**Ad hoc.** Library media staff members have staff development experiences "as needed."

Communication

Principal	**Shared vision.** The principal envisions the library media program as an integral part of the school.	**Supportive.** The principal supports the library media program with resources and communications to constituencies.	**Passive.** The principal takes no action to support the library media program.

Parents	**Involved.** Parents participate in the library media program through volunteerism, committees, and programs.	**One-way.** Parents receive information from the library media program through newsletters and other communication media.	**Indirect.** Parents learn about the library media program through their children or classroom teachers.
Business	**Involved.** The library media program has active partnerships with businesses.	**Informative.** The library media program targets relevant information to local businesses such as bookstores or electronics dealers.	**Indirect.** Businesses only know about the library media program from general communication.
Public Library	**Collaborative.** The school library media specialist and the public librarian communicate regularly and frequently about programs and resources	**Informative.** The school library notifies the public library about specific programs or activities on an *ad hoc* basis.	**Indirect.** Libraries only know about each other's programs and resources through publicly disseminated communication.

Resources

Budget	**Comprehensive.** The annual budget includes specific line items for training, new hardware, replacement hardware, hardware upgrades, repair, new software, software upgrades, replacement and new print resources, supplies, and professional, clerical and technical staff.	**Basic.** Line items are included in the annual budget for print resources, hardware, and software.	**Ad hoc.** As money becomes available, it is spent on technology and other media resources.

Scheduling

Integration	**Integrated.** Based on collaborative planning, classes are scheduled when activities require lessons on seeking or using information. Classes come to the center several days in a row for information work.	**Reserved.** Each class has a block of time reserved for their use as needed.	**Fixed.** Each class comes to the library media center on a regular basis; lessons may or may not be aligned with classroom activities.
Access	**Open access.** Both library media and classroom policies allow students to access the library media center whenever they need to.	**Controlled.** Students have regularly scheduled opportunities to access the library media center.	**Limited.** Students can access the library media center when their class is scheduled there.

For Further Reading

This list is a selective compilation of books for enriching the professional collection of the school library media center. The resources were selected specifically to facilitate the connection between the library media program and its educational community.

STUDENTS

Dame, Melvina Azar. *Serving Linguistically and Culturally Diverse Students: Strategies for the School Library Media Specialist.* Neal-Schuman, 1993. Includes strategies and suggested resources for locating appropriate materials for diverse populations.

Glasser, William. *The Quality School; Managing Students Without Coercion.* New York: Harper & Row, 1990. Presents a practical, yet theory-based, approach to motivating students and creating a productive school climate.

Kohn, Alfie. *Punished by Rewards; The Trouble with Gold Stars, Incentive Plans, A's, Praise, and Other Bribes.* New York: Houghton Mifflin, 1993. Discusses the dangers of extrinsic rewards.

Wesson, Caren, and Margaret J. Keefe, eds. *Serving Special Needs Students in the School Library Media Center.* Westport, Conn.: Greenwood Press, 1995. Organized according to the three roles of the library media specialist—teacher, information specialist, and consultant. Strategies for supporting students with special needs are described.

CURRICULUM

Lounsbury, John H., ed. *Connecting the Curriculum Through Interdisciplinary Instruction.* Columbus, Ohio: National Middle School Association, 1992. Describes how teaching teams work, what skills and attributes are needed for team work, and what benefits teamwork offers for learning.

Mehlinger, Howard D. *School Reform in the Information Age.* Bloomington, Ind.: Center for Excellence in Education, 1995. Summarizes educational theories and trends in educational reform.

COMMUNITY

Feinberg, Sarah, and Sari Feldman. *Serving Families and Children Through Partnerships: A How-to-Do-It Manual for Librarians.* New York: Neal-Schuman, 1996. Designed primarily with public libraries in mind, many of these strategies and approaches for partnering can be applied to school library media programs as well.

INFORMATION SKILLS

Blake, Michael, et al. *Teaching the New Library: A How-to-Do-It Manual for Planning and Designing Instructional Programs.* New York: Neal-Schuman, 1996. Describes practical techniques for developing instruction.

California School Library Association. *From Library Skills to Information Literacy.* Castle Rock, Colo.: Hi Willow Research and Publishing, 1997. Describes an information literacy curriculum and strategies for implementing it.

Eisenberg, Michael B., and Robert E. Berkowitz. *Information Problem-Solving: The Big Six Skills Approach to Library and Information Skills Instruction.* Norwood, N.J.: Ablex, 1990. Describes a model for information problem solving and includes teaching strategies and sample lessons.

Harmon, Charles, ed. *Using the Internet, Online Services, and CD-ROMS for Writing Research and Term Papers.* New York: Neal-Schuman, 1996. This is a practical guide to helping students use electronic resources.

Kuhlthau, Carol Collier. *Seeking Meaning: A Process Approach to Library and Information Services.* Norwood, N.J.: Ablex, 1993. Includes a description of an information processing model on which an information skills curriculum can be based.

Miller Donna, and J'Lynn Anderson. *Developing an Integrated Library Program.* Worthington, Ohio: Linworth, 1996. Describes a step-by-step method for integrating information skills into classroom curriculum.

Tarquin, Patti, and Sharon Walker. *Creating Success in the Classroom; Visual Organizers and How to Use Them.* Englewood, CO: Teacher Ideas Press, 1997. Includes a set of visual organizers to represent frameworks that help students manage information. Examples include semantic feature analysis frameworks, flowcharts, webbing, and Venn diagrams.

Teaching Electronic Information Skills: A Resource Guide Series. McHenry, Ill.: Follett Software Company, 1995. Three notebooks (grades K–5, 6–8, and 9–12) are included in the series. Each notebook begins with an information skills model designed by Marjorie Pappas; the model is then applied to examples of integrated lessons for classroom and library media center collaboration.

COLLABORATION

Austrom, Liz, et al. *Implementing Change: A Cooperative Approach to Initiating, Implementing and Sustaining Library Resource Centre Programs.* Vancouver, B.C.: British Columbia Teacher–Librarians' Association, 1989. Based on the Concerns-Based Adoption Model for initiating change, strategies for developing an integrated library media program are described.

Costa, Arthur, and Robert J. Garmston. *Cognitive Coaching: A Foundation for Renaissance Schools.* Norwood, Mass.: Christopher-Gordon, 1994. Describes a coaching model of collegial support.

Holcomb, Edie L. *Asking the Right Questions: Tools and Techniques for Teamwork.* Thousand Oaks, Calif.: Corwin Press, 1996. Presents specific and practical techniques for facilitating group process, shared decision making, and teamwork.

Vandergrift, Kay E. *Power Teaching: A Primary Role of the School Library Media Specialist.* Chicago: American Library Association, 1994. Presents teaching strategies for library media specialists, always with an emphasis on the importance of close collaboration with classroom teachers.

COLLECTION

Owens, Genevieve, ed. *Electronic Resources: Implications for Collection Management.* Binghamton, N.Y.: Haworth Press, 1996. Reviews strengths and weaknesses of electronic resources and includes selection criteria.

Pastine, Maureen, ed. *Collection Development: Past and Future.* Binghamton, N.Y.: Haworth, 1996. Covers selection and evaluation of electronic resources.

van Orden, Phyllis. *The Collection Program in Schools: Concepts, Practices, and Information Sources.* 2d ed. Englewood, Colo.: Libraries Unlimited, 1995. Presents a review of philosophy and decision-making strategy for collection development and maintenance, with consideration for the educational context.

READING

Carletti, Silvana, et al. *The Library/Classroom Connection.* Portsmouth, N.H.: Heinemann, 1991. Describes ways to integrate instructional activities of the library media program and the classroom.

Senator, Rochelle B. *Collaboration for Literacy; Creating an Integrated Language Arts Program for Middle Schools.* Westport, Conn.: Greenwood Press, 1995. Presents practical strategies and real-life examples to demonstrate how to integrate the library media program and the literature program in a middle school.

TECHNOLOGY

Campbell, John, and Mary Campbell. *The Student's Guide to Doing Research on the Internet.* Reading, Mass.: Addison-Wesley, 1995. Serves as a guide to selected World Wide Web sites. Also includes a basic introduciton to html.

Crawford, Walt, and Michael Gorman. *Future Libraries; Dreams, Madness and Reality.* Chicago: American Library Association, 1995. Discusses ways in which technology can improve library services. Cautions readers not to become overzealous about technology's role.

Dewing, Martha. *Beyond TV: Activities for Using Video with Children.* ABC-CLIO, 1992. Serves as a practical compilation of activities for using television in instruction to develop critical thinking and viewing skills.

Kuhlthau, Carol Collier, ed. *The Virtual School Library; Gateway to the Information Superhighway.* Englewood, Colo.: Libraries Unlimited, 1996. Includes a collection of essays on the integration of information technologies into the school library media program.

Mendrinos, Roxanne. *Building Information Literacy Using High Technology; A Guide for Schools and Libraries.* Englewood, Colo.: Libraries Unlimited, 1994. Based on research into the teaching of information literacy in a technological environment, includes what needs to be taught, what electronic resources are necessary in a school media center, and what the library media specialist must know. Sample lessons exemplify integration of information technologies into the curriculum.

ASSESSMENT

Hibbard, K. Michael. *A Teacher's Guide to Performance-Based Learning and Assessment.* Alexandria, Va.: Association for Supervision and Curriculum Development, 1996. Serves as a complete introduction to performance-based assessment. Includes extensive coverage of rubrics.

Joyce, M., and J. Tallman. *Making the Writing and Research Connection with the I-*

Search Process: A How-to-Do-It Manual for Teachers and School Librarians. New York: Neal-Schuman, 1996. Presents strategies for using the I-Search process and incorporating it into the information skills curriculum.

Kuhlthau, Carol Collier, ed. *Assessment and the School Library Media Center.* Englewood, Colo.: Libraries Unlimited, 1994. Provides a general overview of assessment issues, particularly as they relate to the library media program.

Marzano, Robert J., Debra Pickering, and Jay McTighe. *Assessing Student Outcomes; Performance Assessment Using the Dimensions of Learning Model.* Alexandria, Va.: Association for Supervision and Curriculum Development, 1993. Summarizes the use of rubrics for assessing students' performances. Includes model sets of rubrics for such dimensions as complex thinking and information processing.

PROGRAM EVALUATION

Crowley, John D. *Developing a Vision; Strategic Planning and the Library Media Specialist.* Westport, Conn.: Greenwood Press, 1994. Presents a model for applying strategic planning steps to the library media program.

Yesner, Bernice L., and Hilda L. Jay. *Operating and Evaluating School Library Media Programs: A Handbook for Administrators and Librarians.* New York: Neal-Schuman, 1998. Serves as a guide to assist in determining strengths and shortcomings in a program. Includes strategies for addressing needs.

Subject Index

Author Index

About the Author

Jean Donham teaches in the School of Library and Information Science at The University of Iowa. Prior to her appointment to the faculty, she was the district coordinator for library media and technology for the Iowa City Community School District, where the library media program recently received the American Association of School Librarians (AASL) School Library Media Program of the Year Award as well as the American Library Association (ALA) John Cotton Dana Award. Donham has been a presenter at conferences in the midwest, as well as at AASL conferences. Active in the Iowa Educational Media Association, she was the first recipient of that organization's Media Professional of the Year Award. She holds a master's degree in library and information services from the University of Maryland and a Ph. D. in educational administration from the University of Iowa.